iMac®

fast&easy®

Revised Editon

Check the Web for Updates

To check for updates or corrections relevant to this book, visit our updates page on the Web at http://www.prima-tech.com/updates.

Send Us Your Comments

To comment on this book or any other PRIMA TECH title, visit our reader response page on the Web at http://www.prima-tech.com/comments.

How to Order

For information on quantity discounts, contact the publisher: Prima Publishing, P.O. Box 1260BK, Rocklin, CA 95677-1260; (916) 787-7000. On your letterhead, include information concerning the intended use of the books and the number of books you want to purchase.

iMac®

fast&easy®

Revised Editon

Ilene M. Hoffman

PRIMA TECH

A DIVISION OF PRIMA PUBLISHING

A Division of Prima Publishing

Prima Publishing and colophon and Fast & Easy are registered trademarks of Prima Communications, Inc. PRIMA TECH is a trademark of Prima Communications, Inc., Roseville, California 95661.

Apple, the Apple logo, AppleWorks, Balloon Help, Charcoal, Chicago, ClarisWorks, ColorSync, Extensions Manager, Finder, iMac, ImageWriter, iMovie, LaserWriter, LocalTalk, Mac, Macintosh, Mac logo, "Moof" and Dogcow logo, QuickTime, Sherlock, Think different, TrueType, VideoSync and VideoEdit are either registered trademarks or trademarks of Apple Computer, Inc., in the U.S. and other countries. EarthLink and the EarthLink logo are service marks of EarthLink, Inc. Microsoft, Microsoft Internet Explorer logo, and Outlook are registered trademarks of Microsoft Corporation in the United States and/or other countries. Netscape and Netscape Navigator are registered trademarks of Netscape Communications Corporation in the U.S. and other countries. Quicken is a registered trademark of Intuit, Inc., in the United States and other countries. Adobe, the Adobe logo, Acrobat, and the Acrobat logo are either registered trademarks or trademarks of Adobe Systems Incorporated in the United States and/or other countries. "AOL" and AOL triangle logo are registered trademarks of America Online, Inc. All rights reserved. StuffIt and StuffIt Expander are trademarks of Aladdin Systems, Inc.

This book is an independent publication of Prima Publishing and is not affiliated with or sponsored by any of the companies mentioned above.

Important: If you have problems running your iMac, go to Apple's Web site at http://www.apple.com. Prima Publishing cannot provide software support.

Prima Publishing and the author have attempted throughout this book to distinguish proprietary trademarks from descriptive terms by following the capitalization style used by the manufacturer.

Information contained in this book has been obtained by Prima Publishing from sources believed to be reliable. However, because of the possibility of human or mechanical error by our sources, Prima Publishing, or others, the Publisher does not guarantee the accuracy, adequacy, or completeness of any information and is not responsible for any errors or omissions or the results obtained from use of such information. Readers should be particularly aware of the fact that the Internet is an ever-changing entity. Some facts may have changed since this book went to press.

ISBN: 0-7615-3136-X

Library of Congress Catalog Card Number: 00-106652

Printed in the United States of America

00 01 02 03 04 DD 10 9 8 7 6 5 4 3 2 1

Publisher:
Stacy L. Hiquet

Marketing Manager:
Judi Taylor-Wade

Associate Marketing Manager:
Heather Buzzingham

Managing Editor:
Sandy Doell

Acquisitions Editor:
Jawahara K. Saidullah

Project Editor:
Brian Thomasson

Technical Editor:
Michael Johnson

Copy Editor:
Gabrielle Nemes

Interior Layout:
Danielle Foster

Cover Design:
Prima Design Team

Indexer:
Sharon Shock

To the late Don Crabb, an extraordinary Macintosh writer, who helped me more than he knew, in his all too short lifespan.

And

To my parents who have unwittingly ended up buying most of my Macintosh computers, Andy Ihnatko, who "knew I could do it," Chris Breen, who "refuses to do it," Bob Levitus who "does it regularly," Ted Landau, who "hates to do it," and to my son Marcus who didn't make it any easier (he made me put that line in!), and of course Dobbyn and Sally, who don't do anything at all. Plus, Sheila, who listened to my ramblings even though she had no idea what a Macintosh is.

Acknowledgments

Many thanks to the people at Prima Tech who worked on this book. Thank you for all the time you gave and for your assistance.

A grateful bow to P.A.M. Borys of Step by Step Training for assisting with the AppleWorks chapter.

A warm thank you also to the press relations staff at the following companies: Apple Computer, Ambrosia Software, Canon, Hewlett Packard, iRez, Dr. Bott, LLC, Intuit, and Belkin for their support and allowing me to use their products in the making of this book.

Special thanks to Bynkii, FirehawkG3, Flowbie, Mcirish, TheMartian, Windsurfer, Nyx, and Bones3D, for their technical assistance and being available by IM and chat all hours of the day and night. And finally, thank you to Brian Thomasson and Jawahara Saidullah for managing this book through the entire editorial process.

About the Author

Ilene M. Hoffman, MSW has been working with and writing about the Macintosh since August, 1984. She runs a Macintosh and Internet-based consultancy in the Boston area. In addition to her writing, she is the Forums Administrator and Senior Editor at MacFixIt.com, a Contributing Editor at MacTech and TechRepublic magazines, and she hosts weekly help conferences on Talk City and AOL. Ilene maintains the Hess Macworld Expo Events List and the People Who Think Different Web sites, and is a recipient of the User Group Connection's User Group Hero award. She started her professional life as a social worker and dancer and found her destiny in the Macintosh.

Ilene has one brilliant son, two not so brilliant dogs, and a house that looks like a bombed-out Macintosh museum.

Contents at a Glance

Contents

PART IV
MULTIMEDIA ON YOUR IMAC 195

Introduction

Prima Publishing's Fast and Easy guides are a highly visual way to get started quickly with computer-related subjects. Using clear directions with illustrations of each step, this series makes it simple and clear how to do tasks without the confusion of long text descriptions or the frustration of trying to "make do" with online documentation. IMac Fast & Easy is an introduction to Apple Computer's new personal computer, the iMac.

Who Should Read This Book?

This book is intended for first-time computer users and for converts to the Macintosh from the Windows world. Those moving up to the iMac from an older Macintosh will also enjoy new features and find the step-by-step approach helpful.

This book has been designed specifically for the iMac. The illustrations in this guide accurately represent what you see on the screen and all software that is discussed is already included in the iMac package.

Special Features of This Book

Besides the detailed descriptions of useful tasks, this book also includes:

- **Tips**. These shortcuts, features, and hints help make your iMac experience even more productive and fun.

- **Notes**. These give background, additional information, or further ideas on how to use various features.

Remember, as the Apple slogan says, "Think different." Have fun with this book and with your iMac!

P A R T   I

iMac Basics

1

Getting Started with Your iMac

If this is your first new computer, you'll probably want to get it set up and running as fast as you can. This chapter helps you do that. In this chapter, you'll learn how to:

- Unpack your iMac and plug in the parts
- Connect your iMac to other devices
- Use the Desktop
- Use the mouse and keyboard
- Identify the two major types of software used on your iMac

Unpacking Your iMac

The iMac is one of the easiest computers to set up. A trifold card titled "Welcome to Your iMac" packed in the iMac's box clearly walks you through the few steps needed to set up your iMac.

1. Lift out the **cardboard accessory box** including the piece of styrofoam and set it aside.

2. Carefully **lift** the **iMac** out of its box and take off the protective wrap.

3. Open the **cardboard accessory box** and find the Welcome to Your iMac folder. This trifold card shows you Apple's easy setup steps. Follow the directions in the trifold card.

4. Unpack the **keyboard** and **mouse** from the accessory box and remove the plastic wrap.

5. Place the **computer** on a desk.

6. Swing the **foot** forward.

7. Look in the accessory box for the power cord, then plug it into the computer and an outlet.

NOTE

Ideally, you should plug your iMac into a surge protector. You can find surge protectors at most computer stores or general merchandise stores, such as Wal-Mart or Sears.

8. **Plug** the **keyboard** into a USB (*Universal Serial Bus*) port. The Apple logo should be on the top. USB ports are discussed later in this chapter.

9. **Plug** the **mouse** into one of the USB ports on the keyboard. If you are left-handed, you may want to put the mouse on the left side. (You can also plug the mouse directly into the second USB port in the computer.)

10. **Plug** a **telephone cord** into the standard telephone jack if you plan to connect to the Internet.

NOTE

In the side panel are a number of connectors. These are known as *ports* and they allow you to plug additional equipment into your iMac. The plugs may differ on your iMac model.

Before we start up the iMac, let's look at all the plugs and components so that you understand how these connections work together.

Ports

When you set up your iMac, you plug the keyboard cable into a port on the side of the computer. Ports are different kinds of plugs used to connect your iMac to other devices, called peripherals. The ports are listed as they appear on your computer from left to right.

- **Audio**. The iMac has both sound input and output ports. You can attach a microphone to the audio input port or other equipment such as a CD player or tape deck. You can attach speakers or headphones to the audio output port.

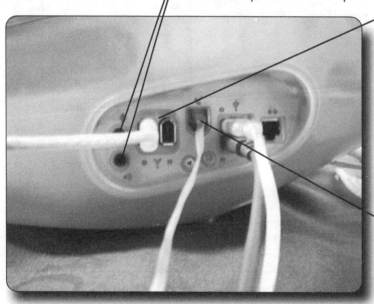

© 1999 Apple Computer, Inc

- **Firewire**. There are two Firewire ports on your iMac DV. The Firewire port allows you to connect up to 63 high-speed devices, daisy-chained together. Devices include digital video cameras, hard drives, printers, etc.

- **Modem.** The *modem* port is where you connect a telephone line so that your iMac can communicate with the Internet. Connection to the modem port requires a standard telephone cord with a typical connector, called an RJ-11 modular connector. Read more about the modem in Chapter 2 "Mac OS Setup Assistant."

- **Reset Button**. Underneath the modem port there is a small button that can be used to restart your computer when it refuses to shut down or restart normally.

- **Programmer's Button**. Underneath the modem port there is also a button that is used by programmers when developing software. Unless you are a programmer, you should never have to use this button.

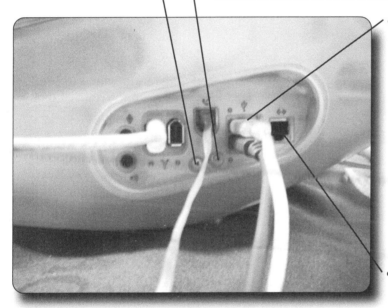

- **Universal Serial Bus (USB)**. There are two USB ports on your iMac. The Universal Serial Bus ports allow you to connect up to 127 devices, daisy–chained together. Such devices include keyboards, mice, scanners, trackballs, disk drives, and printers. This is the iMac's primary means of connecting devices.

- **Ethernet**. The word *Ethernet* describes a way that computers can talk to each other and pass files back and forth. It looks just like a larger version of the modem port. The iMac's Ethernet port is designed for connecting to multiple computers (called a network) or connecting cable modems and Digital Subscriber Line modems. Unless you plan to connect your iMac to other computers at home or work, or plan to purchase high speed Internet service, you don't need to use the Ethernet port.

- **Headphones**. There are two headphone ports on the front of the iMac, located at the left edge of the right speaker.

Turning on Your iMac

Turning on the iMac is as easy as pressing a single button.

1. Press the **Power button** (⏻). The first image you will see is the "Happy Mac."

TIP

The Power button (⏻) is a round button located just to the right of the CD slot on the computer. There is also a Power button at the top of the keyboard, between the F12 and Help keys on older iMac keyboards.

2. Wait until the computer loads all of its startup software.

NOTE

Along the bottom of the screen you'll see several icons appearing one after the other. These icons are called *system extensions* and they indicate additions to the Mac OS that are being loaded.

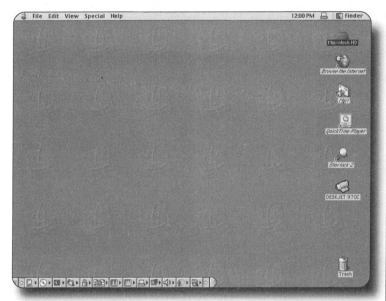

Once everything is loaded, the screen changes to the Desktop. Your computer has now *booted*, or started up. In the next chapter, you will learn how to set up your computer environment.

> **NOTE**
>
> The term *boot* comes from the idea of "pulling yourself up by your bootstraps." In fact in the early days of computing, starting a computer was called *bootstrapping* and the program that managed the self-startup was known as a *bootstrap loader*.

Using the Keyboard

The keyboard is the primary way you talk to your iMac. Your keyboard comes with a keypad on the right side for easy typing of numbers. The keys labeled F1 through F12 are function keys, which are discussed below.

Special Keys on Your Keyboard

All Macintosh keyboards contain some special keys. These keys help you work with your iMac more easily. Even if your keyboard looks a little different than the one pictured here, the keys perform the same functions.

- **Command ⌘ key**. The *command key* is a *modifier key*. It does nothing when pressed by itself. You press it in combination with another key on the keyboard to do special things with your keyboard. ⌘ plus another key will not type anything on the screen. Instead, command key combinations are used to send commands to the computer using the keyboard rather than the mouse. With practice, you may find these shortcuts faster and easier to use.

- **Option key**. The *option key* is another modifier key that, when pressed along with a letter, number, or symbol key, produces a character different than the letter, number, or symbol the key normally types. For example: Option plus the number 8 will type a bullet (•) character.

- **Control key**. The *control key* is yet another modifier key. Like the ⌘ key, when used with another key it produces nonprinting characters.

- **Escape (esc) key**. The *escape key* does exactly what its name implies. It allows you to escape from some action. The use of the escape key varies from one program to another.

- **Function keys**. *Function keys* allow you to send a command by pressing a single key. The tasks performed by each key vary from one program to another. You can also assign commands to these keys.

- **Arrow keys**. The *arrow keys* are used to move your cursor around a document. You can move one space, character, or item at a time. The *cursor* is the symbol, such as an arrow, a large I, or a line that lets you know where your next typed character will be placed on a page, or where a mouse click will work.

- **Navigation keys**. There are three *navigation keys*: Home, Page Up (pg up), and Page Down (pg dn). Pressing Home moves you to the beginning of the document on which you are working. Pressing Page Up moves you one page backward; pressing Page Down moves you one page forward.

- **Caps Lock key**. The *Caps Lock key* only locks the caps for the letter keys; the number and symbol keys are not affected. For example, if you press the Caps Lock key and type a number, you will see that number. To get a dollar sign, you must still hold down the Shift key and then press the symbol key.

Using the Mouse

Now is a good time to learn about using your mouse. You use the iMac's mouse to interact with items on the Desktop and to work with programs. As you read this book and software documentation, you will find references to several basic mouse skills.

Moving the Mouse Pointer

1. Place the **mouse** on a firm, dry surface such as a mouse pad.

2. Push or pull the **mouse** in the direction you want the mouse to go. The mouse pointer will move on the screen in the same direction that you move the mouse on your desk.

TIP

The mouse does not move in the direction you want unless it is oriented correctly. Make sure that the cord is facing toward the computer and away from you.

Point and Click

Many of the things that you do with the iMac involve a *mouse click*, or simply a *click*. To perform a click use the following steps:

1. **Move** the **mouse pointer** to the item you want to click.

NOTE

If you have a new iMac, your entire mouse is a button. Apply even pressure with your hand to the top surface of the mouse until you feel a soft click.

---

2. Press and release the **mouse button** once. You will hear the mouse make a soft clicking sound and the item you clicked is highlighted, or *selected*. The result of selecting something depends on the type of item, and you will learn more about specific results throughout this book.

Double-clicking

You can sometimes simplify commands with windows, folders, and files by *double-clicking*.

1. Move the **mouse pointer** to the item you want to double-click.

2. Press and release the **mouse button twice** in rapid succession. The mouse button will make two quiet clicking sounds. As with a click, the result of a double-click depends on exactly what was double-clicked. The results are discussed throughout this book.

Dragging

Dragging your mouse lets you move a folder or file from one place to another, or text and other selected items from one place to another.

1. **Move** the **mouse pointer** to the item you want to move.

2. **Press and hold** the **mouse button**. The item will be selected.

3. **Move** the **mouse pointer** to the new location for the item. The item will move along with the mouse pointer to the new location.

4. **Release** the **mouse button**. The item will appear in its new location.

TIP

Don't click the mouse too slowly or move the mouse accidentally while clicking, as it may not do what you want. You learn how to adjust the mouse settings later (see Chapter 6, "Customizing Your iMac").

Types of Software

The term *software* refers to the programs that your iMac uses. A program, also called an application, contains instructions that a computer follows. Without software, a computer is nothing more than an expensive, but pretty, doorstop.

There are two major types of software that you use with your iMac: application software and system software. Each has its own specific job.

Application Software

Application software (more commonly referred to as "programs") is specialized software that performs useful work for you—the reason you bought your iMac. Once you have started up your iMac, you can run one or more programs of your choice.

A file created in an application is called a *document*. You run an application, but you store the result of your work in a document wherever you like on the computer. You usually have only one copy of an application on your hard disk, but any number of documents. As you will see later in this chapter, the iMac makes it easy to tell the difference between an application and a document.

Application software includes the following:

- **Word processor**. A *word processor* is a program that allows you to enter, edit, and format text. Many of today's word processors(such as AppleWorks and Microsoft Word) can also handle graphics.

- **Spreadsheet**. A *spreadsheet* is the electronic equivalent of an accountant's journal. You use a spreadsheet to manage numeric data, as when analyzing a budget. Most spreadsheet programs (such as AppleWorks and Microsoft Excel) can also draw graphs from stored data.

- **Graphics**. Graphics programs (such as Adobe PhotoShop and Kai's PhotoSoap) allow you to create and edit pictorial images.

- **Data management**. Data management software (such as FileMaker Pro) allows you to store, organize, and retrieve data. You may hear the terms *database management* or *file management* applied to data management application software.

- **Communications**. Communications software lets you connect your computer to other computers or the Internet so you can exchange information. There are many types of communication software, such as e-mail applications, chat software, Web browsers, and video conferencing software.

- **Games**. Game software lets you have fun with your computer. There are many different games you can play on your iMac, including traditional card and board games, car racing games, strategy games, and almost any other kind of game you can imagine.

You will also find that there is a great deal of specialized software, such as Intuit's Quicken, that accompanies your iMac. Quicken is designed to help you manage your finances.

System Software

System software is software that manages the computer. It allows you to name and store files, use the hard drive, and use the modem. The most commonly-used example of system software is a collection of programs known together as an *operating system*. The iMac's operating system, known as the Macintosh Operating System or Mac OS, is on your Desktop. It comes pre–installed on your iMac. It includes a number to tell you which version of the Mac OS you are using.

The Desktop is a visual metaphor for how the parts of the computer are presented on your screen. The parts are supposed to resemble items on a desk. When you use items on the Desktop, you are working with the Mac OS.

NOTE

Programs and documents are stored in *files*. A file is a document on a computer. You learn much more about files in Chapter 5, "Using Folders and Files."

Introduction to the Desktop

Today, the Desktop is generally accepted as the easiest way for people to interact with their computer. The pictures on the Desktop represent elements of the computer and are known as *icons*. Icons represent disks (hard disks, CD-ROMs, and any other disks you may have attached to your computer), programs, and documents. Icons also represent *folders* that help you organize the storage of your files on disks.

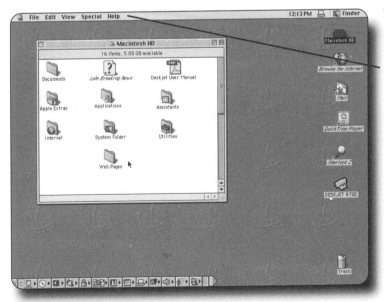

The basic elements of the iMac Desktop are:

- **Menu bar**. A *menu* is a list of options from which you can choose. The Mac OS uses one *main menu bar* that always appears at the top of the screen. Other menus appear depending on the specific program you use. You will learn about menus and making menu choices in Chapter 4, "Using Menus."

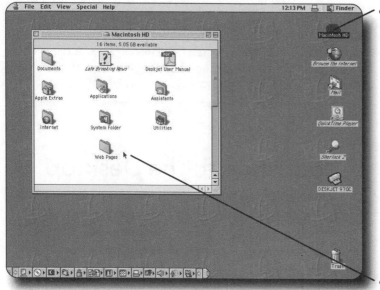

- **Hard disk**. A *hard disk* is a device that provides permanent storage for programs and documents. It is internal storage for all the files on your iMac, so you will only see it represented as an icon on your desktop. You will learn a great deal about viewing and manipulating the contents of a hard disk in Chapter 5, "Using Folders and Files."

- **Mouse pointer**. The *mouse pointer* lets you point to items on the Desktop and work with elements such as icons and menus. The mouse pointer moves on the screen as you move your mouse. It is also called a *cursor*.

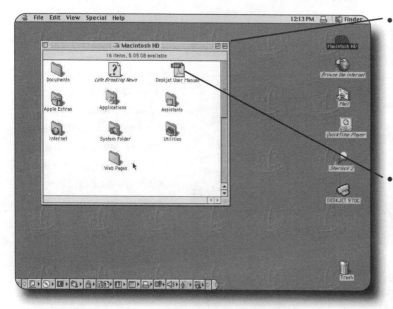

- **Window**. A *window* is a box-like container that lets you see the contents of an item, such as a folder. As you will see throughout this book, windows also display the contents of documents.

- **Document icon**. A *document icon* represents a document that is stored on a disk. A document is usually associated with the program used to create it, but may be opened in another similar type of program.

- **Folder icon**. A *folder* is a receptacle for documents, programs, and other folders. You will learn more about folders in Chapter 5, "Using Folders and Files."

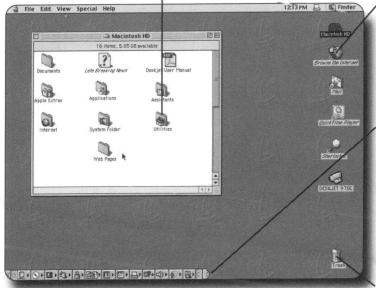

- **Alias icon**. An alias points to a file on your computer. It represents a file or folder on your hard disk and opens that file or folder when double-clicked.

- **Control strip**. The *Control strip* allows you to easily change the various settings that you'll use frequently, such as speaker volume. It sits at the bottom left of your computer screen.

- **Trash**. The *Trash* is used to delete items. Although it appears as an icon on the Desktop, it is actually a folder. Any item in the Trash folder is deleted from your hard disk when you empty the trash.

2

Mac OS Setup Assistant

This chapter helps you get your iMac up and running. The instructions take you through the first steps towards turning your iMac into a personal tool. In this chapter, you'll learn how to:

- Set up your work environment with Mac OS Setup Assistant
- Set up your Internet connection with Internet Setup Assistant
- Shut down your iMac

NOTE

You can find all the Setup Assistant's files inside the Assistants folder on your hard drive. To start one, just double-click on the file's icon.

Setting up with Mac OS Setup Assistant

The first time you boot your iMac, the Mac OS Setup Assistant greets you. The Mac OS Setup Assistant walks you through a series of questions and you click on the buttons or type the answers to set up your Macintosh. Each question appears in its own box, called a screen. This section walks you through each of those screens so that you can understand everything your Macintosh is asking of you.

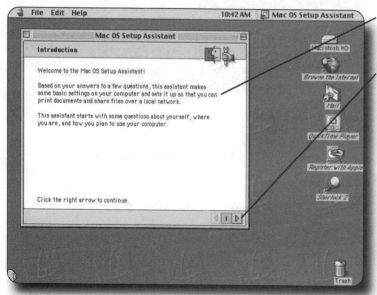

1. **Read** the **Mac OS Setup Assistant Introduction**.

2. **Click** on the **right arrow** on the bottom of the Mac OS Setup Assistant screen. You will continue to the Regional Preferences screen.

Regional Preferences

People around the world use different formats for items like dates and currency. Fortunately, the iMac offers several choices.

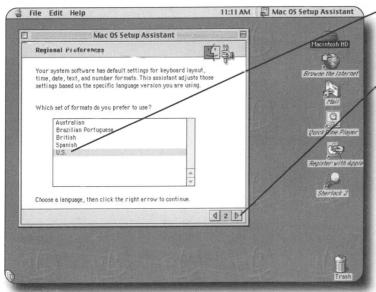

1. **Click** on the **country** in which tou live. The country you choose will be selected.

2. **Click** on the **right arrow**. You will proceed to the Name and Organization screen.

Name and Organization

A flashing line, called *the insertion point* appears in the What is your name box. The insertion point shows you where the next text character you type will appear.

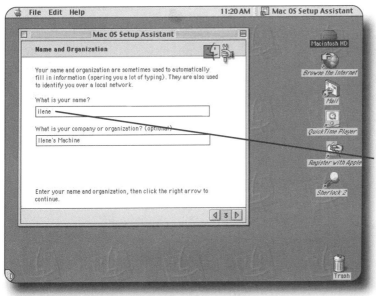

After you type in your name and organization, the iMac automatically inserts them for you when they are needed—for example, when you set up your Internet account.

1. **Type** your **name**. The highlighting will disappear when you start to type.

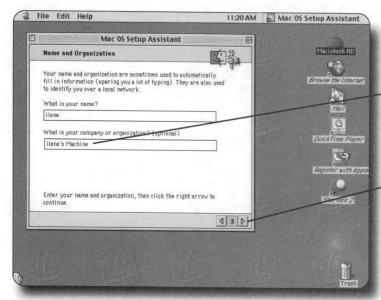

2. **Press** the **Tab key**. The insertion point will move to the next text box.

3. **Type** your **company** or **organization name** in the second box. This is not required.

4. **Click** on the **right arrow** on the bottom of the Mac OS Setup Assistant screen. You will continue to the Time and Date screen.

Time and Date

Your Macintosh keeps track of the correct time and date. There is a special battery inside the computer that is always on. This allows the computer to keep track of the time when you create or change a file or document. The time and date are also useful when you send e-mail messages to people.

1. **Click** on **Yes** if Daylight Savings time is currently in effect in your town. The radio button will be selected.

OR

1b. **Click** on **No** if you are not observing Daylight Savings time. The radio button will be selected.

NOTE

The round button is called a *radio button*. When it is selected, a black dot will appear in the center.

---

2. **Click** in the **hour area**. It will be highlighted.

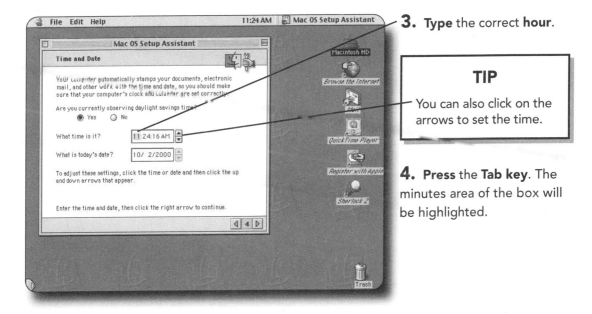

3. **Type** the correct **hour**.

TIP

You can also click on the arrows to set the time.

---

4. **Press** the **Tab key**. The minutes area of the box will be highlighted.

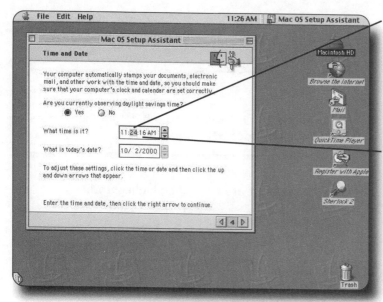

5. **Type** the correct **minutes**.

6. **Press** the **Tab key.** The seconds area of the box will be highlighted.

7. **Type** the correct **seconds**.

8. **Press** the **Tab key.** The AM/PM area of the box will be highlighted.

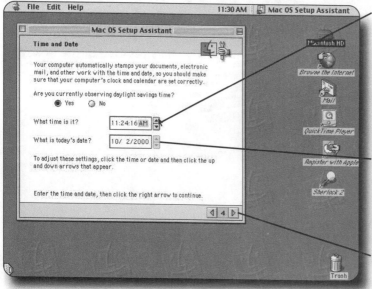

9. **Click** on the **arrows** to choose AM or PM. The correct choice will be displayed in the box.

10. **Press** the **Tab key.** The date box will be highlighted.

11. **Follow** the same **steps** to change the current month, day, and year. The date will be set.

12. **Click** on the **right arrow.** You will continue to the Geographic Location screen.

Geographic Location

1. **Click** on the **arrows** to find the city that is closest to where you live. When you press the arrow buttons, the highlighting will move in the same direction as the arrow.

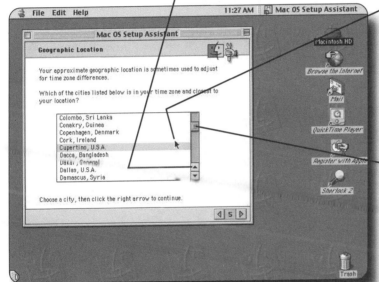

2. **Click** on the **city name**.

3. **Click** on the **right arrow**. You will proceed to the Finder Preferences screen.

TIP

When you click on the arrow keys to move through the choices in the window, it is called scrolling. You can also use the scroll box, to move through a document. Drag the square box up and down to view the choices. The area containing the up and down arrows and the scroll box is called the *scroll bar*.

Finder Preferences

The Finder is the program that starts first when you turn on your iMac. It gives you access to the computer's files, folders, and other programs, plus it keeps track of where these files are on the hard disk. In short, its job is to manage the Desktop. The Simple Finder preference limits the choices you see in the menu bar at the top of your screen. In order to follow all of the instructions in this book, do not choose the Simple Finder preference.

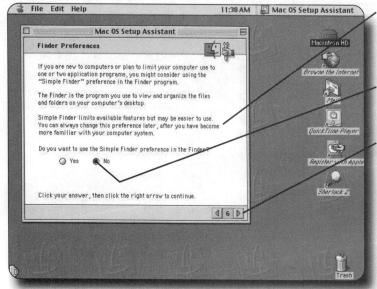

1. **Read** the **instructions** on the Finder Preferences screen.

2. **Click** on **No**. The radio button will be selected.

3. **Click** on the **right arrow.** You will continue to the Local Network Introduction screen.

NOTE

The Simple Finder is recommended for young children. Many important functions are disabled when you choose the Simple Finder.

Local Network Introduction

Very simply, a local network consists of several connected computers or a computer and a printer connected with network cabling. Setting up the local network information is most useful if your iMac will be attached to a network with other Macintosh computers. If not, you are still required to fill in your name and password to proceed.

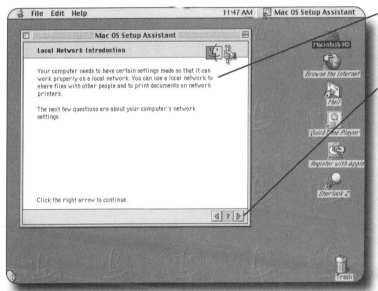

1. **Read** the **Local Network Introduction** screen.

2. **Click** on the **right arrow**. The Computer Name and Password screen will appear.

Computer Name and Password

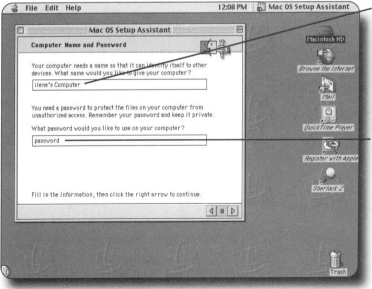

1. **Type** a **name** in the first text box.

2. **Press** the **Tab key**. The insertion bar will appear in the password text box.

3. **Type** a **password**. You can see the password the first time you enter it. When you return to this screen later, it will appear as a series of dots.

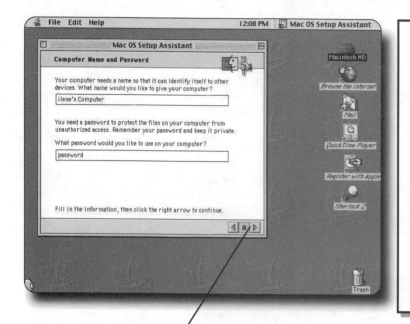

TIP

The password is case sensitive. To avoid someone guessing your password, use a mixture of numbers and letters. Do not use special characters, such as #, @, or *. Choose a password that you can remember, but is hard for someone else to guess. Store your password in a safe place where you can find it later.

4. Click on the **right arrow**. The Shared Folder screen will appear.

Shared Folder

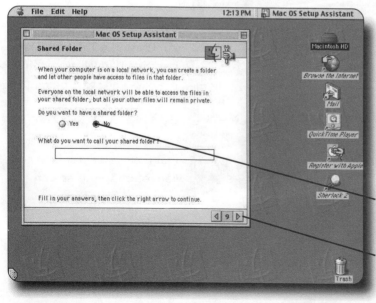

Shared folders are useful if another computer is connected to your iMac. This allows other computer users in your local network to share and access the files that reside in that folder. Most households do not use the shared folder feature.

1. Click on **No**. The radio button will be selected.

2. Click on the **right arrow**. The Printer Connection screen will appear.

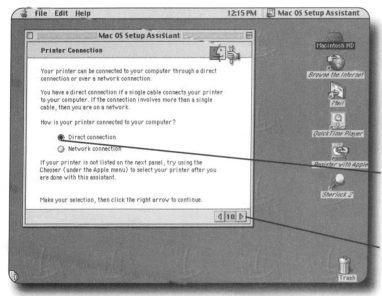

Printer Connection

Most printers are connected to your iMac with one cable. This is called a *direct connection*.

1. **Click** on **Direct Connection**. The radio button will be selected.

2. **Click** on the **right arrow**. The Printer Type screen will appear.

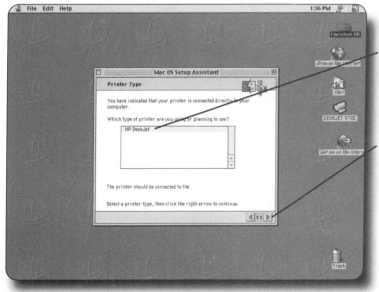

Printer Type

1. **Click** on the **type of printer** connected to your iMac. The printer you choose will be highlighted.

2. **Click** on the **right arrow.** You will proceed to the Conclusion screen.

Finishing with Mac OS Setup Assistant

Once you have selected your options, you need to save them with the assistant.

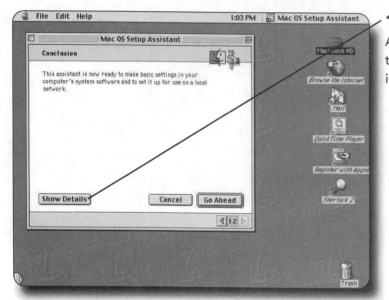

1. **Click** on **Show Details**. A list of all of the settings that you entered will appear in the Conclusion screen.

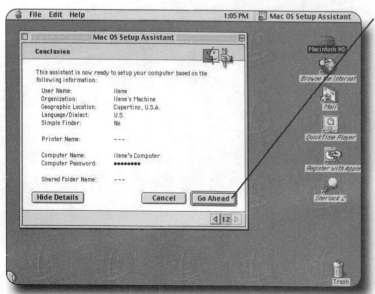

2. **Click** on **Go Ahead** if your settings are correct. The computer will tell you what it is doing as it sets up all the options you've chosen.

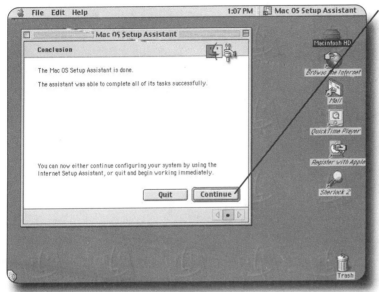

3. Click on **Continue**. The Internet Setup Assistant will appear.

Congratulations, you have just set up your computer for your unique home setting. Go have a cup of coffee! Next, you will learn how to set up your Internet access and how to shut down your computer safely.

Using Internet Setup Assistant

To get on the Internet you must configure your system software. The software to access EarthLink is preinstalled on your iMac. EarthLink is a national ISP (*Internet Service Provider*) that has access phone numbers all across the United States.

Once you have an EarthLink account (at a fee), your iMac calls EarthLink and connects to the Internet. That's all an ISP does: it provides the Internet connection. You can use any Internet software you choose; for example, you can use Microsoft Outlook for e-mail and either Microsoft Internet Explorer or Netscape Navigator as Web browsers and also for e-mail.

Internet Access

This section assumes that you do not have an Internet account and that you will be setting up your access to the

Internet for the first time. This tutorial walks you through signing up with EarthLink.

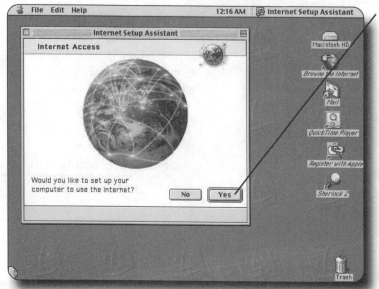

1. Click on **Yes**. You will be guided through another set of questions. The next screen will appear.

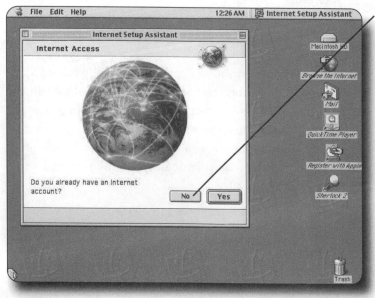

2. Click on **No**, because you need to set up an Internet account. The EarthLink TotalAccess Agreement will appear.

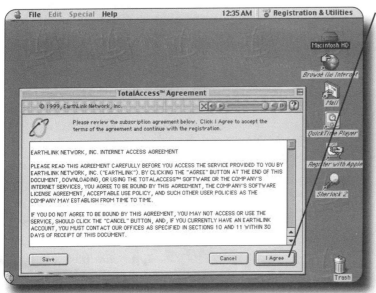

3. Click on **I Agree** after you have read the TotalAccess Agreement carefully and listened to the spoken message. The Welcome to TotalAccess screen will appear.

Setting up EarthLink

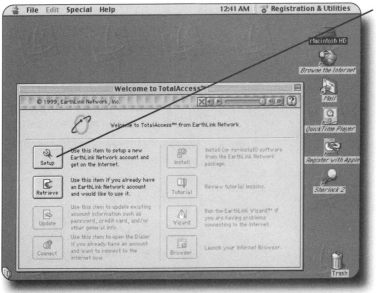

1. Click on **Setup** to create a new EarthLink Network account. The Setup New Account screen will appear.

2. **Type** the **name** you want to use as your e-mail address. Do not use spaces or the at (@), semicolon (;), period (.), pound (#), or backslash (/) symbols in your name.

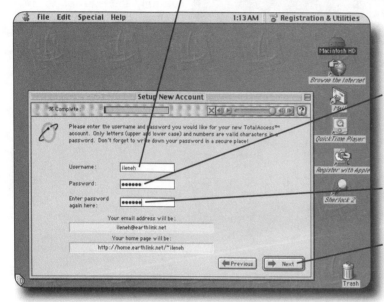

3. **Press** the **Tab key**. The cursor will move to the Password box.

4. **Type** your **password** in the box. Do not use the at (@), pound (#), or backslash (/) symbols in your password.

5. **Type** your **password** again, to verify the spelling.

6. **Click** on **Next**. You will continue to the General Information screen.

General Information

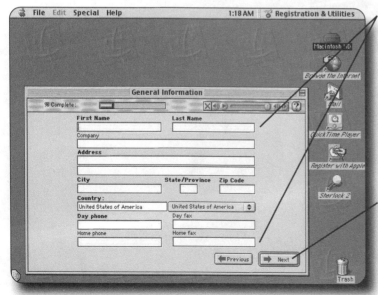

1. **Type** your **information** into the boxes on the provided form. Use the Tab key to move from one item to the next. You can also use your mouse and click in the form line to correct an entry. Leave the entries blank that do not apply to you.

2. **Click** on **Next**. The Phone Setup screen will appear.

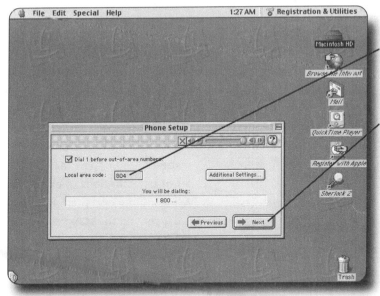

Phone Setup

1. Check that the **area code** in the Local area code box is correct.

2. Click on **Next**. A dialog box will open that informs you an 800 number will be called.

3. Click on **OK**. The Communications Status message box will appear.

Communication Status

The modem will dial out and the message box will inform you of the status of the connection.

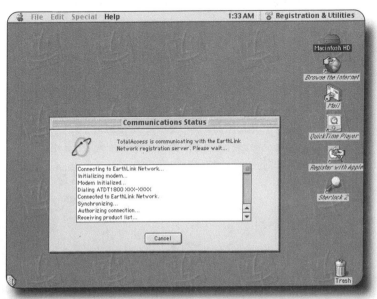

EarthLink Network will look up a local access number for you, and check for software updates you might need. The modem will automatically hang up when completed and the Product Info screen will appear.

Product Info

Earthlink provides three types of accounts. The first is for unlimited access through a local access number. The second provides the same local access, but adds five hours of access through a toll-free 800 number. This is a good choice if you travel frequently. The third account is for those who have ISDN access; a high-speed connection that does not use standard telephone lines. Only one plan may be presented to iMac users with an internal modem, using a regular phone line to connect.

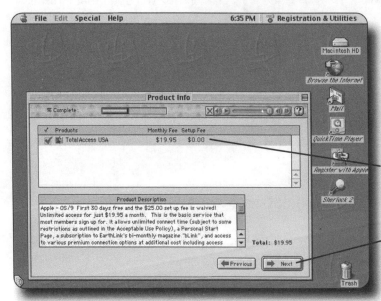

1. Click the **plan** you desire for Internet access. The plan will be selected.

2. Click on **Next**. The Credit Card Information screen will appear.

Credit Card Information

EarthLink bills you monthly for your Internet access. Check the TotalAccess Agreement to view information on the security of providing Earthlink with confidential data.

1. **Type** your **credit card number** in the first text box.

2. **Press** the **Tab key** to go to the Expiration date box.

3. **Type** your **credit card's expiration date**.

4. **Click** on the **radio button** for the type of credit card you want to use.

5. **Click** on **Next**. A dialog box will appear.

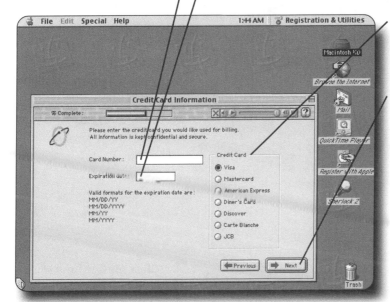

6. **Click** on **OK**. TotalAccess will dial an 800 number to register your new account and a Communications Status message box will appear.

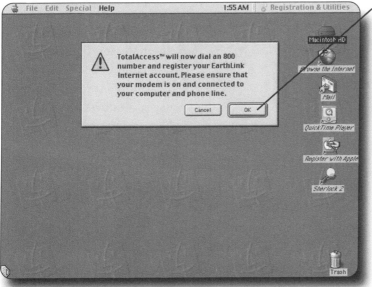

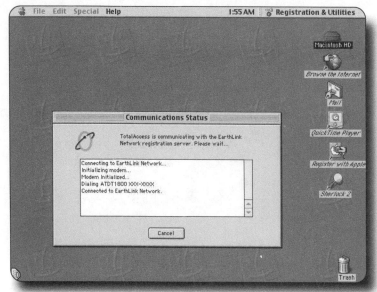

The Communication Status message box allows you to monitor your connection. Once the Order Accepted dialog box opens, if you do nothing, EarthLink will find a local access number for you.

7. **Click** on the **number** closest to your home area.

8. **Click** on **Next**. The Installation screen will appear.

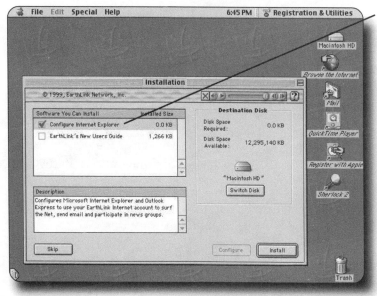

9. **Click** on **Configure Internet Explorer**.

You are now done setting up Internet access. Before we go out on the Internet, there are many features of your iMac that you should review. Chapters 3 through 5 cover using windows, menus, and files and folders.

Turning off Your iMac

Your iMac needs to be shut down properly to prevent possible data loss. When the shut down command is sent, all open files are closed, and the file directories are updated with any changes.

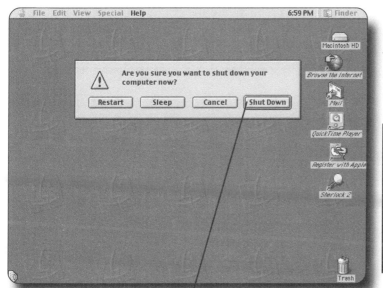

1. Press the **Power button** ⏻ on the keyboard or on the computer. A small message box known as an *alert* will appear.

NOTE

An alert is different from other message boxes because you must click a button and make a choice before you can continue.

2. Click on **Shut Down**. The computer will turn off.

TIP

You can also choose Shut Down from the Special Menu on the menu bar to shut down your iMac.

NOTE

If you let your computer sit for about 30 minutes without touching it, the screen goes dark and the Power button turns orange. Your computer has gone into Energy Saver mode or "sleep." This mode uses only a little power to keep the electronics warm. The screen actually turns itself off and the hard disk stops spinning. You reactivate the computer by pressing the Power button or any key (other than a modifier key) on the keyboard.

3

Working with Windows

Almost everything you do with your iMac happens within a *window*. A *Finder window* displays the contents of a disk or folder; a *document window* displays the contents of the document. In this chapter, you will learn how to:

- Identify the parts of a window
- Open, close, move, and resize a window
- Scroll through the contents of a window
- Change the way in which the contents of a Finder window are viewed
- Distinguish between Finder windows, document windows, dialog boxes, and alerts

Understanding the Parts of a Window

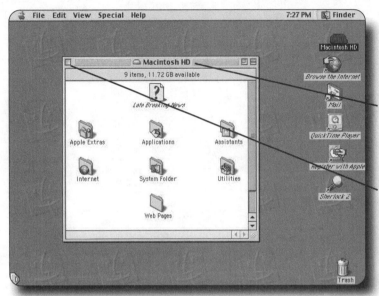

Finder windows and standard document windows have many things in common.

- **Title bar**. The *title bar* is the strip along the top of the window that contains the name of the window.

- **Close box**. The *close box* can be found at the far-left edge of the title bar. You click on the close box to close the window.

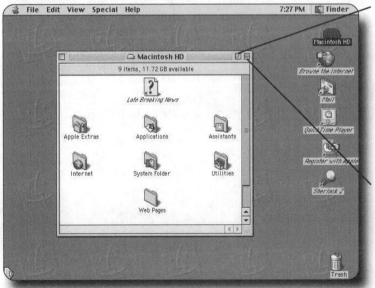

- **Zoom box**. The *zoom box* is the leftmost square at the right edge of the title bar. You click on the zoom box to expand the window to show all items in the window. Click on it again to return the window to its original size.

- **Rollup box**. The *rollup box,* also called the *window shade,* is found at the right edge of the title bar. You click on the rollup box to hide the entire window except its title bar. Click on it again to show the full window.

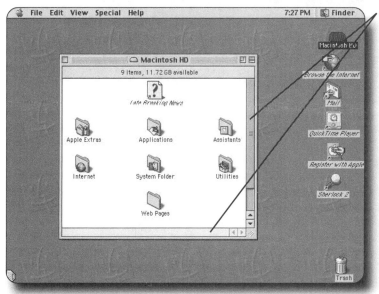

- **Scroll bars**. A window can have a *vertical scroll bar* and a *horizontal* scroll bar, both of which are used to bring hidden portions of the window's contents into view.

TIP

The scroll bar area is grey when everything inside a window is visible.

- **Up and down arrows**. The *up and down arrows* found in a scroll bar also help bring parts of a window's contents into view. Click and hold on the up or down arrow to scroll through a window one line at a time.

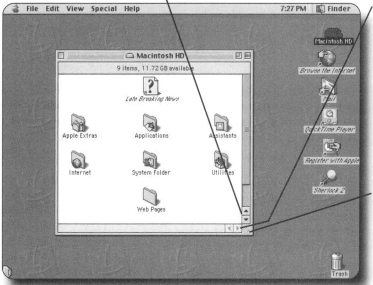

- **Left and right arrows**. The *left and right arrows* found in a scroll bar also help bring parts of a window's contents into view. Click and hold the left or right arrow to scroll through a window sideways.

- **Size box.** The *size box* is the lower-right corner of the window. You drag it to resize the window. As you drag, the top-left corner of the window is fixed in place.

Opening a Finder Window

The programs that run on your iMac are usually stored on your hard drive or on a CD-ROM. To open the disk containing the program you want to run, open a Finder window on the Desktop.

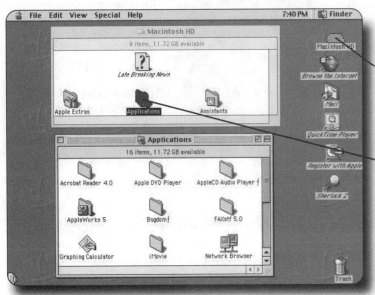

1. Double-click on the **Macintosh HD icon**. The files and folders on the hard disk will appear in a window.

2. Double-click on the **Applications folder** in the Macintosh HD window. The folder will open into another window, displaying its contents.

NOTE

You can also open a document by double-clicking on its icon on the Desktop. The program used to create the document automatically opens. You will learn more about opening applications in Chapter 8, "Working with AppleWorks."

Making a Window Active

The Mac OS allows you to have many windows open at once. However, you can work with only one window at a time—the *active window*. All other open windows are *inactive*.

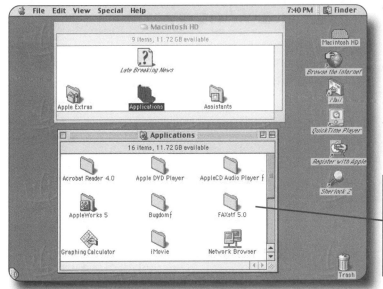

The active window always appears on top of all other open windows. An active window has horizontal lines in its title bar and its scroll bars are filled in. An inactive window has a gray title bar and empty scroll bars.

TIP

To make a window active, click anywhere on the window.

Closing a Window

You can have many windows open at a time, but your Desktop will become very cluttered if you don't close some windows when you finish with them.

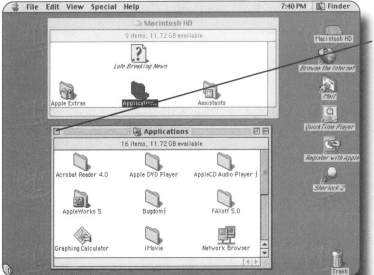

1. Click on the window's **close box**. The window will close.

TIP

You can also close a window by pressing the key combination Command+W.

Moving a Window

Windows can overlap one another on the iMac screen. You may want to move a window to make its contents easier to see.

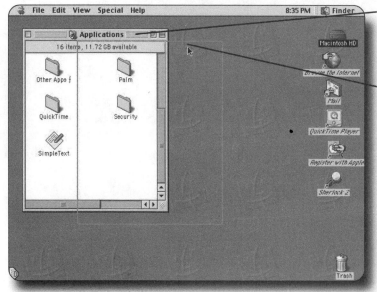

1. **Click** on the **window** you want to move. The window will become active.

2. **Click** on the **title bar** and **drag** the **window** to its new location. As you drag, an outline of the window will follow the mouse pointer.

3. **Release** the **mouse button.** The window will appear in its new location.

Resizing a Window

There are two ways to resize a window; one gives you complete control over the resulting size, whereas the other makes the window as big as possible.

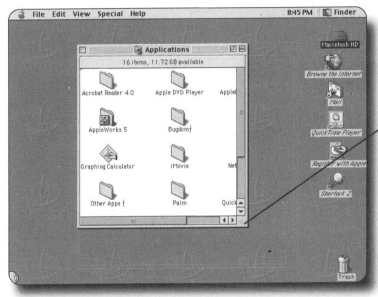

Using the Size Box

Using the size box is the most precise way to resize a window.

1. **Drag** the **lower-right corner** of the window in any direction. An outline of the window will become larger or smaller as you drag.

2. **Release** the **mouse button.** The window will be resized.

Zooming a Window

Clicking on the zoom box that appears at the far right of a window's title bar resizes the window to fill the entire screen. Ideally, the window is large enough at full screen size so that you can see its entire contents without scrolling. Click the zoom box a second time to return the window to its original size.

1. **Click** on the **zoom box**. The window will be resized either to show all its contents without scrolling or, if the entire contents won't fit on the screen, to fill the entire screen.

2. **Click** on the **zoom box again**. The window will return to its original size.

Using Pop-up Windows

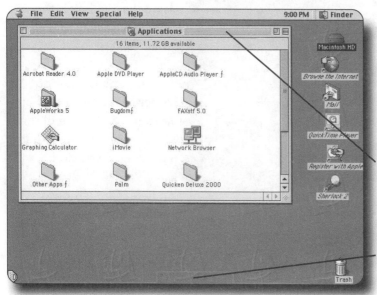

If you want a Finder window to be out of the way but easily accessible, you can turn it into a pop-up window at the bottom of the screen. You can also expand the window back to its original size.

1. Drag the window's **title bar** to the bottom of the Desktop screen. You will see an outline of a tab.

2. Release the **mouse button**. The tab will appear at the bottom of the screen.

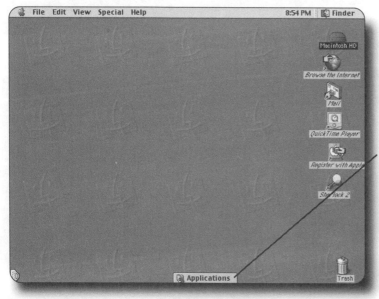

Expanding a Pop-up Window

Once you have created a pop-up window, opening it is simple.

1. Click on the **tab**. The pop-up window will expand. Its title will appear as a tab at the top of the window.

TIP

To return a pop-up window to a tab at the bottom of the screen, just click on the tab again.

Changing a Pop-up Window into a Regular Window

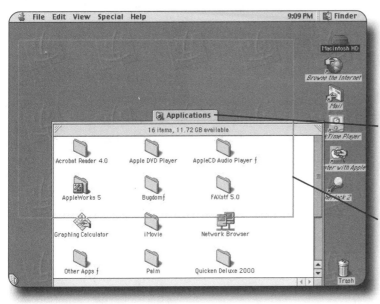

When you are through working with a window as a pop-up window, you can change it back to a regular window.

1. Drag the window's **tab** until an outline of the window is visible on the screen.

2. Release the **mouse button**. The window will appear as a regular window.

Rolling up a Window

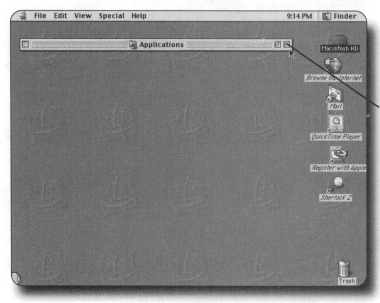

Another way to keep a window out of the way without closing it is to roll it up into a window shade.

1. **Click** on the **rollup box**. The window will roll up, leaving only its title bar visible.

2. **Click** on the **rollup box** again. The window will return to its original size.

Special Types of Windows

The windows that you have seen so far have all been either standard Finder windows or document windows. However, the iMac has two additional types of windows that you will encounter frequently: dialog boxes and alerts.

Dialog Boxes

A *dialog box* is a window that tells you something or asks you to make a choice among various options. Dialog boxes usually have buttons to click on indicating what action will be taken.

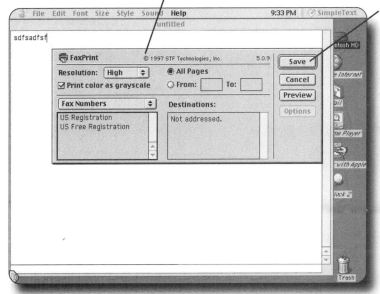

In most cases, there is a button with a heavy outline. This is the *default* button. A default button is usually the most common choice. You select the default button by clicking on it with the mouse pointer or by pressing either the Return or Enter keys. Usually a Cancel button that allows you to cancel the dialog and the action is also included.

Alerts

An *alert* is a window, similar to a dialog box, which displays a warning or notifies you that something has happened. The alert is usually accompanied by a sound from the computer's speaker (the *system beep*).

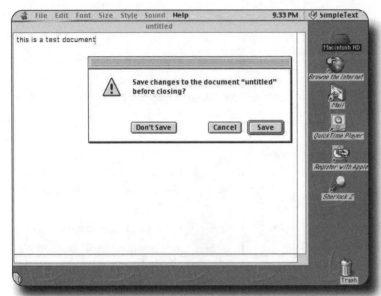

You must remove an alert from the screen before you can perform any another action on your iMac. Clicking on one of the choices removes the alert.

NOTE

If you leave an alert on your iMac screen without closing it for a short period of time, the iMac will read the contents of the alert aloud.

4

Using Menus

A *menu* is a list of options from which you can choose. By clicking on menu options, you can tell your iMac to perform a command or change a program's setting. In this chapter, you will learn how to:

- Make menu choices
- Use Command-key combinations for menu choices
- Use the items in the Apple menu
- Work with pop-up menus
- Work with contextual menus

Working with the Menu Bar

Nearly all iMac programs have a single menu bar across the top of the screen. (The exception is some games, which hide the menu bar until you press some key combination.) The leftmost three menus are nearly identical in almost all programs. Any remaining menus are specific to the program in which you are working.

Working with Standard Mac OS Menus

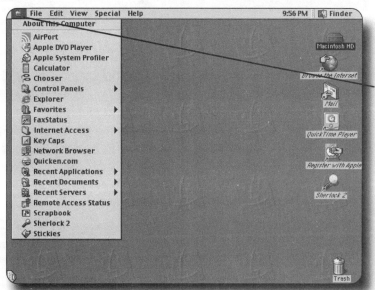

From the left, the three standard Mac OS menus are as follows:

- **Apple menu**. The Apple menu is always at the far-left edge of the menu bar. The options in the Apple menu are the same regardless of the program with which you are working. You will read much more about this menu later in this chapter.

NOTE

The first item in the Apple menu is usually the "About box" for the active program. When in the Finder, About This Computer is the first item. You can find out the version number of the active program from the About box.

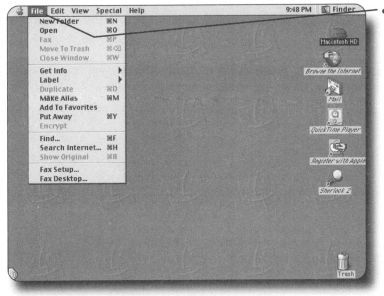

- **File menu.** The File menu contains options with which to manage files, such as creating new documents, opening documents, or printing documents. Although the specific contents of the menu change from one program to another, the File menu is always just to the right of the Apple menu.

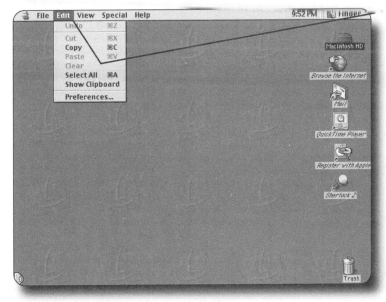

- **Edit menu.** The Edit menu contains options that allow you to edit parts of a document. The first two sections of the menu are the same in most programs (Undo, Cut, Copy, Paste, and Clear). You will learn to use these options throughout this book.

The Undo command always reverses the last action you did, such as retyping the last text you deleted, or removing the last paste you performed.

The Cut command removes the item you selected, such as text or a piece of a picture.

The Copy command creates a copy of the item you selected, which can then be placed elsewhere using the Paste command. Only one item can be copied at a time.

The Paste command inserts copied or cut items into a document.

NOTE

If you look at the File and Edit menus, you will notice that some of the options are followed by ellipses (...). This indicates that a dialog box with extra options will appear when that menu option is chosen.

Making Menu Choices

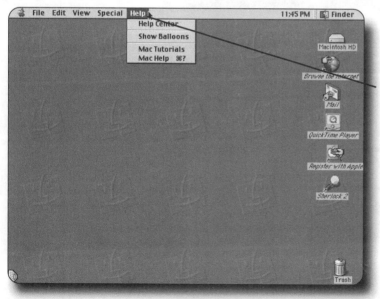

The most common way to choose an option from a menu is to use the mouse.

1. **Click** on **Help**. The Help menu will appear.

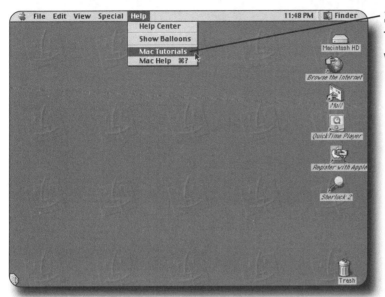

2. Click on **Mac Tutorials**. The Mac Tutorials window will open.

TIP

If you have never used a mouse before, it is recommended that you click on the Desktop Skills tutorial and complete the exercises.

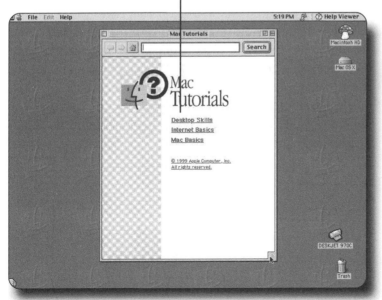

3. Click on **File.** The File menu will appear.

4. Click on **Close.** The Mac Tutorials window will close.

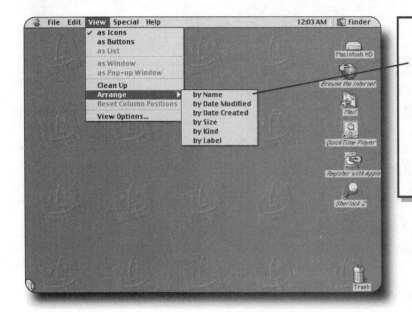

NOTE

Related menu options are often grouped under a single heading and then displayed as a *submenu*. Menu options that have submenus have a right arrow next to them.

Working with Command-Key Combinations

As you become familiar with using your mouse, you might find that choosing menu options with it takes too long. A *command-key combination* allows you to press a key or combination of keys to make a quick menu selection. You may remember from Chapter 1, "Getting Started with Your iMac," that there are four modifier keys on the iMac keyboard. One or more of these keys can be combined with any of the other keys on the keyboard to produce a useful shortcut.

- The Command key

- The Option key

- The Control key

- The Shift key

You can see the key combinations that are available by looking at each menu. The key combinations are visible at the right edge of each menu item.

TIP

To make a menu selection using a command-key combination, press and hold the needed modifier key(s) and then press the associated letter, number, symbol, or function key. Some key combinations are consistent for all Macintosh programs. For example, Command+Q always quits the program in which you are currently working.

Using the Apple Menu

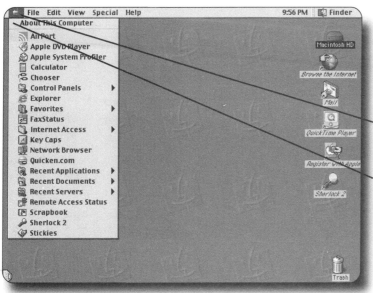

The Apple menu lists programs and documents that you may need to access regardless of the application in which you are working.

1. Click on the **Apple icon**. The Apple menu will appear.

2. Click on **About This Computer**. The About This Computer window will appear.

3. **Read** the **information** provided, as it contains useful facts about your computer. You can see which operating system version you are running, how much memory is installed, and how much room on your drive is filled.

4. **Click** on the **close box**. The About This Computer window will close.

The Apple DVD Player

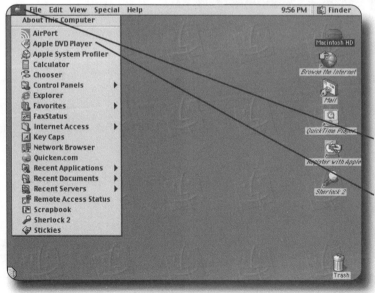

iMac computers with DVD-ROM drives installed come with the Apple DVD Player installed in the Apple menu. These iMacs can play DVD movies.

1. **Click** on the **Apple icon**. The Apple menu will appear.

2. **Click** on **Apple DVD Player**. The DVD Controller will appear.

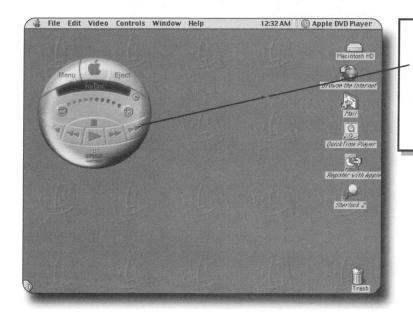

File Edit Video Controls Window Help   12:32 AM   Apple DVD Player

Menu   Eject

No Disc

NOTE

None of the options
in the Apple DVD
Player are available
unless a DVD is in the
DVD-ROM drive.

Macintosh HD

Browse the Internet

Mail

QuickTime Player

Register with Apple

Sherlock 2

Trash

Playing a DVD Movie

Look in your iMac box and find the DVD movie *A Bug's Life*,
which is shipped with the iMac DV.

1. Carefully **remove** the **DVD disc** from its case and insert
it into the slot on the front of your iMac.

TIP

The controls on the DVD Controller work the same
way as on a typical VCR; they are just presented in a
more artistic way. Use the forward arrow to play and
the two bars to stop the DVD movie. The play/stop
button toggles back and forth.

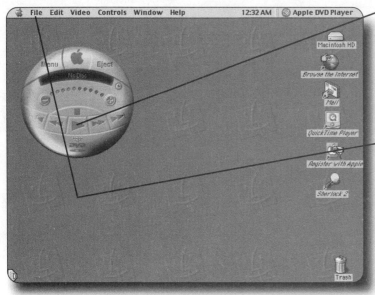

2. **Click** on the **Play button**. The DVD Viewer will open and the movie will begin.

3. **Click** on the **Stop button** when you are done.

4. **Click** on **File**. The File menu will appear.

5. **Click** on **Quit**. The DVD Controller and the movie will close.

The Apple System Profiler

The Apple System Profiler contains useful information about your iMac, such as the model name and number, version number of your system software, amount of memory, and the processor speed. You may be asked for this kind of technical information if you ever need to call in for Apple's technical support.

1. **Click** on the **Apple icon** on the menu bar. The Apple menu will appear.

2. **Click** on **Apple System Profiler**. The Apple System Profiler window will appear.

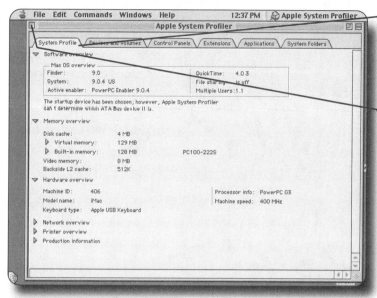

3. **Click** on the **tabs** to see detailed information about your iMac. The tabs will move to the front.

4. **Click** on the **close box.** The Apple System Profiler window will close.

The Calculators

The Mac OS is accompanied by two calculators—one that is easy to use but limited in function and another that is extremely powerful but rather complex. The simple calculator is in your Apple menu; the Graphing Calculator is stored in the Applications folder.

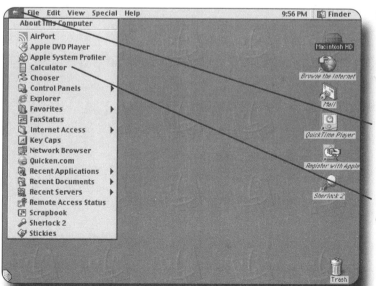

1. **Click** on the **Apple icon** on the menu bar. The Apple menu will appear.

2. **Click** on **Calculator**. The Calculator will appear.

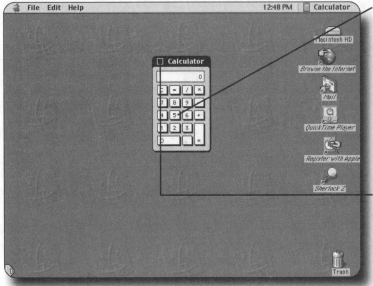

3. **Click** on the **Calculator buttons** with the mouse pointer. The results of your calculations appear at the top of the Calculator window. You can also use the numeric keypad on the right side of your keyboard to enter numbers.

4. **Click** on the **close box.** The Calculator will close.

NOTE

The Graphing Calculator is a very powerful program that can handle exponents, compute square roots, solve algebraic equations, and graph polynomials. You can copy and paste the calculated results into any document.

The Chooser

The Chooser is the application that allows you to select a printer. You must choose your printer prior to printing for the first time.

1. Click on the **Apple icon.** The Apple menu will appear.

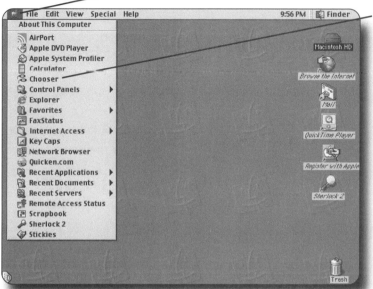

2. Click on **Chooser**. The Chooser window will appear.

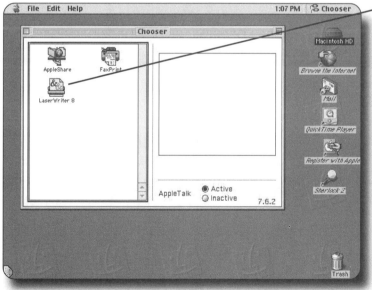

3. Click on a **printer icon** in the left side of the window. The printer icon will be highlighted.

4. Click on the **close box.** The Chooser window will close.

Favorites

The Favorites folder stores aliases of applications, documents, and Internet locations you use frequently. You can access these aliases quickly from the Favorites submenu.

1. **Click** on an **icon** on the Desktop. The icon will be highlighted.

2. **Click** on **File.** The File menu will appear.

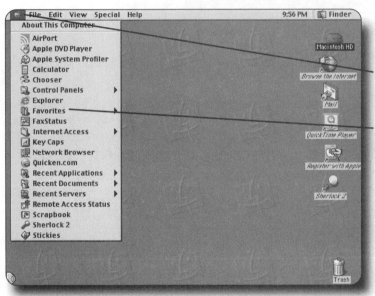

3. **Click** on **Add to Favorites**.

4. **Click** on the **Apple icon**. The Apple menu will appear.

5. **Click** on **Favorites**. The Favorites window will appear.

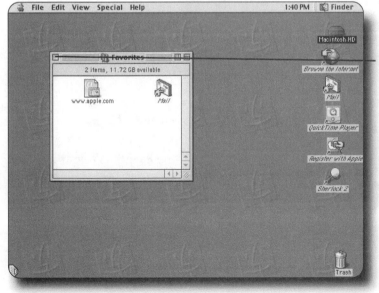

You will see an alias of the icon you selected.

6. **Click** on the **close box.** The Favorites window will close.

Key Caps

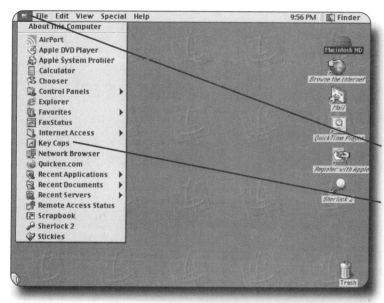

Using the Key Caps program, you can modify the keys on your keyboard to represent other symbols—Greek letters or even small images—for example.

1. **Click** on the **Apple icon**. The Apple menu will appear.

2. **Click** on **Key Caps.**

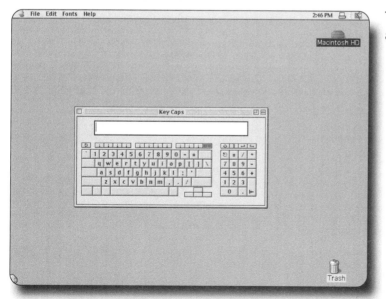

The Key Caps window will appear.

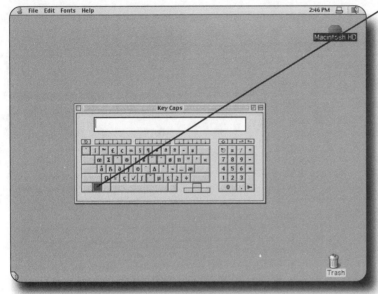

3. Press the **Option key** on your keyboard. The Key Caps display will change to show you the characters that would appear if they were pressed in conjunction with the Option key.

Take some time to see what effect each of the different modifier keys have on the characters.

4. Click on the **close box.** The Key Caps window will close.

NOTE

Changing the appearance of text is discussed in Chapter 8, "Working with AppleWorks."

The Network Browser

The Network Browser is used to access other computers on your network or to connect to your Internet server.

1. **Click** on the **Apple icon.** The Apple menu will appear.

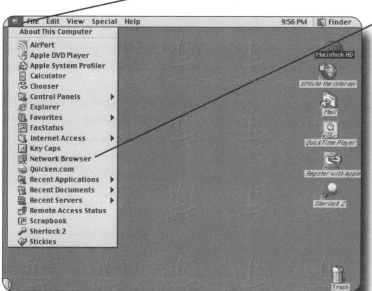

2. **Click** on **Network Browser**. The Network window will appear. If you arc on a network, you will see an AppleTalk icon.

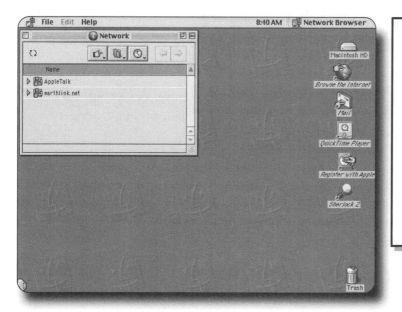

NOTE

If you have Earthlink installed, your computer automatically dials into the EarthLink network when the Network Browser is opened. You can disconnect by choosing Remote Access Status from the Apple menu and clicking on Cancel.

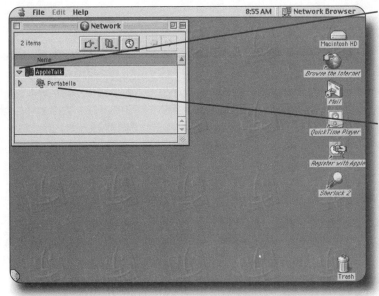

3. **Click** on the **arrow** to the left of the AppleTalk icon. You will see the names of any other computers connected to your network.

4. **Double-click** on the **computer name** or server to which you want to connect. A file server connect dialog box will open.

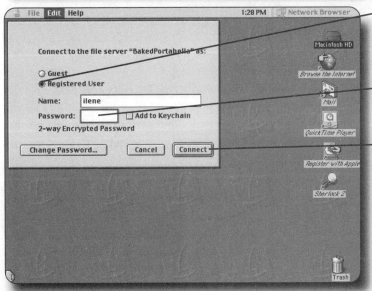

5. **Click** on the **Registered User radio button.** The radio button will be selected.

6. **Type** your **password** into the Password text box.

7. **Click** on **Connect.** A connection will be established and the other computer will appear as an icon on your Desktop.

NOTE

You can buy a simple crossover Ethernet cable to connect most older Macintosh computers to your new iMac. You can transfer files from one machine to another using the Network Browser to establish a connection.

Working with Recently Used Items

The Apple menu includes three submenus—Recent Applications, Recent Documents, and Recent Servers—that provide quick access to items that you've recently used.

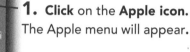

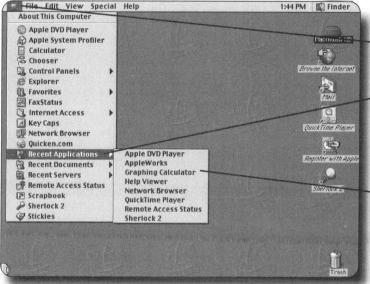

1. **Click** on the **Apple icon.** The Apple menu will appear.

2. **Move** the **mouse pointer** to Recent Applications. A submenu will appear.

3. **Click** on the **application** that you wish to open. The application will launch.

NOTE

You can modify the number of items that appear in the submenus or even the appearance of submenus in the Apple menu. You will read about configuring the contents of the Apple menu in Chapter 6, "Customizing Your iMac."

Using Remote Access Status

Remote Access Status is used to check the status of your Internet connection. You can quickly connect to the Internet or disconnect.

1. Click on the **Apple icon**. The Apple menu will appear.

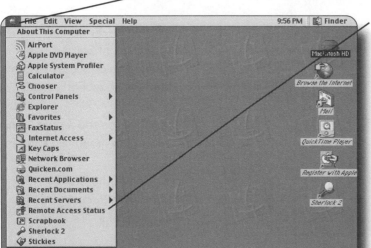

2. Click on **Remote Access Status**. The Remote Access window will open.

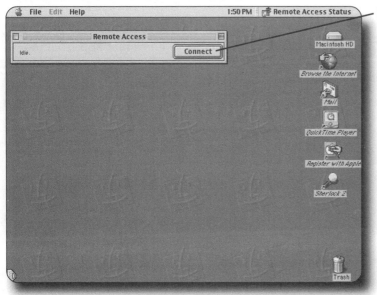

3. Click on **Connect**. Your modem will dial your Internet Service Provider and establish a connection to the Internet.

Stickies

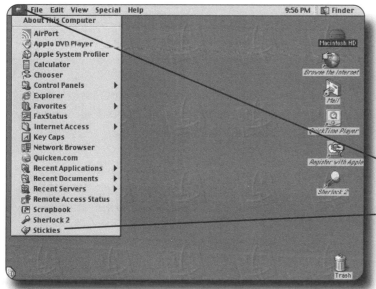

Stickies are the electronic version of a Post-It note. You can place them all over your Desktop and have them pop up automatically whenever you start up your iMac.

1. Click on the **Apple icon**. The Apple menu will appear.

2. Click on **Stickies**. Any Stickies that you have previously created will appear on the Desktop.

3. Click on **File**. The File menu will appear.

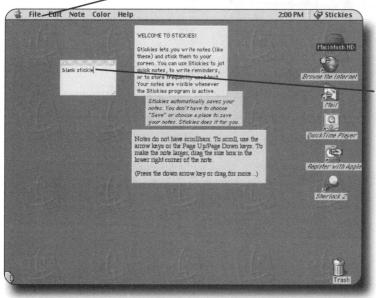

4. Click on **New Note**. A new, blank stickie will appear on the Desktop.

5. Type some text into the active Stickie.

NOTE

Stickies are really small text documents. You can use them the same way you use text files, which you will learn about in Chapter 8, "Working with AppleWorks."

6. Press Command+Q. The iMac will display an alert asking if you would like Stickies to be started automatically each time you start your computer.

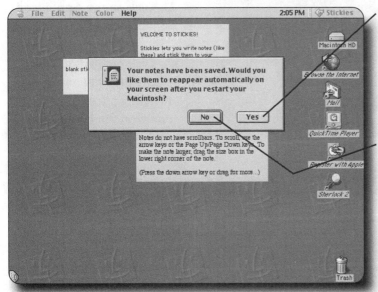

7. Click on **Yes**. Stickies will be set to start automatically every time you start up your iMac.

OR

7b. Click on **No**. Stickies will need to be activated from the Apple menu the next time you wish to use them.

TIP

To delete a stickie, click on the close box in the upper left corner. A dialog to save the stickie as a text file appears. Click on the Save or Don't Save button and continue working.

Using Pop-up Menus

A *pop-up menu* provides another way to select a single option from a list. Double arrows at the right edge of a visible menu option indicate that a pop-up menu is available.

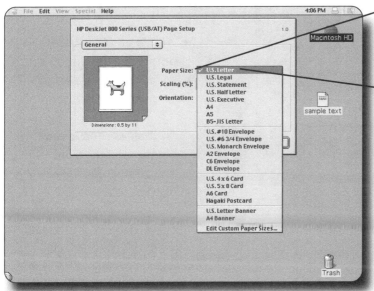

1. **Click** on the **pop-up menu**. The menu options will appear.

2. **Move** the **mouse pointer** to the option you want. The option will be highlighted.

3. **Release** the **mouse button**. Only the option you selected will appear.

Using Contextual Menus

A *contextual menu* is a pop-up menu that can appear for most items on the Desktop. The major benefit of such a menu is that you don't need to move the mouse pointer to the menu bar to gain access to commands.

1. **Move** the **mouse pointer** over the item for which you want to display a contextual menu.

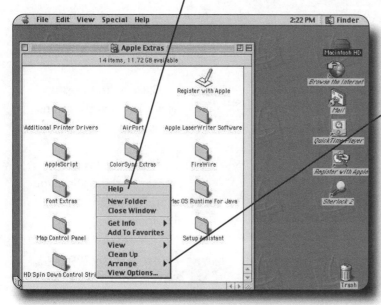

2. **Click** the **mouse button** while holding down the Control key. The contextual menu will appear.

3. **Move** the **mouse pointer** to the option you want. The menu option will be selected.

4. **Release** the **mouse button and** the **Control key**. The contextual menu will disappear.

5

Using Folders and Files

Items stored on disks or hard drives are saved as files. You'll work with and accumulate many files, so knowing how to organize them into folders and find them again is very important. In this chapter, you'll learn how to:

- Organize folders and files
- Create, open, and put items into folders
- Copy, move, and rename a file
- Delete files and folders
- Find items using Sherlock 2
- Work with aliases

It is not unusual for there to be over 10,000 files stored on your iMac's hard disk. If all those files were placed together in a single area would be extremely time consuming to locate the one that you want. The iMac has a way of organizing these files that can help get around that problem. Begin by looking at an overview of the organization used by your iMac; you'll then learn to manipulate the folders and files.

> **NOTE**
>
> The Desktop is actually a folder. On the iMac's screen, though, the hard disk appears on the Desktop. Internally, however, the iMac thinks of the Desktop as a folder on the hard disk.

Understanding Disk Organization

Each disk that the iMac can access is called a *volume.* A volume can be an entire disk or part of a larger disk, whether that is a hard disk, a Zip disk, or a CD-ROM. When a volume appears on the Desktop, it is *mounted,* that is, accessible for storing and retrieving files.

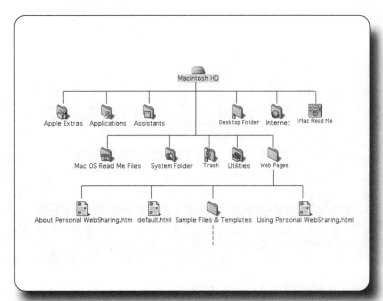

Each volume contains a hierarchy of folders and files. As you can see in the illustration, the iMac's hard disk is at the top of the hierarchy. It is the top-level container. Each level in the hierarchy can contain folders or files. A folder can hold other folders and files. You can use folders to organize the contents of any volume.

Working with Folders

Folders act as containers in which you store other folders and files on a disk. They are most commonly created and manipulated in the Finder.

NOTE

CD-ROMs have a folder and file hierarchy to organize their contents just like hard disks. However, because a CD-ROM is a read-only disc, you can open its folders but you cannot make any permanent changes to them.

Creating and Naming Folders

You open folders on all types of disks (for example, hard disks and CD-ROMs) the same way.

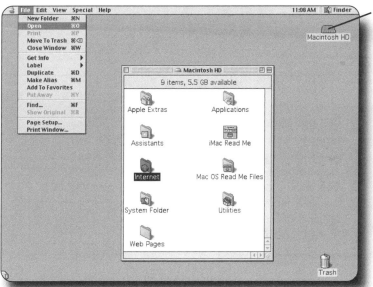

1. Double-click on the **Macintosh HD icon**. The Macintosh HD window will open.

TIP

You can use a keyboard shortcut instead of using the mouse. Simply click on the Macintosh HD icon and press Command+O.

You can create folders on the hard disk to help you organize your files at any time. Give folders names that reflect their contents to make it easier to remember where you have stored things.

2. **Click** on **File**. The File menu will appear.

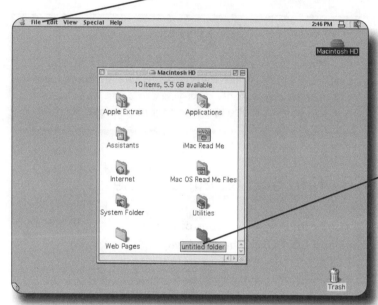

3. **Click** on **New**. A new folder will appear with the name "untitled folder." The characters in the name will be highlighted and a rectangle will appear around the name.

4. **Type** a **name** for the folder. Your typing will replace the highlighted text.

5. **Press Return**. The new name will appear.

TIP

To rename a hard disk, folder, or file, click on its name, wait a few seconds for a rectangle to appear around the name, then type the new name in the box. You cannot rename a hard disk when file sharing is turned on.

NOTE

File and folder names can contain any characters except a colon and can be up to 32 characters long. Slash (/) characters are not recommended because they confuse some programs. File names cannot start with a period. Names must also be unique within a folder. This means that you can have more than one file or folder with the same name as long as they are inside different folders.

Moving Files and Folders around

The organization of a hard disk is not fixed except for those items in the System Folder. You can move items into and out of folders as needed.

Dragging

The easiest way to put an existing file or folder inside another folder is to drag it there.

1. Drag the **file** or **folder** onto a folder's icon. The folder's icon will be highlighted. The item being moved will still appear in its original location and a gray version of the file or folder will appear over the destination folder.

2. Release the **mouse button**. The file or folder will appear in its new location.

NOTE

When the destination is on the same volume as the file or folder's original location, the Mac OS actually *moves* a dragged file or folder. But if you move a file to a different volume, the iMac *copies* the item being moved, leaving the item unchanged in its original location. Do not forget to delete the original item, unless you want two copies of your file or folder. To make a copy of an item in a different folder on the same volume, hold down the Option key when you drag the item to its new location.

Spring-Loaded Folders

When something is stored many levels down in a folder hierarchy, it can be awkward to open all the folders until you reach the one you want. The Mac OS provides *spring-loaded folders*, which open automatically as you drag.

1. **Drag** the **folder** or **file** you want to move onto the top folder in the destination hierarchy. The folder will be highlighted.

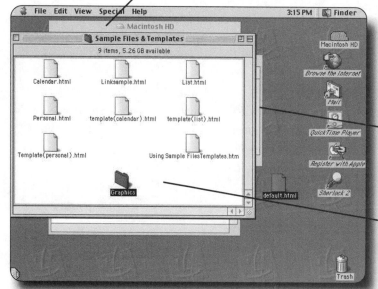

2. **Hold** the **folder** or **file** in place for a couple of seconds. The folder underneath it will automatically open.

3. **Drag** the **folder** or **file** on top of the next folder in the hierarchy. The folder will open after a few seconds.

4. **Repeat steps 2** and **3** until the item being moved is over the folder that will be its final destination.

5. **Release** the **mouse button**. All the folders that sprung open while you were dragging will close.

NOTE

Using the spring-loaded folder feature can take a bit of practice. If it doesn't work for you, don't worry. Come back and try it again when you have spent more time with your iMac. If you accidentally open a folder, simply drag the file outside that folder's window, and the incorrect folder will close.

Changing the Way You See the Contents of a Folder

Up until this point, all of the Finder windows you have seen have shown you large icons for the items within a folder. However, big icons, as attractive as they can be, aren't a very efficient use of window space. The iMac lets you change the way in which you display folder contents.

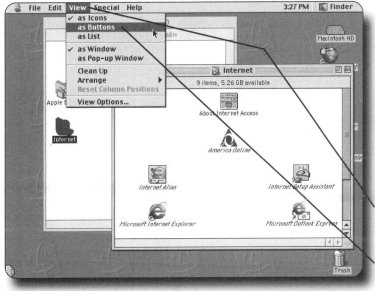

As Buttons

To view the items in a folder as buttons, open the folder and follow these steps:

1. Click on **View**. The View menu will appear.

2. Click on **as Buttons**. The icons in the window will change to buttons and a check will appear by the as Buttons option in the View menu. Each item in the window can now be opened with a single click.

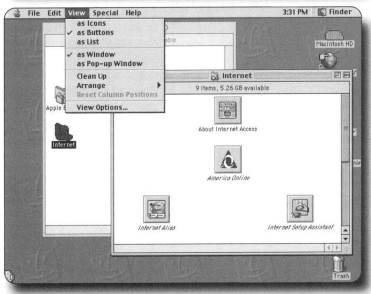

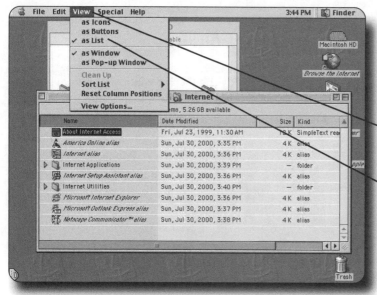

As List

To see the items in a folder as a list, open the folder and follow these steps:

1. **Click** on **View**. The view menu will appear.

2. **Click** on **as List**. The icons in the window will change to a list and a check will appear by the as List option in the View menu.

A List view provides much more information about the contents of a folder. By default, you see the date on which the item was last modified, the size of a file, and the type of file.

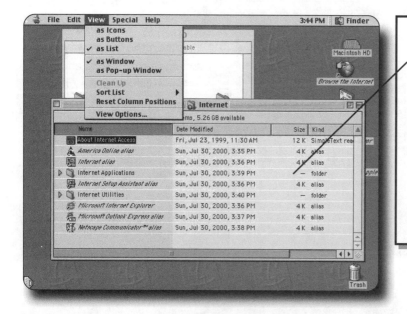

NOTE

You can also set the iMac to display the size of a *folder* in the View Options. However, doing so significantly slows the speed of your iMac because it has to calculate each folder size. It is better to leave that option turned off.

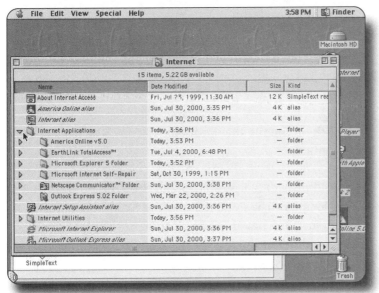

To expand a folder shown in List view, click on the right arrow just to the left of the folder's name. The List view will expand to include the contents of the folder. To collapse an expanded List view of a folder's contents, click on the down arrow to the left of the folder's name.

NOTE

You can change the way you view the contents of CD-ROM windows, but the change is temporary. The next time you use the disc, you will notice that the folders have returned to their original view.

Working with Files

A file is a document (for example, a letter, a graphics image, or a database) or a program (instructions that the computer can follow). The iMac distinguishes between these two types of files by calling them *documents* and *applications* (or *programs*). A document is a file that you create with a program.

Copying a File

Copying a file is very much like copying a folder. The following procedure applies to copying a file on the same volume.

1. Click on the **file** that you want to copy. The file will be highlighted.

2. Hold down the **option key** and **drag** the original file to a new location. The iMac will give the file the same name as the original. You now have two copies of the same file stored in different folders.

Copying a File within a Folder

Making a copy of a file within the same folder requires a slightly different procedure.

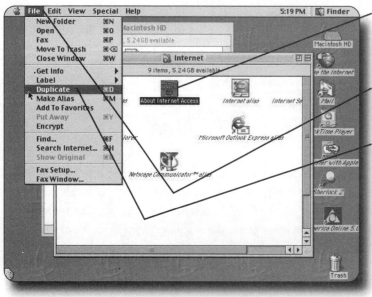

1. Click on the **file** that you want to copy. The file will be highlighted.

2. Click on **File**. The File menu will appear.

3. Click on **Duplicate**. The iMac will make a copy of the file and add "copy" to the file name.

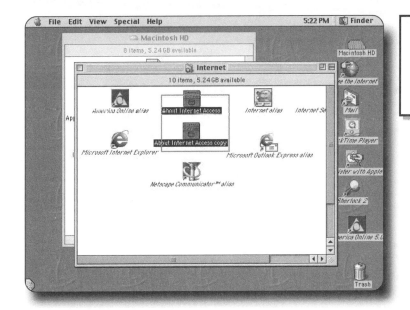

TIP

You can also make a copy of a file by pressing Command+D.

Deleting Files and Folders

When you no longer need a file or folder, you can delete it from a volume. There are several important things to consider before you delete a file or folder:

- Once an item has been deleted, you can't undelete it without special software such as Norton Utilities or Tech Tool Pro. Such software is only somewhat successful, and if you have modified another file or saved a new file on the disk after performing the delete, recovery of a deleted file is nearly impossible.

- Deletion does not actually erase a file. The iMac merely marks the space used by the deleted file as available for reuse. Once the space is reused, you can no longer recover the file.

- When you delete a folder, you also delete all of its contents.

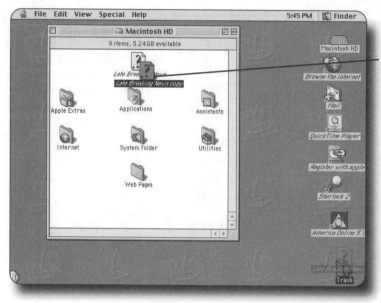

Deleting a File

1. Drag the **file** that you want to delete to the Trash icon on the Desktop. If the Trash was empty, the icon will change into a full trash can.

TIP

You can also move an item to the Trash by clicking on the item and then pressing Command+Delete.

---

2. Click on **Special**. The Special menu will appear.

3. Click on **Empty Trash**. An alert will appear asking you to confirm the deletion.

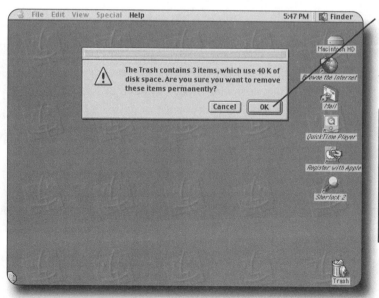

4. Click on **OK**. The iMac will complete the deletion and the Trash icon will return to its empty state.

NOTE

If you drag a CD-ROM icon to the Trash, the iMac removes the icon from the Desktop and ejects the disc.

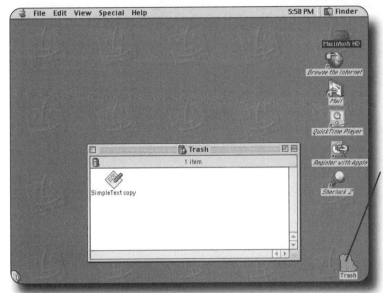

Removing Items from the Trash

If you have not emptied the Trash, you can return whatever is in the Trash to its original location.

1. Double-click on the **Trash icon**. The Trash window will open.

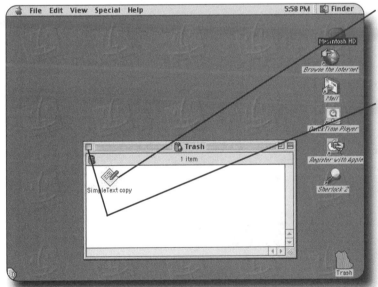

2. Drag the **item** out of the Trash folder to the Desktop. The item will appear in the new location.

3. Click on the **close box.** The Trash folder will close.

TIP

You can place an item back in its original location by clicking on it to select it and then choosing Put Away from the File menu, or by pressing Command+Y.

Finding Files and Folders Using Sherlock 2

Even if you give files and folders meaningful names you may sometimes misplace them. The iMac has a program called Sherlock 2 that can search all mounted volumes to look for files and folders. Mac OS 8.6 and below use Sherlock, while Mac OS 9.0 and above use Sherlock 2.

Performing a Search

It is easy to search for a file or folder by name with Sherlock.

1. **Click** on the **Apple icon**. The Apple menu will appear.

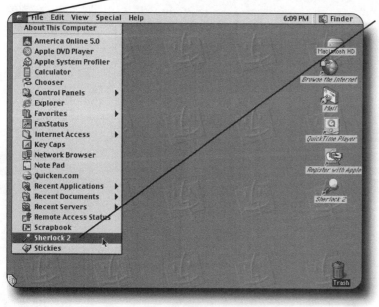

2. **Click** on **Sherlock 2**. Sherlock 2 will appear.

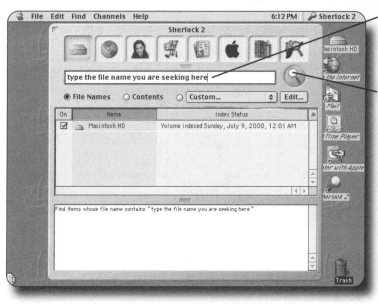

3. Type any part of the **file name or folder name** you want to find in the text box.

4. Click on the **Magnifying glass icon**. Sherlock 2 will perform the search and display the results.

Using the Results of a Search

Once Sherlock 2 has found files and folders with names containing the text you entered, you can do several things.

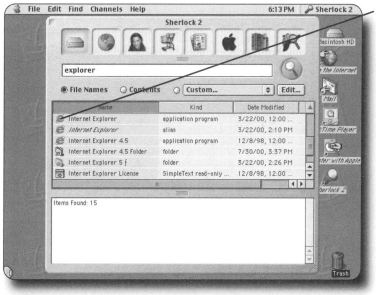

1. Click on the **file** or **folder** in the search result box to find out where it is located on the hard drive. The bottom box will show where the file is on the hard disk.

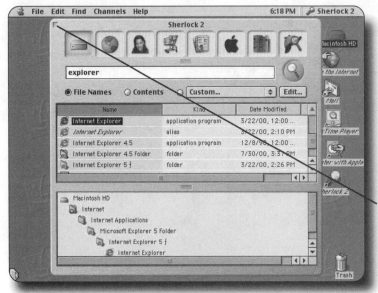

TIP

If you double-click on the file or folder the iMac either opens the folder's window on the Desktop or opens the document using the program that created it.

2. Click on the **close box** when you are finished with your search. Sherlock 2 will close.

Using Aliases

An *alias* is a placeholder that points to the actual location of a file or folder. Once you create an alias, you can leave the original file or folder in its current location and place the alias somewhere that is more convenient to access. For example, you might place an alias of a frequently-used file or folder on the Desktop.

Creating an Alias

Making aliases is very simple and using them will make using your iMac much more convenient.

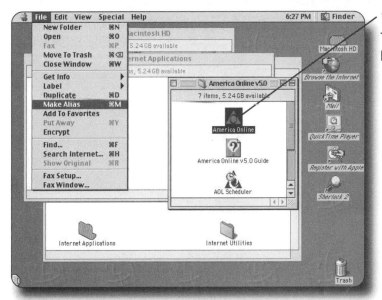

1. Click on a **file** or **folder**. The file or folder will be highlighted.

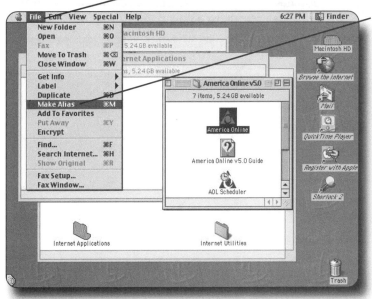

2. Click on **File**. The File menu will appear.

3. Click on **Make Alias**. The iMac will create an alias with "alias" added to the file name. The alias' file name will be highlighted so that it can be easily renamed. All alias file names appear in italics.

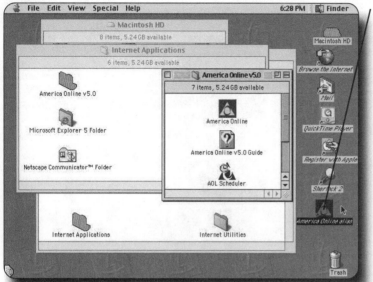

To open and use an alias, just double-click on it.

NOTE

You can rename or move the alias at any time without affecting the original. However, if you move or rename the original to which an alias points you should delete the old alias and create a new one.

6

Customizing Your iMac

The iMac's operating system is designed to let you personalize your working environment. For example, you can change the color or pattern of the Desktop, the volume of the speakers, and the way in which software acts. In this chapter, you'll learn how to:

- Use control panels to configure your system
- Customize the contents of the Apple menu
- Enable and disable extensions with the Extensions Manager

Introducing Control Panels

Control panels are small programs that let you to configure software. Usually, the customized settings are stored in a Preferences file, which is found in the Preferences folder inside the System folder.

Control panels load into your computer's memory when it boots and appear as icons, which you see loading across the bottom of your screen. Control panels can be found in the Control Panels folder inside the System folder, but there is a much easier way to access them—through the Apple Menu.

Exactly what appears in the Control Panels submenu depends on what is inside of the Control Panels folder.

Using Basic Control Panels

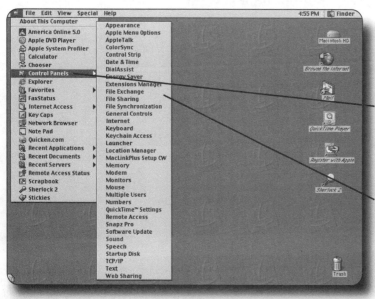

In this section, you'll be introduced to the control panels that configure the look and feel of your iMac.

1. Choose Control Panels from the Apple menu. The Control Panels submenu will appear.

2. Click on a **control panel** in the submenu. The control panel you selected will appear.

3. Click on the **close box**. The control panel will close.

Setting General Controls

The General Controls cover system-wide preferences, such as the rate of cursor and menu blinking, where files are stored automatically, warning you when your computer wasn't shut down properly, and whether your System Folder is protected. These preferences can be changed at any time.

1. Choose General Controls from the Control Panels submenu of the Apple menu. The General Controls control panel will open.

You can control several aspects of the iMac environment from this control panel:

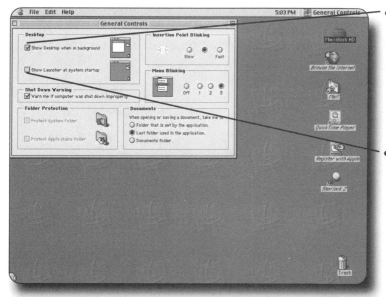

- The Show Desktop when in background check box lets you choose whether the icons on the Desktop are visible when you are working with another application.

- The Show Launcher at sytem startup check box determines whether the *Launcher* appears when you start your iMac.

NOTE

The Launcher helps you personalize your iMac by giving you quick access to the programs you use frequently.

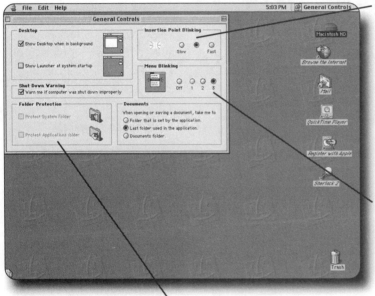

- The Insertion Point Blinking radio buttons control the flashing rate of the insertion point, which is seen when working in text or word processing programs. The sample blinking cursor on the left shows how fast you've set the blink rate.

- The Menu Blinking radio buttons control the rate at which menu options blink when selected. The sample menu shows what the blinking rate looks like.

- The Folder Protection check boxes prevent changes to the contents of the System Folder and/or the Applications folder. When checked, padlocks appear on the chosen folders.

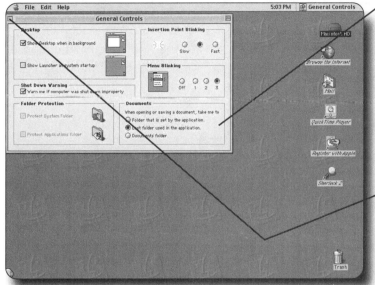

• The Documents radio buttons set the default folder used by a program the first time an Open File or Save File dialog box is displayed. These settings can really help you keep the documents you create organized.

2. **Click** on the **close box**. The General Controls control panel will close and automatically save your settings.

NOTE

All control panel setting changes are saved into a file located in the Preferences folder inside the System Folder.

Adjusting Your Mouse Settings

If using your mouse seems difficult at first, you can modify the dragging speed and clicking tempo by accessing the Mouse control panel. Remember to hold the round mouse so that the cord is at the top when it is on the mouse pad. Even though the round mouse is pictured, this control panel works with any mouse.

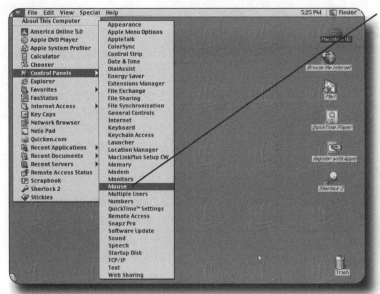

1. Choose Mouse from the Control Panels submenu of the Apple menu. The Mouse control panel will open.

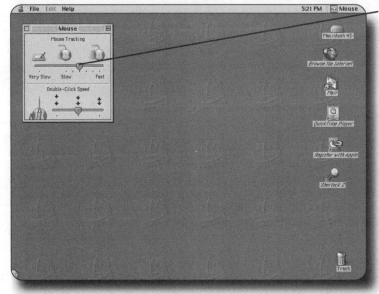

2. Drag the **Mouse Tracking slider**. You will notice that your mouse pointer will speed up or slow down. Choose the speed of mouse movement across the screen that is most comfortable to you.

NOTE

If you find that your mouse is moving too fast when you select text while typing, then slow the mouse tracking down. iMacs are so fast that sometimes it is easier to work with the mouse tracking set to a slower speed.

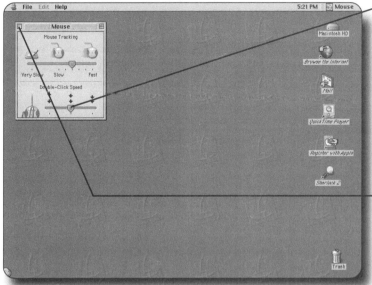

3. **Drag** the **Double-Click Speed slider.** The speed at which you must double-click for a command to be executed will be adjusted. The mouse diagram on the left shows you the speed of the double-click for each of the three choices.

4. **Click** on the **close box**. The Mouse control panel will close and automatically save your changes.

Changing the Desktop Appearance

You can have a lot of fun changing the appearance of your Desktop. The Appearance control panel allows you to customize it to your liking. You can change Desktop patterns and colors, add or remove sound, and choose system fonts.

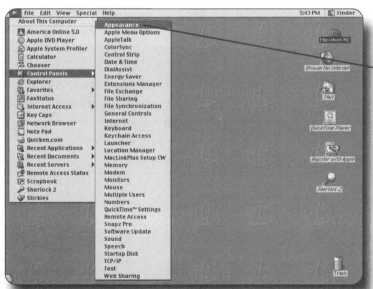

1. **Choose Appearance** from the Control Panels submenu of the Apple menu. The Appearance control panel will open.

The Appearance control panel organizes groups of Desktop settings into *themes*. You can either use one of the themes provided by the iMac or create your own custom theme. The tabs at the top of the control panel provide access to all the elements that make up a theme. When you are through with your settings, you can give your custom theme a name so that you can access all the settings as a unit.

Choosing an Existing Theme

A theme is a color and design preference which applies to all of your windows, menus, and sometimes your cursor too. Many users have developed themes you can download from the World Wide Web also. You can find other themes by searching for them at http://www.versiontracker.com, after you cover connecting to the Internet in Chapter 11, "Wandering the World Wide Web."

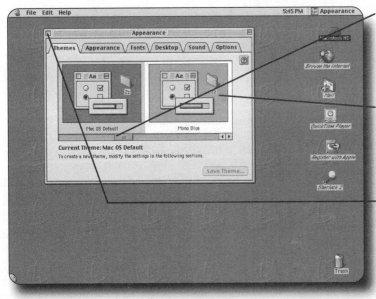

1. **Click and drag** the **scroll box** below the themes. A sample of each theme will appear as you scroll.

2. **Click** on the **sample** of the theme you want to use. The theme will be applied to your Desktop.

3. **Click** on the **close box**. The Appearance control panel will save the last theme you chose as your default theme.

OR

3b. **Keep** the **Appearance control panel** open and continue to the next section.

Creating a Custom Theme

You can create a custom theme using the other tabs of the Appearance control panel.

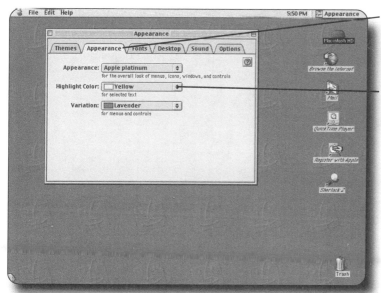

1. Click on the **Appearance tab**. The tab will move to the front.

2. Click on the **Highlight Color pop-up menu.** The pop-up menu will open.

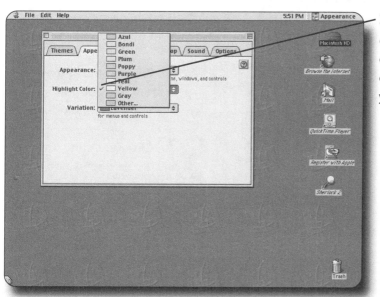

3. Click on a **color**. A check will appear by the color you chose and that color will be used whenever you select text.

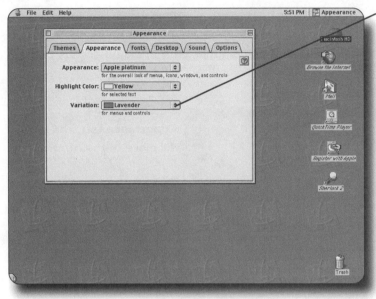

4. Click on the **Variation pop-up menu.** The pop-up menu will open.

5. Click on a **color.** A check will appear by the color you chose and that color will be used to highlight menus and controls.

Changing Theme Fonts

Under the Fonts tab, you can use pop-up menus to set which fonts you want the iMac to use for the system.

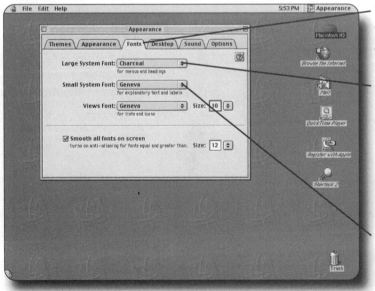

1. Click on the **Fonts tab.** The tab will move to the front.

2. Click on the **Large System Font pop-up menu.** The pop-up menu will open.

3. Click on a **font.** The font will be used for window title bars and menus.

4. Click on the **Small System Font pop-up menu.** The pop-up menu will open.

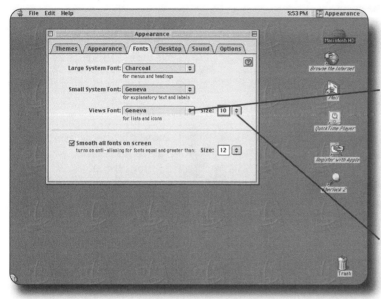

5. **Click** on a **font**. The font will be used for text and labels.

6. **Click** on the **Views Font pop-up menu**. The pop-up menu will open.

7. **Click** on a **font**. The font will be used for list view and icon names in icon view.

8. **Click** on the **Size pop-up menu**. The pop-up menu will open.

9. **Click** on the **size** of the Views font. The size will appear in the text box and the Views font will be set at the size you chose.

Changing Theme Desktop Patterns and Pictures

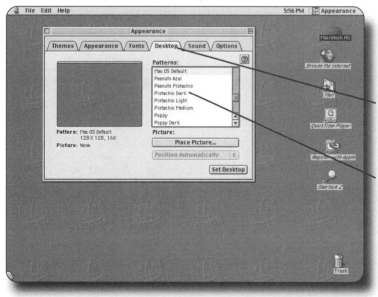

The Desktop pattern or picture you choose is an important element of your custom theme.

1. **Click** on the **Desktop tab**. The tab will move to the front.

2. **Click** on a **Desktop pattern** from the Patterns list box. A sample of the pattern will appear on the left.

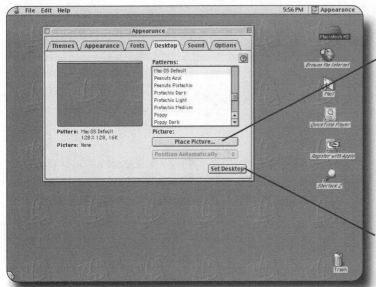

NOTE

If a desktop picture is active, you must click on Remove Picture before you can see the patterns or to place a new picture. When no desktop picture is active, the Place Picture button appears.

3. Click on **Set Desktop.** The pattern will appear on your Desktop.

TIP

You can also use a picture as the background of the Desktop. Click on Place Picture and select a picture from the list that appears from the Desktop Pictures folder. Click on Choose to return to the Desktop tab, then choose Set Desktop. To use your own photograph, just drop it into the Desktop Pictures folder inside the Appearance folder inside your System folder.

Changing Theme Sounds

Using a sound track with your theme is a great way to make using your iMac more interactive.

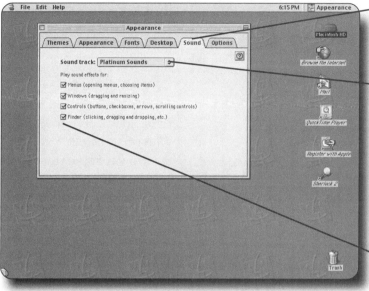

1. **Click** on the **Sound tab**. The tab will move to the front.

2. **Click** on the **Sound track pop-up menu.** The pop-up menu will open.

3. **Click** on a **sound track.** The track will be selected and you will hear the sounds while you work on your iMac.

4. **Click** in the **check boxes** for each event that you wish to hear a sound with. A check will appear in the check boxes that you select.

NOTE

You can choose None from the Sound track pop-up menu to turn off the sound effects.

Changing Theme Options

The Options tab offers some settings to make your theme more convenient to use.

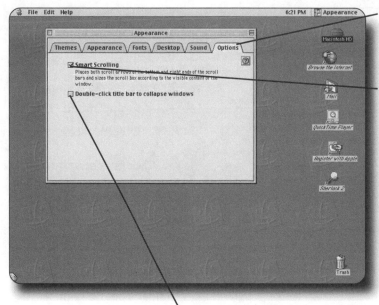

1. **Click** on the **Options tab**. The tab will move to the front.

2. **Click** in the **Smart Scrolling check box.** Smart scrolling will be turned off. With smart scrolling off, the up arrow is at the top of a vertical scroll bar and the scroll box is a small, fixed size. Leave the check box checked if you want to use smart scrolling.

3. **Click** in the **Double-click title bar to collapse windows check box**. You will be able to roll up a window by double-clicking on its title bar.

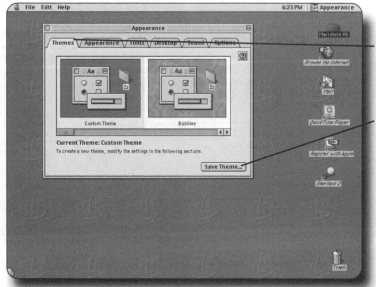

Saving Your Theme

1. **Click** on the **Themes tab.** The tab will move to the front.

2. **Click** on **Save Theme.** The Save Theme dialog box will open.

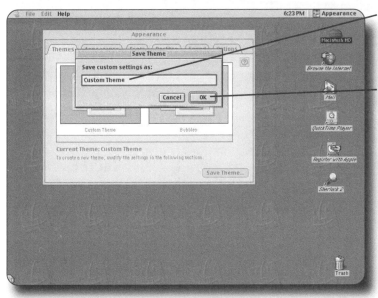

3. Type a **name** for the theme in the Save custom settings as text box.

4. Click on **OK.** The theme will be saved using the name you entered.

5. Click on the **close box.** The Appearance control panel will close.

Configuring Your Monitor

The Monitors control panel lets you change how your screen looks.

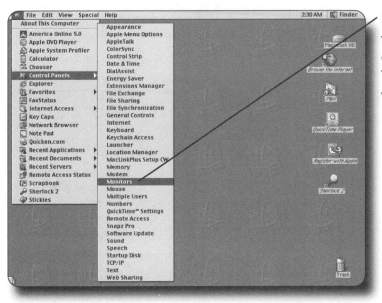

1. Choose Monitors from the Control Panels submenu of the Apple menu. The Monitors control panel will open.

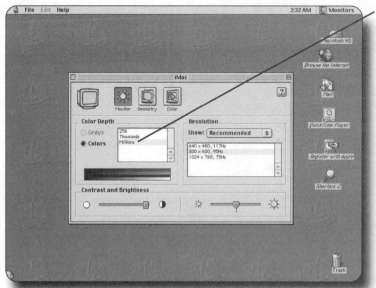

2. Click on an **entry** in the Color Depth list box. Your choice will be highlighted and the monitor will adjust to display only the number of colors you selected.

NOTE

For most uses, you can leave the setting at millions of colors. However, you may run across some software—games in particular—that will only run if the color depth is set to 256.

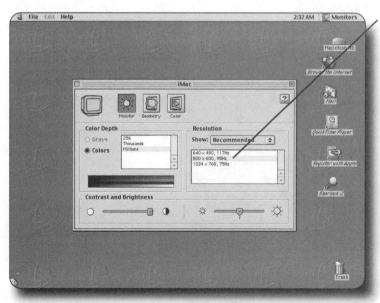

3. Click on an **entry** in the Resolution list box. The iMac will immediately reset the screen resolution.

NOTE

Resolution refers to the detail of an image on the screen. In general, a higher resolution means a larger Desktop area and smaller images.

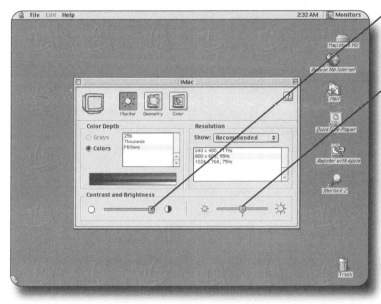

4. **Click and drag** the **Contrast slider.** The screen contrast will be adjusted.

5. **Click and drag** the **Brightness slider**. The screen brightness will be adjusted.

6. **Click** on the **close box** when you have chosen the resolutions you find most comfortable for your eyes. The Monitors control panel will close.

Adjusting Sound

Your iMac makes sounds whenever it wants your attention, or to let you know something has been completed (such as saving a file in Microsoft Word 98). In addition, you can change the input and output devices for sound. You can also set the sound volume from this control panel.

1. **Choose Sound** from the Control Panels submenu of the Apple menu. The Sound control panel will open.

Choosing an Alert Sound

The iMac lets you choose what sound you'll hear when an alert appears on the screen.

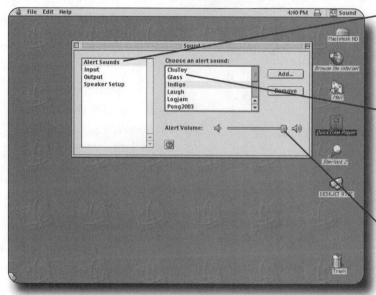

1. **Click** on **Alert Sounds** in the list box. The Choose an alert sound list box will appear.

2. **Click** on a **sound** in the list box. The sound will be selected and the iMac will play the sound the next time it needs your attention.

3. **Click and drag** the **Alert Volume slider.** The alert volume will be set.

Sound Input

You can put sounds into your iMac from a CD or record them from the built-in microphone. Usually, the iMac listens to the CD-ROM drive for sound. However, if you are recording sounds or if you have added voice recognition software to your iMac, the iMac needs to listen to the built-in microphone for sound.

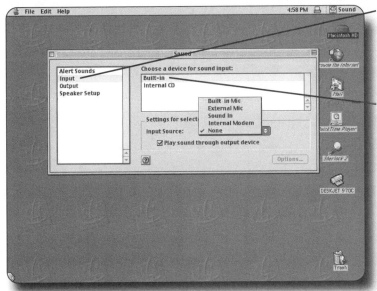

1. **Click** on **Input** in the list box. The Choose a device for sound input list box will appear.

2. **Click** on **Built-in** in the list box. The built-in microphone will be selected for sound input.

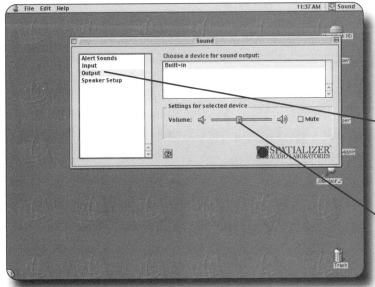

Sound Output

Your iMac has built-in stereo speakers. These are your sound output devices.

1. **Click** on **Output** in the list box. The Choose a device for sound output list box will appear.

2. **Click and drag** the **Volume slider**. The volume will be adjusted.

3. **Click** on the **close box**. The Sound control panel will close.

Using the Control Strip

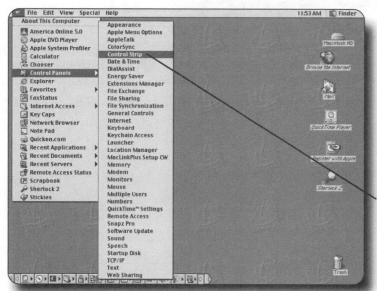

The control strip appears across the bottom of the iMac's screen. Each small portion in the Control Strip is a pop-up menu. When you click on a portion, the pop-up menu appears with options that are ordinarily accessible through control panels.

1. **Choose Control Strip** from the Control Panels submenu of the Apple menu. The Control Strip control panel will appear.

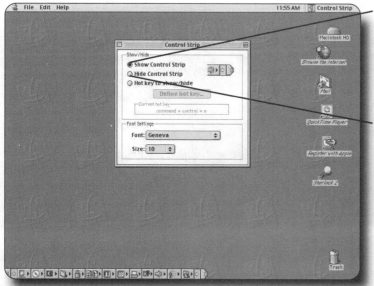

2. **Click** on the **Show Control Strip radio button**. The radio button will be selected and the Control Strip will appear.

3. **Click** on the **Hide Control Strip radio button**. The radio button will be selected and the Control Strip will disappear.

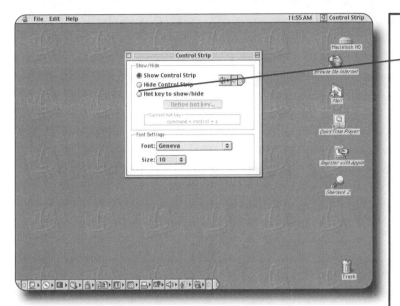

4. Click on the **close box**. The Control Strip control panel will close.

Configuring the Date and Time

When you used the iMac Setup Assistant to configure your iMac, you set the date and time. You will probably never need to change them unless you move to another time zone. However, the Date & Time control panel does give you some control over the format of date and time displays.

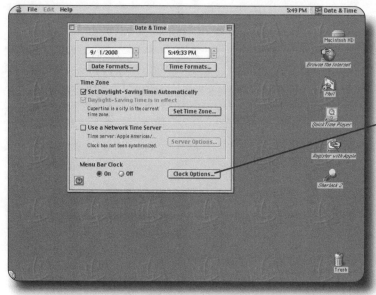

1. Choose Date & Time from the Control Panels submenu of the Apple menu. The Date & Time control panel will appear.

2. Click on **Clock Options**. The Clock Options dialog box will open.

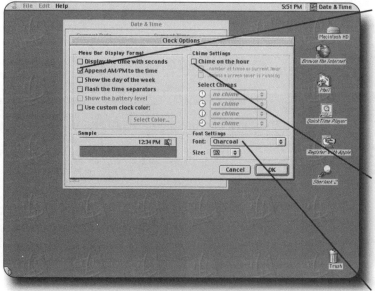

3. Click on the **Menu Bar Display Format check boxes** that you wish to. Your menu bar clock display will be adjusted and your changes will appear in the Sample box at the bottom of the dialog box.

4. Click in the **Chime on the hour check box** if you want to hear your clock strike the hour. A check will appear in the box.

5. Click on the **Font pop-up menu** if you want to choose a new a font for the menu bar clock. The pop-up menu will open.

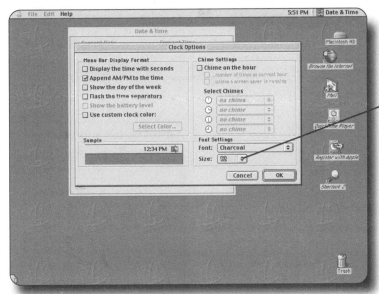

6. **Click** on a **font**. Your changes will appear in the Sample area at the bottom of the dialog box.

7. **Click** on the **Size pop-up menu** if you want to choose a type size for the menu bar clock. The pop-up menu will open.

8. **Click** on a **size**. Your changes will appear in the Sample area at the bottom of the dialog box.

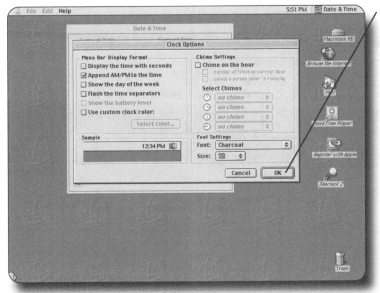

9. **Click** on **OK**. The Clock Options dialog box will close.

10. **Click** on the **close box**. The Date & Time control panel will close.

Setting Speech Characteristics

The Speech control panel handles settings for talking alerts and other applications that speak. You can change the speaking voice and configure how talking alerts work.

1. **Choose Speech** from the Control Panels submenu of the Apple menu. The Speech control panel will open.

The Speech control panel has two options. The Voice panel sets the speaking voice and rate of speech. The Talking Alerts panel configures what is spoken when an alert appears.

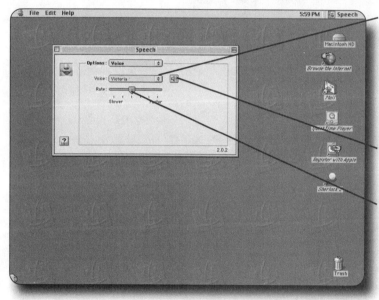

2. **Click** on the **Voice pop-up menu**. The pop-up menu will open.

3. **Click** on a **voice**. The voice will be selected.

4. **Click** on the **sound icon**. You will hear the voice.

5. **Click and drag** the **Rate slider**. The speed at which the voice speaks will be adjusted.

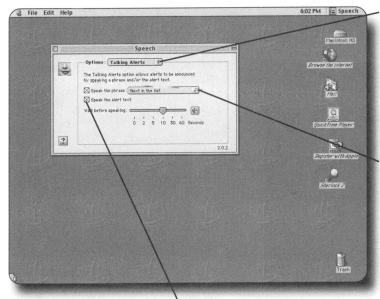

6. Click on the **Options pop-up menu**. The pop-up menu will open.

7. Click on **Talking Alerts**.The Talking Alerts panel will open.

8. Click on the **Speak the phrase pop-up menu**. The pop-up menu will open.

9. Click on the **phrase** to be spoken when an alert appears. The phrase will be selected.

TIP

To hear a sample of your talking alert settings, click on the speaker icon.

10. Click in the **Speak the alert text check box** if you don't want the iMac to read all alert messages aloud. The check will be removed.

11. Click on the **close box**. The Speech control panel will close.

Modifying the Apple Menu

The programs and other items that appear in the Apple menu are found in the Apple Menu Items folder, which is inside the System Folder. Programs, documents, aliases, or folders can be accessed from the Apple menu. Small programs that are accessible only from the Apple menu—such as the Chooser, Key Caps, or the Graphing Calculator—are placed directly in the Apple Menu Items folder when you install the operating system. Other programs, such as the AppleCD Audio Player, are referenced by aliases. The names of aliases appear in italics inside the folder, but not when listed in the Apple menu.

Adding and Removing Items from the Apple Menu

Any item can be easily added to the Apple menu.

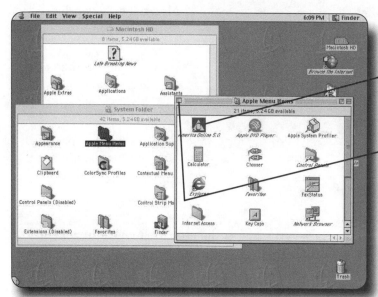

1. **Create** an **alias** for the item.

2. **Drag** the **alias** into the Apple Menu Items folder inside the System Folder.

3. **Click** on the **close box** of the Apple Menu Items window. The window will close and the new item will appear in the Apple menu.

To remove an item from the Apple menu, simply drag the alias out of the Apple Menu Items folder.

Configuring the Apple Menu

Some of the configuration of the Apple menu is handled by the Apple Menu Options control panel.

1. **Choose Apple Menu Options** from the Control Panels submenu of the Apple menu. The Apple Menu Options control panel will open.

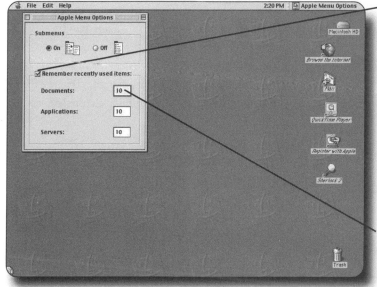

2. **Click** in the **Remember recently used items check box** if you no longer want to access Recent Documents, Recent Applications, and Recent Servers from the Apple menu. The check will be removed from the check box.

OR

2b. **Type** the **number** of recent items to be added to the submenus in the text boxes. Ten is the default.

3. **Click** on the **close box**. The Apple Menu Options control panel will close and the iMac will save any changes you made to the Apple menu.

Using the Extensions Manager

The Extensions Manager helps you manage all of the add-on programs that are automatically loaded into memory when you boot your iMac. Extensions, control panels, and items which launch when you shut down or start up your computer can be turned on or off in the Extensions Manager.

Occasionally, extensions may not work correctly with each another in main memory (called an *extension conflict*). Typical symptoms of an extension conflict can include unexpected program crashes or a sudden computer freeze (sometimes while attempting to load the extensions).

This problem often occurs after new software has been installed making the problem extension easier to identify.

One of the main purposes of the Extensions Manager is to help you identify extension conflicts. By turning them off one-by-one, you'll be able to identify which extension is causing the problem.

1. **Choose Extensions Manager** from the Control Panels submenu of the Apple menu. The Extensions Manager control panel will open.

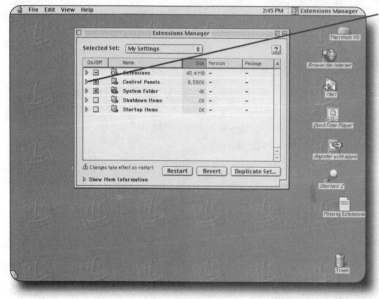

2. **Click** on the **right arrow** next to a folder of items. The folder will expand so you can see its contents. Folders with enabled contents (those that contain items that are being loaded at system startup) have an X in the check box that appears to the left of the folder icon.

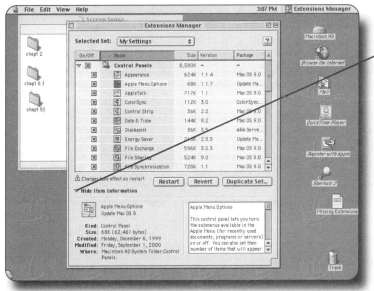

If you want to find out more information about any item listed in the Extensions Manager, click on any item and then click on the Show Item Information right arrow.

You can also disable an item to prevent it from being loaded at system startup.

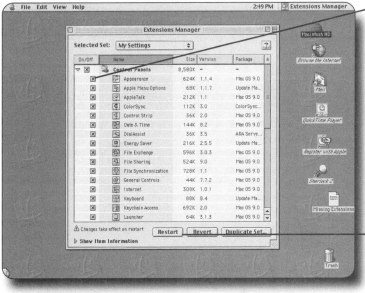

3. Click on the **X** to the left of an item. The X will be removed from the box and the iMac will disable the item, preventing it from being loaded into memory.

4. Repeat step 3 until you have disabled all items that you don't want to load.

5. Click on **Restart**. Your iMac will restart so that your changes will take effect.

TIP

One way to check for an extension conflict is to start up without extensions. To do so, hold down the Shift key while restarting the iMac. You can release the Shift key as soon as you see Extensions Disabled appear underneath the Mac OS logo. If your iMac starts up correctly with no extensions but then crashes or hangs with extensions on, you probably have an extension conflict. Your modem and other peripherals will not work when some extensions are turned off.

PART II

How to Get Help

7

Getting Help

The iMac is designed for computer users of all levels, so there are many different ways you can find help and information. The Help menu provides easy access to various types of help. Like the Apple menu, it is available with all programs. However, the Help menu's options change depending on the program with which you are working. In this chapter, you'll learn how to:

- Use the basic tutorials
- Turn on Balloon Help
- Use the Help Center
- Get help with the Apple Guides

Viewing the Tutorials

Apple has included two interactive multimedia presentations with your iMac that reinforce the basics you learned in the previous chapters. The first presentation deals with using the mouse; the second focuses on the Desktop. You can view these tutorials at any time, although it's a good idea to go through them before you start working with application software. Tutorials and presentations may be different on older iMacs that shipped with Mac OS 8.6.

1. **Click** on the **Desktop**. The Finder will become the active application.

2. **Click** on **Help**. The Help menu will appear.

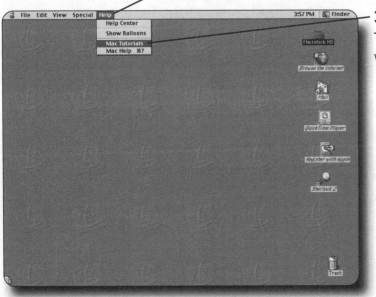

3. **Click** on **Mac Tutorials**. The Mac Tutorials window will appear.

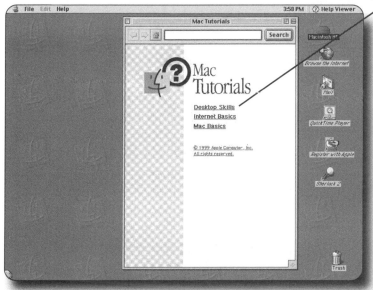

4. Click on **Desktop Skills**. The screen will go black as the iMac launches the tutorial. An introductory screen will appear.

5. Read the **screen** and **press** the **space bar** when finished. The First things first tutorial will begin.

NOTE

You can click on Exit to end the tutorial on any screen.

Each time you finish a tutorial you will return to the Mac Tutorials window where you can select which tutorial you want to watch next. Take your time walking through each tutorial.

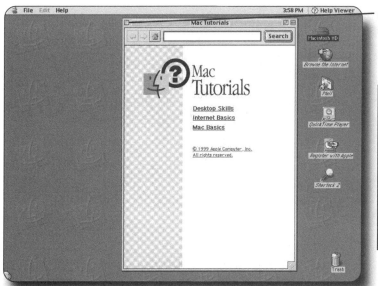

6. Click on the **close box**. The Mac Tutorials window will close.

NOTE

The Mac Basics link leads you to a table of contents in which you can read about different operating system and software features.

Using Balloon Help

Balloon Help, which is available with many programs, provides cartoon-like balloons that appear when you move the mouse pointer over objects on the screen. A balloon contains information that identifies the object and gives you information about how to use it. Balloons are most useful when you are just learning to use your iMac or a new program.

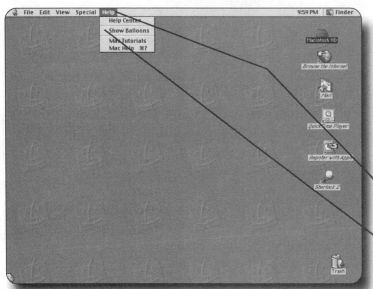

1. **Click** on **Help.** The Help menu will appear.

2. **Click** on **Show Balloons**.

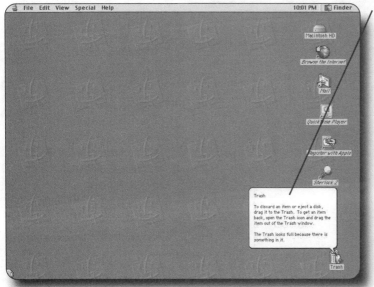

3. **Move** the **mouse pointer** over an item on the screen that you want to know more about. A balloon will pop up with information about the item.

4. Click on **Help**. The Help menu will appear.

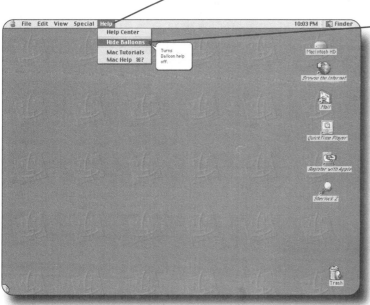

5. Click on **Hide Balloons**. Balloon Help will be turned off.

Visiting the Help Center

The Help Center is a reference that helps you learn more about your iMac. It contains documents in six areas, including Apple DVD Player, AppleScript, and QuickTime Help. The Mac Help item contains valuable information for the new user. You can search through all the documents in The Help Center by browsing topics.

1. Click on **Help**. The Help menu will appear.

2. Click on **Help Center**. The Help Viewer will launch and the Help Center window will appear.

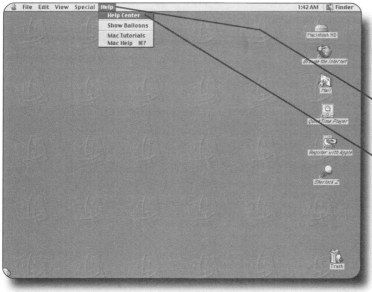

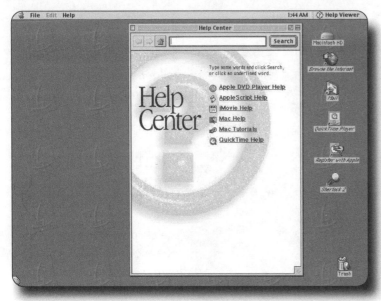

The first Help Center page has a table of contents that lists the main Help Center documents. The titles of these documents appear as blue underlined text on your iMac screen. They are *hyperlinks*—text that, when clicked on, displays another part of the document. This is the same convention used in Web pages, which you will learn more about in Chapter 11 "Wandering the World Wide Web."

Searching in Help Center

One way to find information in the Help Center is to ask the iMac to match search phrases that you type.

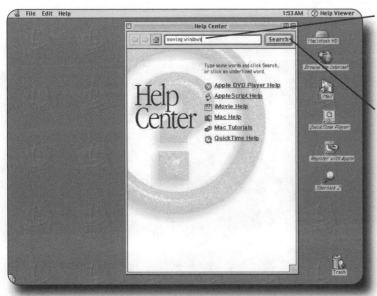

1. Type a **word or phrase** describing a subject about which you want to learn into the text box.

2. Click on **Search**. The Help Center window will show you the results of the search.

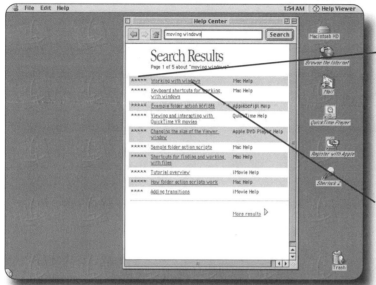

NOTE

On the left side of each listing one to five stars appear that represent how well each document matches your search—five stars being the best match.

3. **Click** on the **topic** that best fits your search. The Help Viewer will take you to that page.

4. **Click** on the **Previous button**. You will move to the previous page.

OR

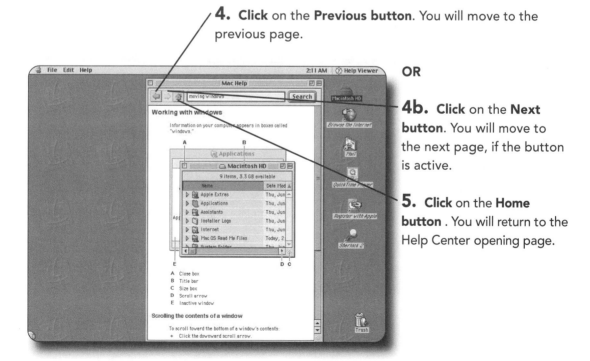

4b. **Click** on the **Next button**. You will move to the next page, if the button is active.

5. **Click** on the **Home button**. You will return to the Help Center opening page.

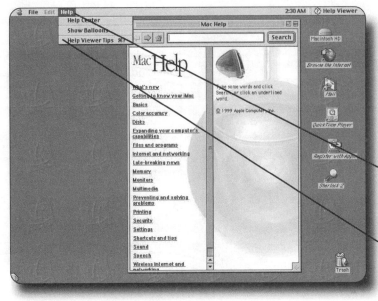

Searching Tips

There are some conventions used to search for multiple words and topics. These conventions are similar to using a search Web page.

1. Click on **Help** while the Help Viewer is still running. The Help menu will appear.

2. Click on **Help Viewer Tips**. The Help Viewer Tips page will open in the Help Viewer.

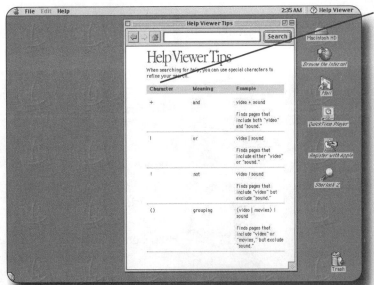

3. Read through the **characters** you can use when searching for specific help.

Browsing the Help Center

You can browse through the Help Center rather than searching for information on a specific topic. This is a good strategy when you are interested in learning a wide variety of iMac techniques.

1. Click on the **Home button**. You will return to the opening page.

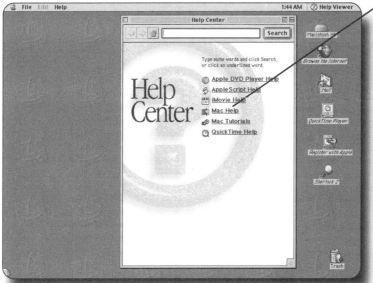

2. **Click** on **Mac Help**. The Mac Help page will open. A list of topics will appear at the left side of the page. Each of these topics is a hyperlink that you can click on to display a list of subtopics.

3. **Click** on a **topic** in the left panel. A list of subtopics will appear in the right panel. Each of the subtopics is a hyperlink that takes you to a page containing information about it.

NOTE

The contents of a Help Center page varies depending on the topic. A Help Center page may also contain a link that opens a control panel, it may contain a Web site link, or even take you to an Apple Guide entry.

4. Click on the **close box** when you are finished with the Help Center. The Help Viewer will close.

> **NOTE**
>
> Apple Guides are also accessible through the Help Center, where documents refer to an Apple Guide section with links that look like blue diamonds.

Using Apple Guides

The Apple Guide takes you step-by-step through various programs. Program-specific guides are accessible from the program's Help menu, usually with the name of the program followed by "Guide" as a menu option.

Opening a Program-Specific Guide

Many of the programs that came with your iMac have Apple Guides available. For the examples in this section, you'll be using SimpleText, the text editor. Access a Guide by using the Help menu.

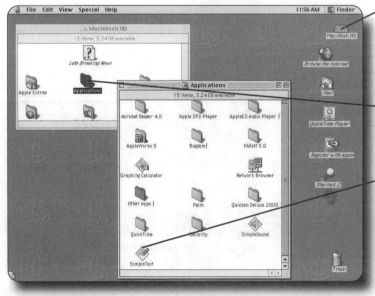

1. Double-click on the **Macintosh HD icon** (your hard drive). The Macintosh HD window will open.

2. Double-click on the **Applications folder**. The Applications folder will open.

3. Double-click on **SimpleText**. SimpleText will open with a blank document window.

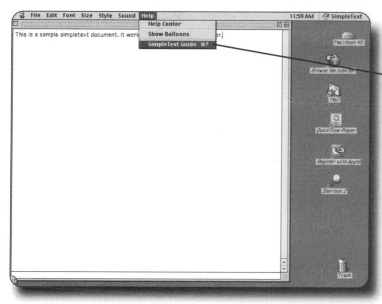

4. Click on **Help.** The Help menu will appear.

5. Click on **SimpleText Guide.** The SimpleText Guide will appear.

Selecting a Topic

The main Guide page allows you to look at the topics available using three different methods: by topic, index, or keyword search. To choose a topic, follow these steps:

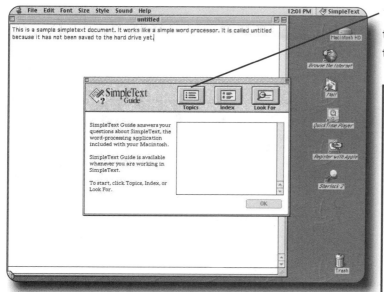

1. Click on **Topics.** A list of topic areas will appear on the left side of the page.

NOTE

Guide windows are different from normal windows. They are called *floating windows* because they stay on top of all other windows as long as they are open. You can still move and close them like normal windows.

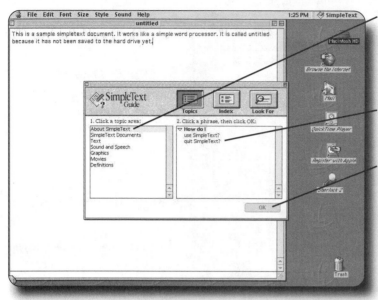

2. Click on a **topic area**. It will be highlighted, and a list of subtopics will appear on the right.

3. Click on a **subtopic**. It will be highlighted.

4. Click on **OK**. The main Guide window will close, and a window for the chosen topic will open.

Guides lead you through a topic step by step, with lots of visual clues to help you along. Don't run ahead of the Guide; if you do, it will force you to back up.

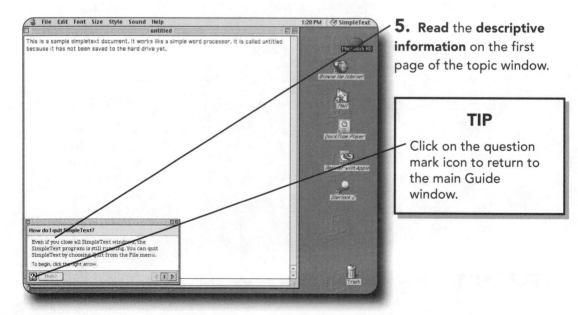

5. Read the **descriptive information** on the first page of the topic window.

TIP

Click on the question mark icon to return to the main Guide window.

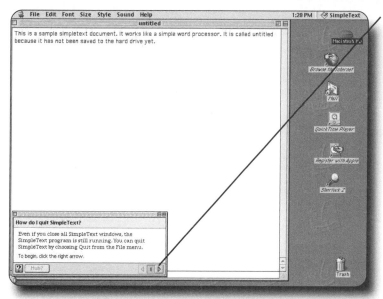

6. Click on the **right arrow button**. You will continue to the next step. If the next step involves a menu that you should open, it will be circled in bright red.

7. Click on the **menu** as directed. The menu will appear. The Guide will show you which option to choose by underlining the correct menu choice and displaying it in red.

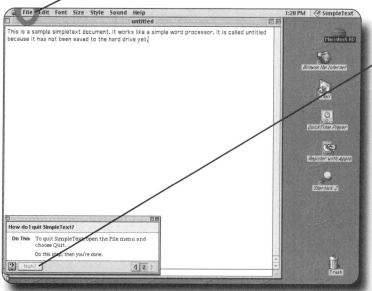

TIP

You can click on the Huh? button if you don't understand a step and want more information.

8. Click on the **close box**. The Guide window will close.

PART III

The iMac's Bundled Programs

8

Working with AppleWorks

To do anything other than the basics on the iMac you need specialized application software designed to perform specific tasks. For example, Quicken is used to manage a checkbook, Netscape is a Web browser, and Photoshop is a graphics editing and creation program. AppleWorks is an integrated program that enables you to create text documents, spreadsheets, databases, and graphics. Macintosh computers appeal to many users because most programs share a common set of commands and similar look and feel. The way in which you interact with documents to create, open, close, save, and print them is generally the same from one program to another. Because of this, this chapter will be helpful for you no matter what application you may be using on your iMac. In this chapter, you'll learn how to:

- Start and quit AppleWorks
- Create and save documents
- Perform essential word processing tasks
- Use an Assistant
- Use a template

Starting AppleWorks

Starting a program is also known as *running* or *launching* it. Depending on the program, you may see a list of templates, a blank workspace may be opened for you, the last document you used may be displayed, or you may simply see a menu bar or toolbars and palettes.

To launch AppleWorks, you must first find its icon on the hard disk.

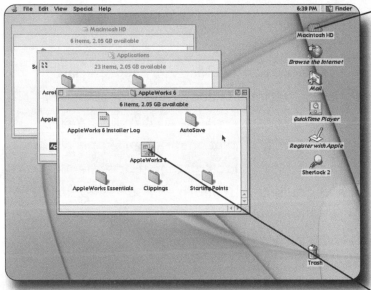

1. Double-click on the **Macintosh HD icon**. The Macintosh HD folder will open.

2. Double-click on the **Applications folder**. The Applications folder will open.

3. Double-click on the **AppleWorks 6 folder**. The AppleWorks 6 folder will open.

4. Double-click on the **AppleWorks 6 icon**. AppleWorks 6 will launch and the Starting Points window will appear.

The AppleWorks Starting Points

AppleWorks is actually a suite of software applications rolled into one program.

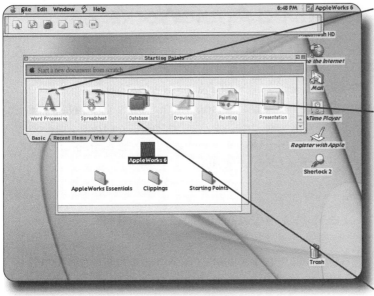

- **Word Processing**. A *word processor* is used to create written documents such as letters, memos, and newsletters.

- **Spreadsheet**. A *spreadsheet* is designed to help you manipulate anything that requires mathematical computations, such as analyzing mortgages, investments, sales, or expenses.

- **Database**. *Database* programs provide the ability to store, organize, and retrieve data.

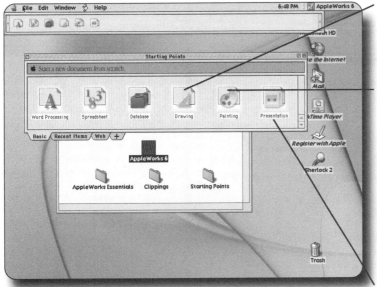

- **Drawing**. A *drawing*, or *object graphics*, program lets you create images from shapes.

- **Painting**. A *paint*, or *bit-mapped graphics*, program is used for artistic graphics and, while sharing some of the tools used in the Drawing module, it provides brushes, special effects, and a greater degree of color management.

- **Presentation**. A *presentation* program is used to convey ideas to a group of people. The slides created in AppleWorks can be printed on transparencies, posted to a Web site, or printed and distributed as handouts.

Handling AppleWorks Documents

The work that you create on your iMac is saved as a document in the Documents folder. Once you save your work to the hard disk, you can close it and then work on it at another time. Unsaved work is not retrievable once the program has been shut down.

Creating a New Document

A new document provides you with a blank surface on which you can type, draw, compute numbers, and so on.

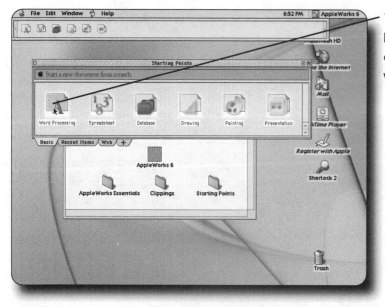

1. **Click** on a **Starting Point**. A blank document of the type you specified will open.

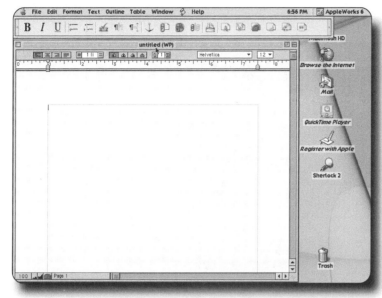

AppleWorks will automatically name the new document "untitled." If you have created more than one new document in this working session the name, "untitled" will be followed by a sequence number, as in "untitled 2." A suffix indicates the type of file:

(WP)word processing

(SS)spreadsheet

(DB)database

(DR)drawing

(PT)painting

(PR)presentation

Opening an Existing Document

When you open a document stored on a disk you can read, edit, or print its contents.

TIP

You can double-click on a document icon to open it. Your iMac launches the program, opens the document, and displays the document's contents in the application in which the document was created.

1. **Click** on **File**. The File menu will appear.

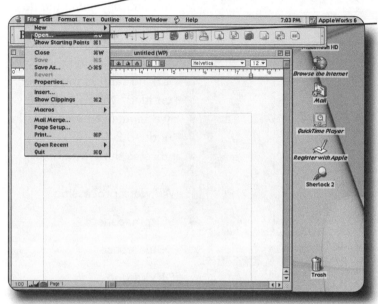

2. **Click** on **Open**. An Open dialog box will appear, showing you the contents of the current folder.

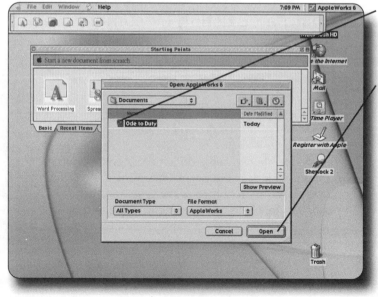

3. **Click** on the **file** that you want to open. The file will be selected.

4. **Click** on **Open**. AppleWorks will open the file.

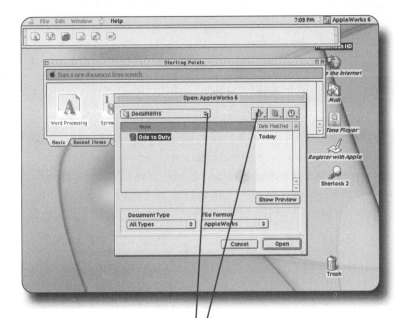

NOTE

You can also use the pop-up menu or the Shortcuts
icon (pointing hand) to navigate through the disk to
find the correct folder. Double clicking on a folder in
the Open dialog box will display the contents of the
folder. After you open or save a file, AppleWorks
returns to the current folder the next time you use the
Open File command.

Working with Text

You need to enter text in many places in your AppleWorks
documents. Whether working on a word processing

document, spreadsheet, or presentation the way you enter and modify text is consistent.

Entering Text

When you open any document where you can type, you see a flashing *insertion point* indicating where text will begin. As you type, the insertion point moves to the right. Notice that the mouse pointer changes to a cursor whenever it is over an area in which text can be typed.

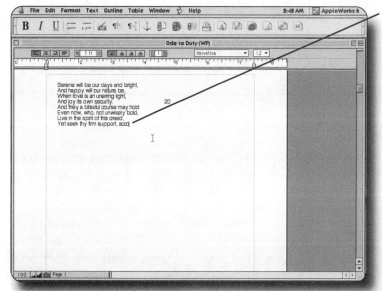

1. **Type** some **text**, pressing the Return key only at the end of a paragraph. The insertion point will move to the right as you type.

NOTE

There's no need to press Return at the end of a line. Most programs use *text wrapping*: if text is too long to fit completely on a line, the program adjusts the line length automatically by *wrapping* the text to the beginning of the next line.

Moving the Insertion Point

If you need to modify text or insert some text in an existing document, you must place the insertion point where you want to start typing.

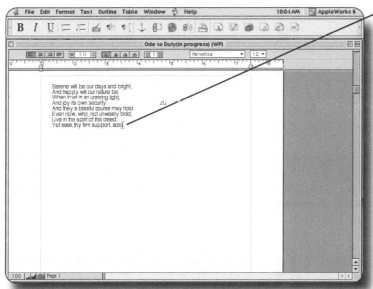

1. Move the **cursor** to the location where you would like to insert text.

2. Click the **mouse button**. The Insertion point will appear in the new location.

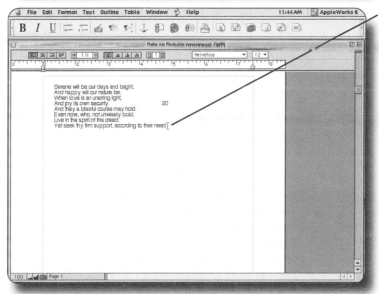

3. Type some **text**. The new text will be inserted at the new location.

Deleting Text

The simplest way to delete text while you are typing is to use the Delete key, which deletes one character at a time to the left of the insertion point.

TIP

You can save time by using the arrow keys to move to a more precise location before using the Delete key.

1. **Click** on the **place** to the right of the text which you wish to delete. The insertion point will appear there.

2. **Press** the **Delete key** once for each character to be deleted. The character to the left of the insertion point will disappear each time you press Delete.

Selecting Text

Before you can change the appearance or position of text, you must first indicate which text you want to modify. You do this by highlighting or selecting the text with your mouse. You can replace, delete, move, and duplicate selected text.

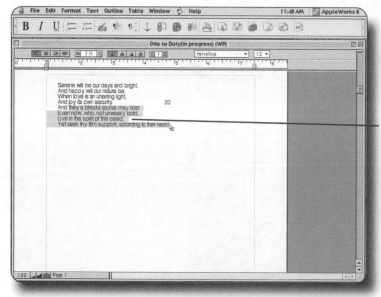

TIP

Double-click on a single word to select it.

1. **Click and drag** the **cursor** over the text you want to select. The text will be highlighted.

Replacing Selected Text

Replacing selected text lets you easily delete a block of text and then replace it with new typing.

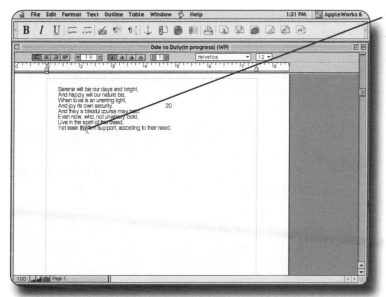

1. Select the **text** you want to replace. The text will be highlighted.

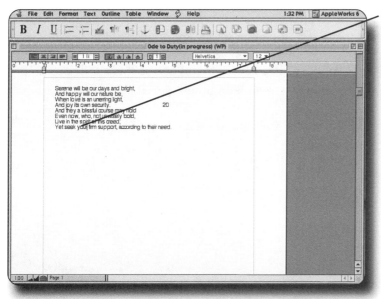

2. Type the **replacement text**. There is no need to delete the selected text before typing. The selected text will be deleted, and the new typing will appear in its place.

Deleting Selected Text

It is simple to delete a block of text without entering replacement text.

1. **Select** the **text** that you want to delete. The text will be highlighted.

2. **Press** the **Delete key**. The selected text will be deleted.

Moving Selected Text

One of the best things about processing text on a computer is that you can easily move blocks of text around without retyping anything. Moving text involves deleting the block of text, storing it somewhere temporarily, and then inserting the text at a new location.

NOTE

This temporary storage area is a system resource known as the *Clipboard*. The Clipboard can hold just about any type of data, text, or graphic. However, it can only hold one item at a time (one image or one block of text). When you place something on the Clipboard, it replaces whatever was there previously.

---

1. **Select** the **text** you want to move. The text will be highlighted.

2. Click on **Edit**. The Edit menu will appear.

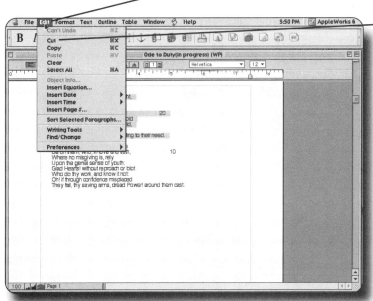

3. Click on **Cut**. The text will be deleted from the document and placed on the Clipboard.

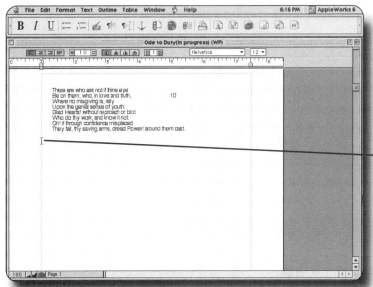

TIP

You can cut (or copy) text from one document and paste it into another.

4. Click on the **place** where you want the text from the Clipboard to be inserted. The insertion point will appear there.

5. **Click** on **Edit**. The Edit menu will appear.

6. **Click** on **Paste**.

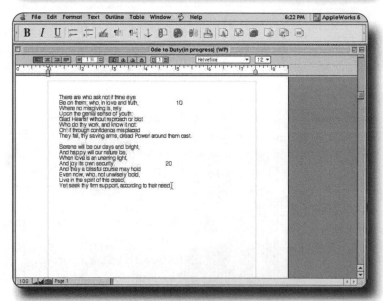

The text on the Clipboard is inserted to the left of the insertion point.

Duplicating Selected Text

Rather than wasting time retyping, use the Copy and Paste commands to duplicate a block of text in another location.

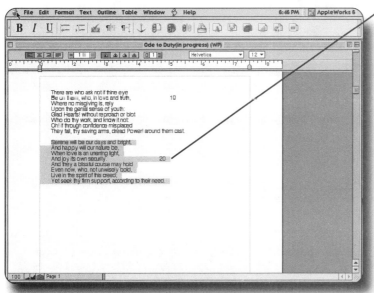

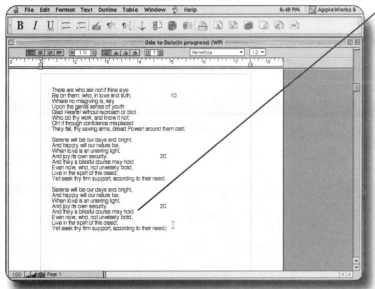

1. Select the **text** to be copied. The text will be highlighted.

2. Press ⌘+**C**. The selected text will be copied to the Clipboard without changing the original document.

3. Click on the **place** where you want to insert the text. The insertion point will appear there.

4. Press ⌘+**V**. The text will be copied from the Clipboard and inserted into the document.

Changing the Appearance of Text

The early popularity of the Macintosh was largely due to the ease with which anyone could produce documents with styled text. With AppleWorks, your iMac has all these capabilities and more. There are three aspects of text over which you have control:

- **Font**. The name of the typeface, such as "Times Roman" that identifies the style of the characters you type on screen.

- **Size**. The height of type is measured in *points*. There are 12 points to 1 inch. Therefore, 12-point type is shorter than 14-point type, which is still smaller than 18 point type. Some fonts may seem bigger because of their design.

- **Style**. Text styles include enhancements such as boldface (heavy text), italic (slanted text), bold italic (slanted heavy text), underline, shadow, outline, etc.

Changing the Font

Your iMac comes with a set of standard Macintosh fonts. You can purchase other fonts to achieve certain effects, type in foreign languages, or typeset mathematical equations. Some software programs install additional fonts as well.

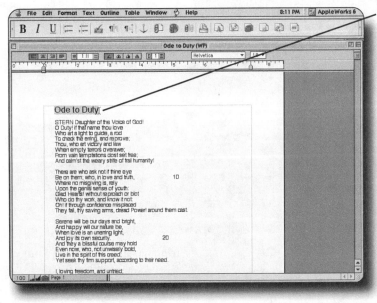

1. Select the **text** for which the font is to be changed. The text will be highlighted.

2. Click on **Text**. The Text menu will appear.

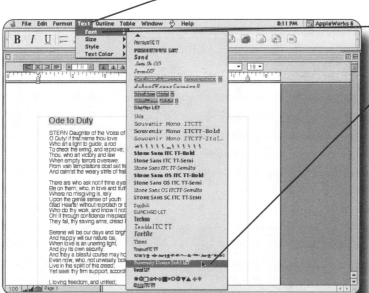

3. Move the **mouse pointer** to Font. The Font submenu will appear.

4. Click on the **name** of the font. The font of the selected text will change

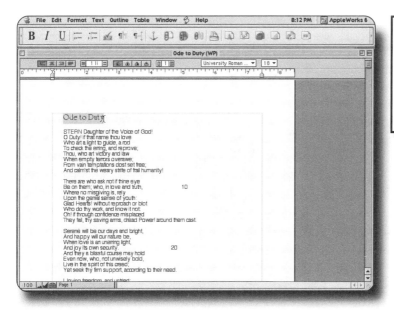

TIP

To start a new document with a font, select the font before you begin typing.

Changing Font Size

When you are typing a letter, you usually type everything in a single font size. However, if you are typing a report or a list with section headings, you may want to use different font sizes to indicate their degree of importance.

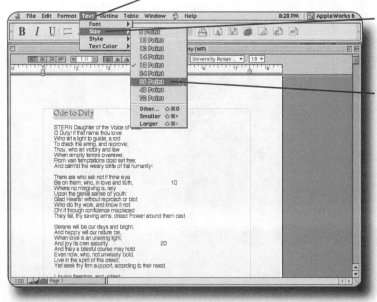

1. **Select** the **text** to which the new size is to be applied. The text will be highlighted.

2. **Click** on **Text**. The Text menu will appear.

3. **Move** the **mouse pointer** to Size. The Size submenu will appear.

4. **Click** on a **font size**. The selected text will be resized.

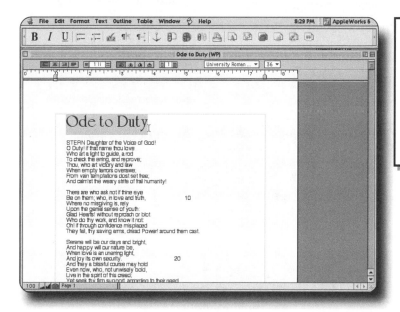

Modifying Style

Styles differ from other text characteristics such as font and size in that they are *additive*. When you choose a new style, it is added to any other formatting currently applied to the selected text. This means that you can use more than one style at a time. Bold italic, for example, is a combination of boldface and italic.

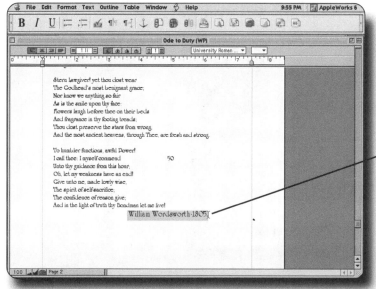

1. Select the **text** to which you want to apply the new style. The text will be highlighted.

2. Click on **Text**. The Text menu will appear.

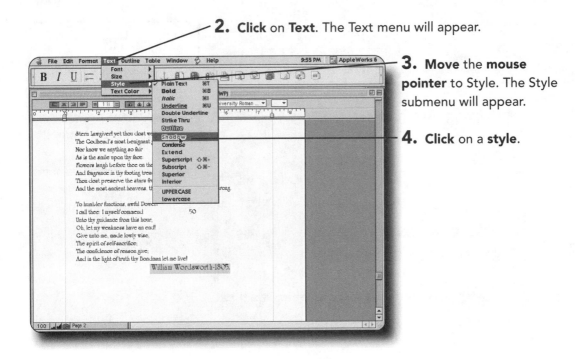

3. Move the **mouse pointer** to Style. The Style submenu will appear.

4. Click on a **style**.

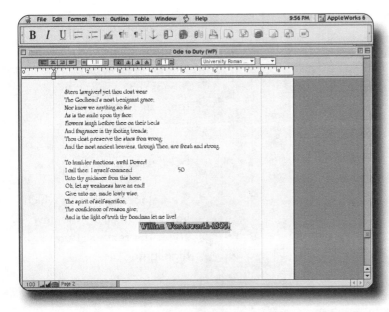

The selected text changes to the new style.

Undoing Changes

Don't panic if you accidentally delete some text or don't like the style you just applied. If you catch the error immediately after making it, you won't have to retype anything or lose any work! You can undo your most recent action with the Undo command.

1. Click on **Edit**. The Edit menu will appear.

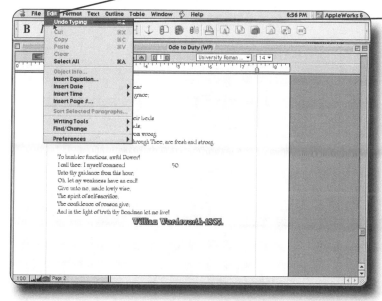

2. Click on **Undo**. The program will undo your most recent action.

Finding and Changing Text

The longer a document becomes, the more difficult it may be to find a specific part of the document. To make that easier, you can search for specified characters and, if desired, replace them with other characters. This is often called *Find and Replace*.

Finding Text

Often you will need to use the Find command to locate words or phrases in long documents.

1. Place the **insertion point** at the location in the document where you want the search to begin.

2. **Click** on **Edit**. The Edit menu will appear.

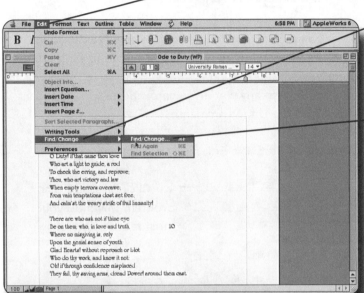

3. **Move** the **mouse pointer** to Find/Change. The Find/Change submenu will appear.

4. **Click** on **Find/Change**. The Find/Change dialog box will appear.

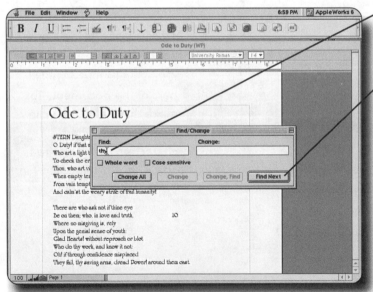

5. **Type** the **text** you want to locate in the Find text box.

6. **Click** on **Find Next**. AppleWorks will locate the first occurrence of the text and highlight that text with a rectangle.

TIP

You can find additional occurrences without displaying the Find/ Change dialog box again. Just choose Find Again from the Edit menu or press ⌘+E.

Replacing Text

The change feature lets you both search for text and replace the found text with new text automatically.

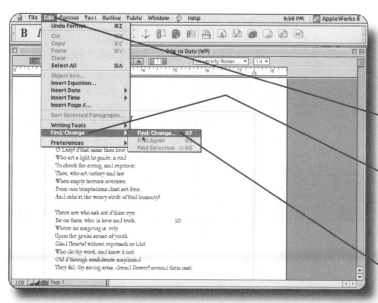

1. **Place** the **insertion point** at the location in the document where you want to find and change text.

2. **Click** on **Edit**. The Edit menu will appear.

3. **Move** the **mouse pointer** to Find/Change. The Find/Change submenu will appear.

4. **Click** on **Find/Change**. The Find/Change dialog box will appear.

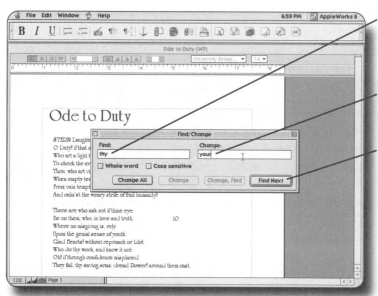

5. **Type** the **text** that you want to find in the Find text box.

6. **Type** the **replacement text** in the Change text box.

7. **Click** on **Find Next**. AppleWorks will locate the first occurrence of the text and highlight that text with a rectangle.

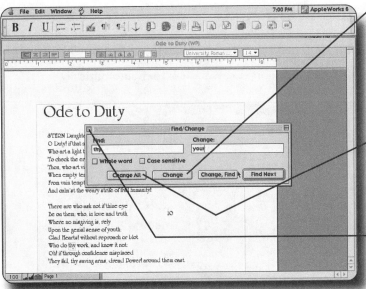

8. **Click** on **Change**. The first instance of the text will be replaced with the replacement text.

OR

8b. **Click** on **Change All**. All instances of the text will be replaced with the replacement text.

9. **Click** on the **close box**. The Find/Change dialog box will close.

NOTE

AppleWorks will display an alert when using the Change All command. You will need to click on OK to proceed. Always be sure to carefully proofread any document that was been edited with the Change All command.

NOTE

A spelling checker doesn't look at the context in which words are used, so you should always proofread for a perfect document. You may inadvertently introduce errors of sense or grammar when using the spelling checker.

Checking Spelling

Spelling checkers typically match the words in a document against a built-in dictionary. Some words, such as technical terms and proper names, may not be in the dictionary and may be indicated as incorrect. You can, however, add words you encounter frequently to your own dictionary. You can use the spelling checker in AppleWorks wherever text appears, whether it's in a word processing document or in text blocks such as those in a newsletter.

1. Click on **Edit**. The Edit menu will appear.

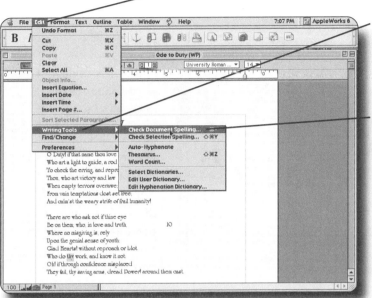

2. Move the **mouse pointer** to Writing Tools. The Writing Tools submenu will appear.

3. Click on **Check Document Spelling**. The Spelling dialog box will appear, displaying the first word that AppleWorks can't find in its dictionary and any recommended alternate spellings.

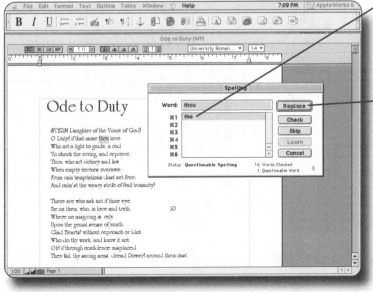

4. Click on the **correctly spelled word** in the list box. The word will be highlighted.

5. Click on **Replace**. The word you chose will replace the misspelled word and the spelling checker will continue to the next incorrect word.

There are several other options available in the Spelling dialog box:

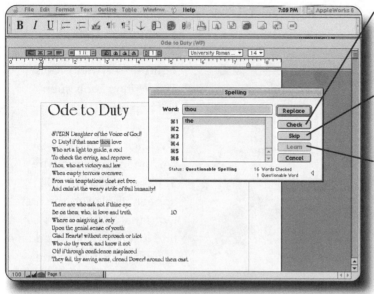

- **Check**. Click on Check if you want enter a word directly into the Word text box.

- **Skip**. Click on Skip if you want to ignore the misspelled word.

- **Learn**. Click on Learn if you want to add this word to your dictionary. AppleWorks will add the word to your personal dictionary so that it won't be caught as misspelled again.

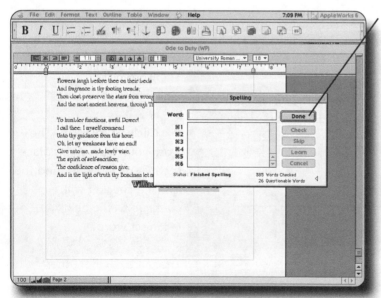

6. Click on **Done** when the spelling checker has reached the end of the text. The Spelling dialog box will close.

TIP

To stop checking spelling at any time, click on Cancel.

NOTE

Since you can never tell when your computer may shut down unexpectedly or you might do something you wish you hadn't, you should get into the habit of saving your documents often.

Saving a Document

A document with which you are working is kept in RAM or temporary memory. Unless you use the Save command to store it permanently on a disk, any changes you have made to the document since it was last saved will be lost when you quit the program.

There are two commands used to save a document: Save and Save As. The way in which you save a document depends on whether you want to save it using the same name (thus replacing the existing, saved version of a document), or whether you want to create a copy of the document (thus saving it under another name).

Save As

To save a document for the first time, use the Save As option.

1. **Click** on **File**. The File menu will appear.

2. **Click** on **Save As**. The Save dialog box will appear.

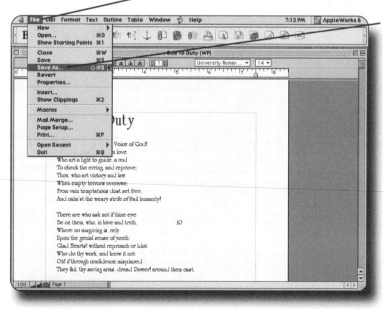

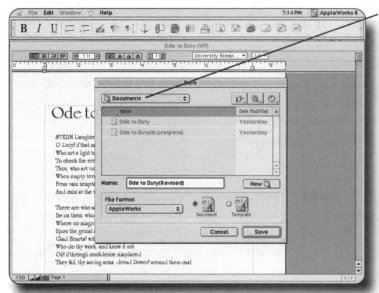

3. Locate the **folder** where you want to save the document. You can use the same techniques that you learned while working with the Open dialog box previously.

TIP

To save changes to a document as you work on it, press ⌘+S.

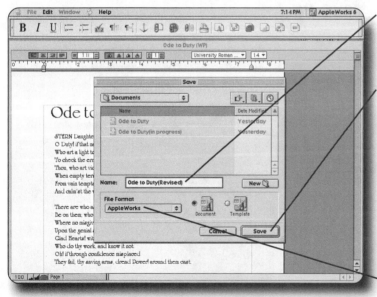

4. Type a **name** for the document in the Name text box.

5. Click on **Save**. The iMac will save the file and close the Save dialog box, returning you to your document. The name of the document will now appear in the title bar.

NOTE

If you need to exchange files with someone who does not own AppleWorks, use the File Format pop-up menu to select a format before saving your document.

Printing a Document

With a printer attached to your iMac, you can print the contents of any document you create, e-mail messages, and documents that you access via the Internet.

Using Page Setup

You use Page Setup to choose print settings such as the size of the paper and the orientation of the page. Once these settings are in place, you do not need to change them unless you switch paper sizes, change document orientation, or choose a different printer.

1. **Click** on **File**. The File menu will appear.

2. **Click** on **Page Setup**. The Page Setup dialog box will appear.

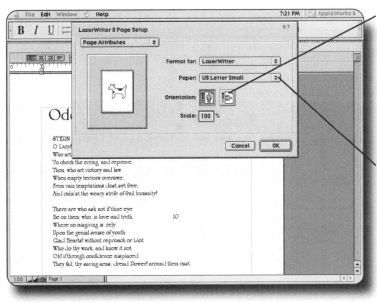

3. **Click** on the **landscape button** if you want to change the page orientation from *portrait* (taller than it is wide) to *landscape* (wider than it is tall). The button will be highlighted.

4. **Click** on the **Paper pop-up menu**. The pop-up menu will open.

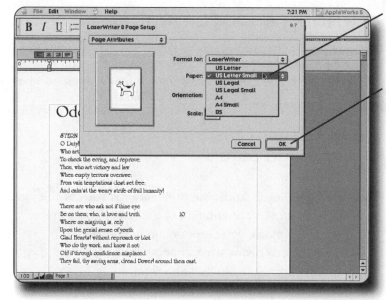

5. **Click** on a **paper size**. The paper size will be selected.

6. **Click** on **OK**. The Page Setup dialog box will close.

Sending a Document to the Printer

After you configure the page settings, you must configure the settings for the printer.

1. **Click** on **File**. The File menu will appear.

2. **Click** on **Print**. The Printer dialog box will appear.

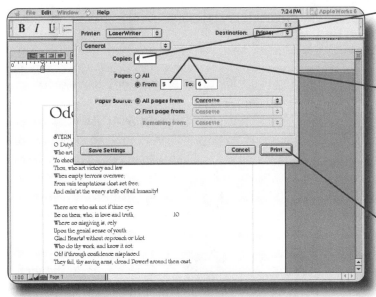

3. **Type** the **number of copies** to be printed in the Copies text box.

4. **Type** the **page range** to be printed in the From and To text boxes if your document has several pages and you don't want to print the entire document.

5. **Click** on **Print**. Your document will be printed.

Creating a Document with an Assistant

AppleWorks comes with Assistants to help you quickly build commonly-used documents that sometimes require a bit of work to get just right. AppleWorks Assistants help you easily create the following documents:

- Address list

- Business cards

- Calendar

- Certificate

- Envelope

- Home Finance

Creating an Envelope with an Assistant

There's nothing like a handwritten envelope to make a polished letter look less professional. You can use the Envelope Assistant to create a great-looking envelope in less than two minutes.

1. **Launch AppleWorks**. The Starting Points window will appear.

2. **Click** on the **Assistants tab**. The Assistants tab will come to the front.

3. **Click** on **Envelope**. The first screen of the Envelope Assistant will appear.

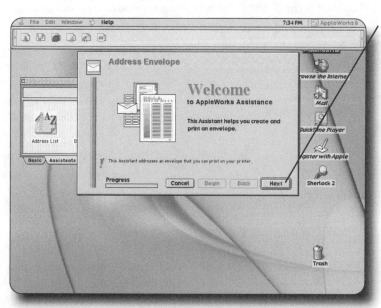

4. **Click** on **Next**. The next screen of the Assistant will appear.

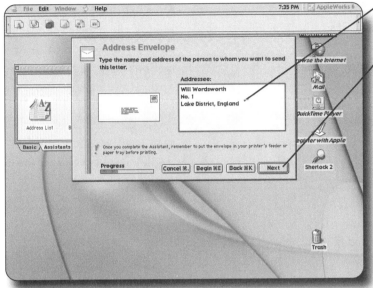

5. **Type** the **name and address** of the addressee.

6. **Click** on **Next**. The next screen of the Assistant will appear.

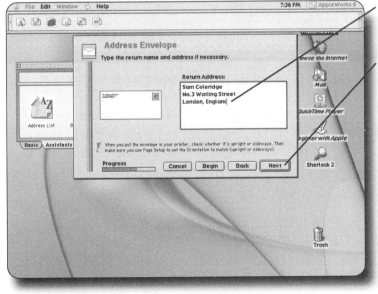

7. **Type** your **name and address**.

8. **Click** on **Next**. The next screen of the Assistant will appear.

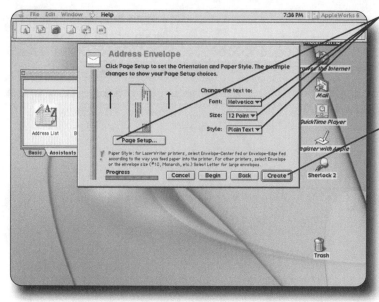

9. **Click** on the **pop-up menus** and **select** the **font, size, style, and orientation options** you like. The options will be selected.

10. **Click** on **Create**. A new, untitled document will display your envelope. You can now save or print your envelope.

Using Templates to Create a Presentation

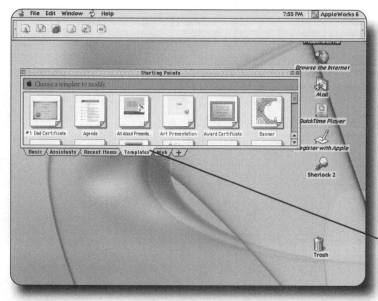

When you open a template, you are working with a pre-formatted pattern. Whenever you open a template, it is displayed as an untitled document until it is saved.

1. Launch AppleWorks. The Starting Points window will appear.

2. Click on the **Templates tab.** The Templates tab will come to the front.

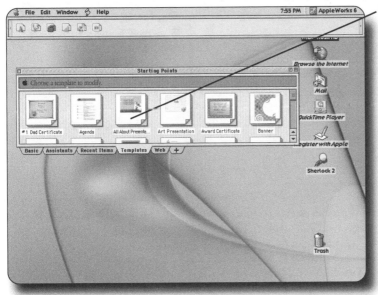

3. Click on a **template icon.** You may need to use the scroll bar on the right to find the template you want. The selected, untitled document will open.

The Presentation module uses some different tools from the word processing module. Below is an explanation of some of the screen elements. Consult the Help menu or a book dedicated to AppleWorks for more detailed information and advanced techniques.

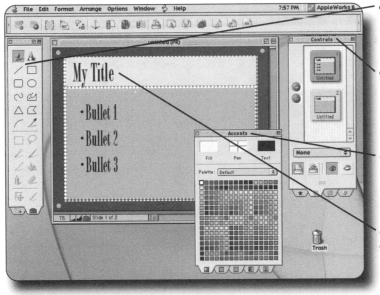

- The Tools pallette provides drawing and painting tools.

- The Controls pallette allows you to reorganize your slides and create a slide slow.

- The Accents pallette allows you to create color, line, and patterns.

4. Click on the **area "My Title."** A rectangular text box will appear.

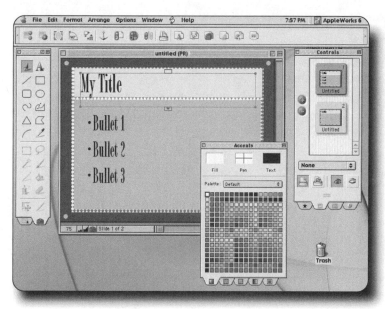

5. **Press** the **Delete key.** The text will be removed.

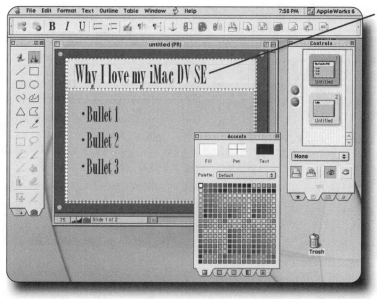

6. **Type** a **title** for your presentation. You may choose to apply a new font and font size.

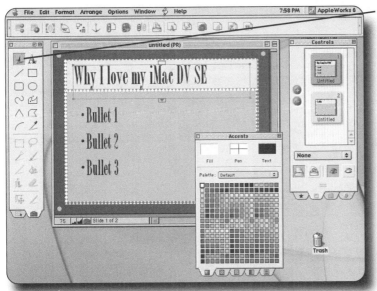

7. Click on the **Selection arrow** in the **Toolbar**. The arrow will be highlighted.

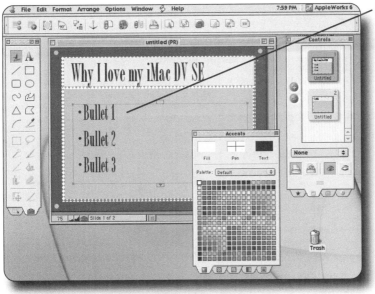

8. Click on the **bulleted text**. A rectangle will surround all of the bullet points.

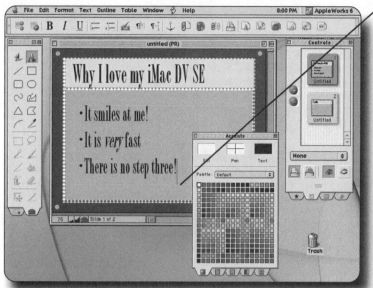

9. **Delete** the **bullet text** and **type new text**. While it may appear that the bullets are disappearing, they will display as you enter the new text.

TIP

You can even add your own artwork by using the drawing tools or using the Insert command from the File menu.

Using AppleWorks Clippings

In AppleWorks, you can create documents that contain elements created by different programs. A clipping file is created when you drag an object or text onto the Desktop of your computer. Your iMac names it with the first 18 characters of the text and gives it an icon with jagged edges. Clippings can be from movies, text, or graphics.

There are several ways to include graphics in an AppleWorks document:

- Use the Insert command from the File menu to insert a clipping

- Create them with either the AppleWorks drawing or painting modules and then use copy and paste, or drag them into your current document.

- Copy and paste graphics from another source into an AppleWorks document. In particular, you may decide to purchase some royalty-free *clip art* images.

- Create a clipping from a source on the Internet and place it into your document.

In this section, you'll be introduced to using the clippings available to you with the AppleWorks.

Adding Clippings to a Document

A picture may be worth a thousand words if it really helps to convey the message or mood of your document. Choose your clippings wisely, taking into account where they will be viewed: onscreen, a color printout, a black and white printout, from far away or close-up.

AppleWorks comes with a number of graphics located in the Clippings folder. You can insert an image from any folder and place it in your document.

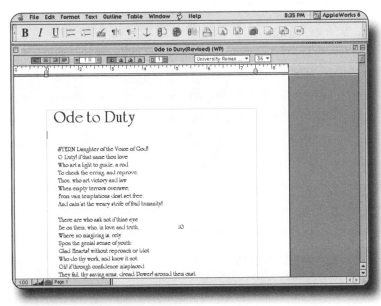

1. **Open** a **document** in which you wish to insert a clipping. The document will appear.

2. Click on **File**. The File menu will appear.

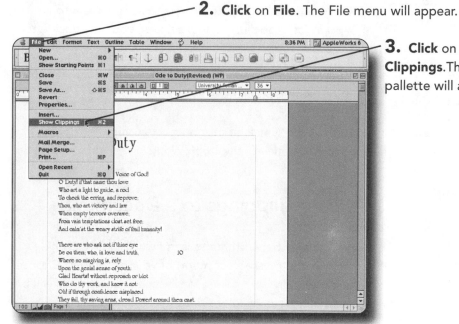

3. Click on **Show Clippings**. The Clippings pallette will appear.

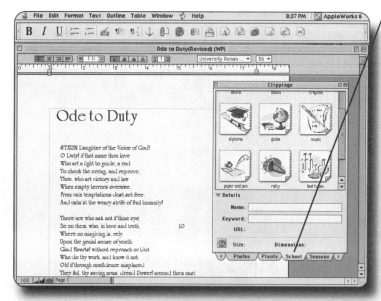

4. Click on the **tabs** if wish to browse the clipping categories. The tabs will come to the front as you click on them.

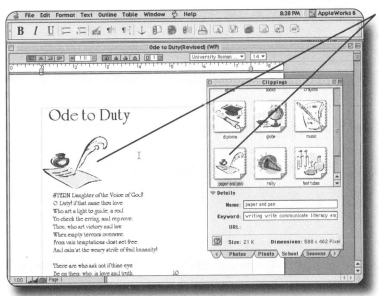

5. Click and drag a **clipping** to your document. The clipping will be placed into your document.

Adjusting Clippings

Once you have placed a graphic in your document, you can drag it to the correct position and adjust the size of the image to fit.

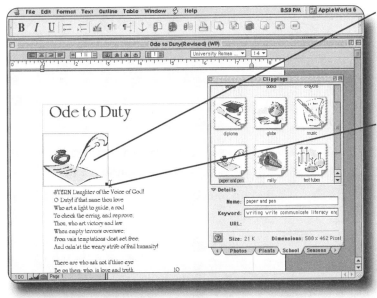

1. Click on the **clipping**. The clipping will be selected and a resizing handle will appear at the bottom-right corner.

2. Click and drag the **resizing handle**. Drag away from the image to enlarge it. Drag to the center of the graphic to reduce it. The image will be resized.

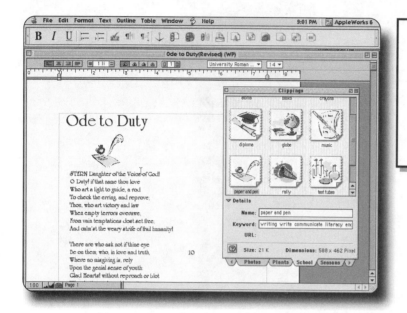

TIP

If you want the image to retain its original proportions as you change its size, hold down the Shift key while you drag a handle.

Using the Zoom Function

AppleWorks lacks the Print Preview command found in many other programs but does give you the ability to zoom in and out of your document.

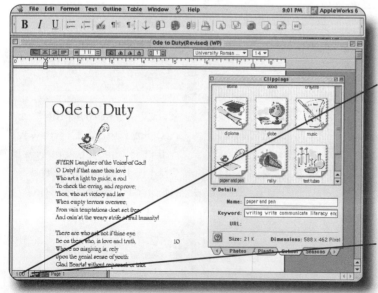

The zoom controls are found in the lower-left corner of every AppleWorks window.

- The bottom-left corner of the window contains a pop-up menu from which you can choose a zoom percentage. The percentage is based on the full size of the document.

- The second button zooms out, making the document smaller.

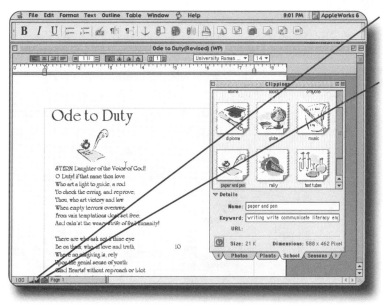

- The third button zooms in, making the document larger.

- The fourth button enables you to show or hide the Paint and Draw tools.

Creating a Drawing Document

The Drawing module can be used to create your own, custom graphics.

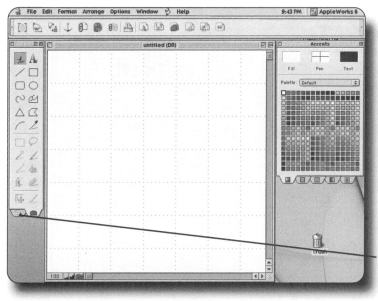

1. Click on **Drawing** from the Starting Points. A new Drawing document with the Tools and Accents palettes will appear.

The Tools pallette (which you have seen earlier when working on a presentation) contains the tools used to create the elements of the drawing.

- **Mode buttons**. The Mode buttons determine the drawing mode. These buttons can be accessed by clicking on the Mode tab at the bottom of the Tool pallette. Select the arrow to work with any of the object graphics tools. Use the A tool to create a text block. The **+** button creates a spreadsheet block, and the brush button creates a painting block. When you are working with text, spreadsheet, or painting blocks within a draw document, all functions of the other modules are available.

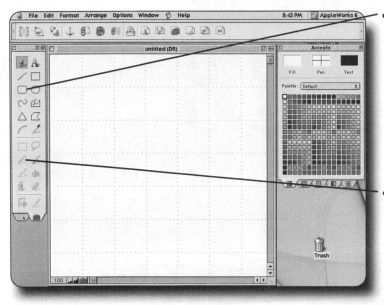

- **Regular shape tools**. These tools draw graphic objects with well-known and predetermined shapes, such as lines, ovals and circles, rectangles and squares, and round-cornered rectangles.

- **Freeform shape tools**. With these tools, you can draw objects, including arcs, polygons, and diamonds. You can also use a freeform drawing tool to draw any shape you need.

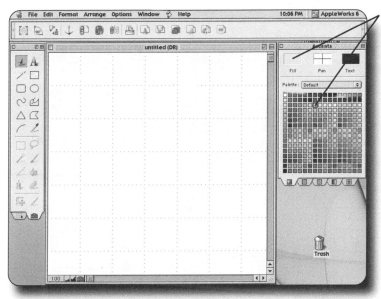

2. **Click** on **Yellow and Fill** on the Accents pallette. The Fill box will turn yellow.

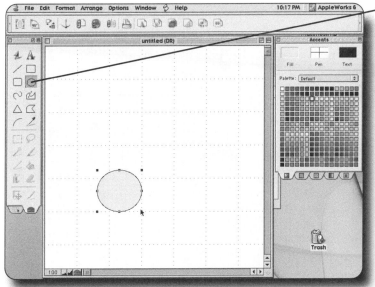

3. **Click** on the **Circle tool.** The circle tool will be selected.

4. **Move** the **mouse pointer** into the drawing area. The mouse pointer will change to a crosshair. When you are drawing a regular shape, the crosshair anchors the top-left corner of the shape.

5. **Move** the **crosshair** to a corner made by the crossing of two grid lines.

6. **Click and drag down** and to the **right** from the crosshair's location. A yellow circle shape will form as you drag.

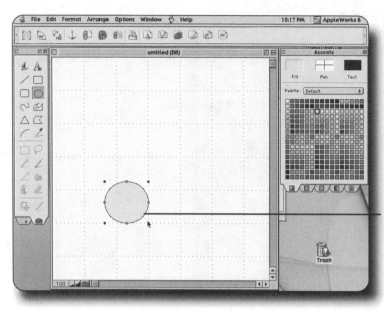

TIP

Holding down the Shift key as you drag constrains the image to a circle instead of an oval, a rectangle instead of a square, or a perfectly straight line.

7. Release the **mouse button**. The circle will have graphic handles allowing you to resize or move it.

8. Click on **Edit**. The Edit menu will appear.

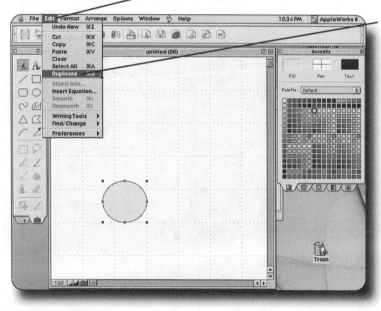

9. Click on **Duplicate**. An exact copy of your circle will appear on top and to the right of the first circle.

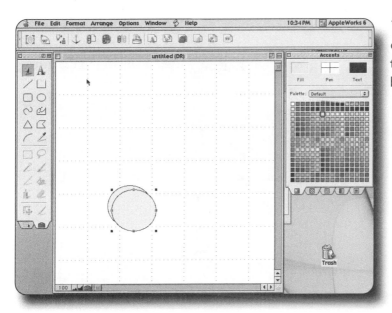

10. **Press** the **arrow keys** on your keyboard to nudge the second circle into a better position.

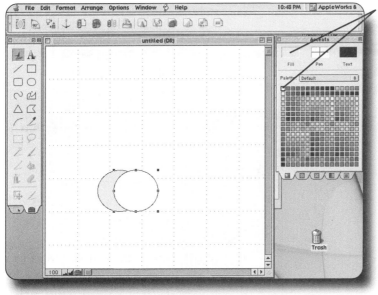

11. **Click** on **White** and **Fill** on the Accents pallette. The top circle (still selected) will become white.

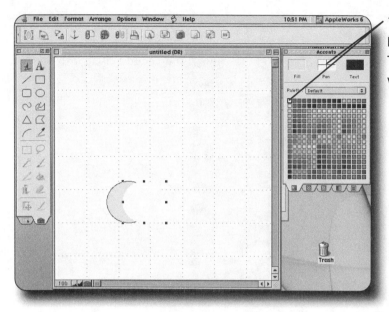

12. **Click** on **White** and **Pen** on the Accents pallette. The outline of the top circle will become white.

Grouping Drawing Objects

The crescent moon created is actually two objects. The various elements must be grouped so that they can be treated as one object, which makes moving and resizing them easier.

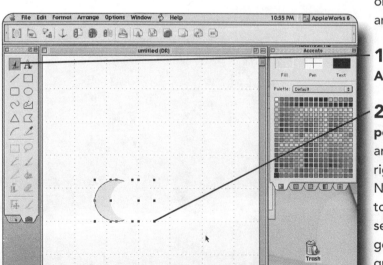

1. **Click** on the **Selection Arrow** on the Tools pallette.

2. **Move** the **mouse pointer** into the drawing area and **click** on the upper-right **edge** of the moon. Now drag across both circles to the right. A marquee will select all objects until you let go of the mouse. The graphic handles (black squares) will appear.

3. **Click** on **Arrange**. The Arrange menu will appear.

4. **Click** on **Group**. The graphic handles will now represent one object, which can be moved or resized.

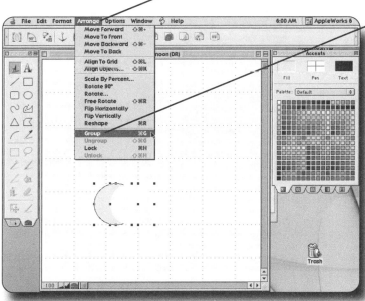

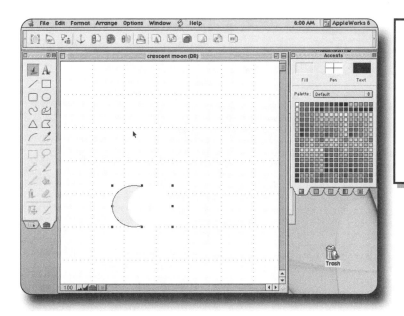

TIP

Holding down the Shift key as you drag constrains the image to a circle instead of an oval, a rectangle instead of a square, or a perfectly straight line.

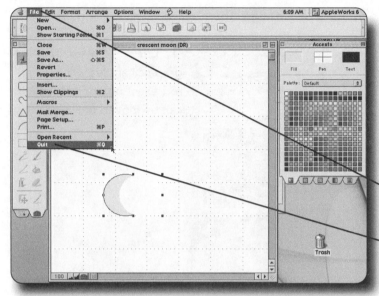

Quitting AppleWorks

Quitting AppleWorks puts away all the documents and toolbars and frees up memory for other programs.

1. Click on **File**. The File menu will appear.

2. Click on **Quit**. AppleWorks will display an alert warning you of unsaved changes and asking you what action you would like to take.

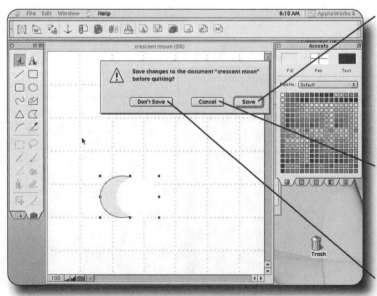

3. Click on **Save**. The document will be saved. If the document has not yet been saved, the Save dialog box will appear.

OR

3b. Click on **Cancel**. You will return to your document so you can continue working.

OR

3c. Click on **Don't Save**. You will exit the program without saving changes to the document. Any unsaved changes will be lost.

PART IV

Multimedia on Your iMac

9

Working with iMovie 2

iMovie 2 is Apple's movie editing software. It is designed for the home movie enthusiast, and is very easy to use. Every iMac DV ships with iMovie 2. You can also purchase it for your iMac from Apple's Web site, at http://www.apple.com/imovie. Some older iMacs were shipped with iMovie 1, which is a free product. Check Apple's Web site for updates and additional plug-ins. In this chapter you will learn to:

- Use the basic controls of iMovie
- Save movies
- Edit movies
- Add enhancements to your iMovie
- Export your movies to QuickTime

iMovie and all of its associated files are pre-installed on your iMac DV. These files are stored in your Applications folder. Although iMovie 2 is jam-packed with editing features, only the basic controls are covered in this chapter. To learn all of iMovie's advanced features and how to import analog video, refer to *iMovie Fast & Easy* (Prima Tech, 2000).

What You Need to Use iMovie 2

To use iMovie 2, you need a digital video (DV) camera (such as the Canon ZR10), or you need to convert movies you have already saved to a digital format. You can use QuickTime Pro to save analog movies in a digital format.

Your iMac DV ships with a 4-pin to 6-pin FireWire cable, which is used to connect your camera to the iMac. You might want to consider purchasing an external hard drive or other large storage capacity peripheral device if you intend to edit a lot of movies. See Chapter 16, "Adding Peripherals" for more information on external storage devices.

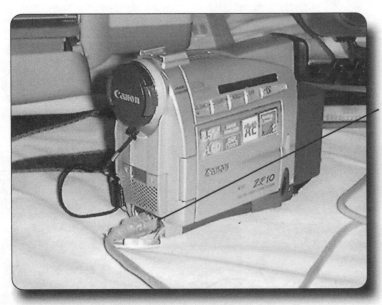

Connecting Your Digital Video Camera

1. **Connect** the **4-pin end** of the FireWire cable to your camera. Make sure you follow any special directions that came with your camera.

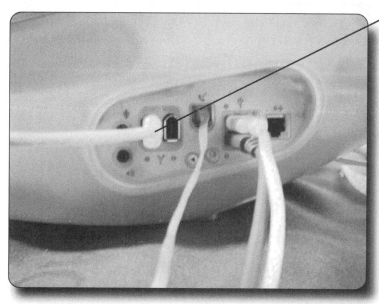

2. Connect the **6-pin end** of the FireWire cable to your iMac.

3. Insert a **tape** with the desired footage into your camera.

Importing Your Video into iMovie

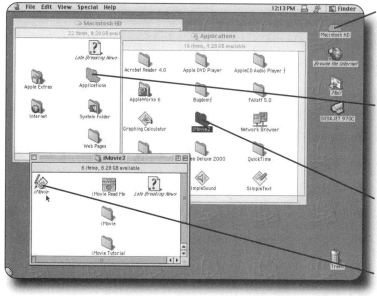

1. Double-click on **Macintosh HD**. The Macintosh HD window will open.

2. Double-click on the **Applications folder**. The Applications window will open.

3. Double-click on the **iMovie 2 folder**. The iMovie 2 window will open.

4. Double-click on the **iMovie alias**. iMovie will start.

5. **Click** on **New Project**. The Create New Project dialog box will open.

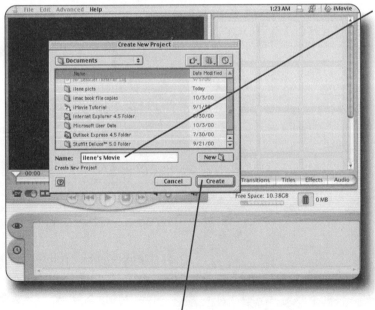

6. **Click** in the **Name box** and **type** a **name** for your movie. The default name is (YourName) Movie.

NOTE

Your file will be saved to the Documents folder by default, but it can be saved anywhere on your hard drive. Remember to give your movie file a distinctive name, so that you'll immediately recognize it when you view a file list.

7. **Click** on **Create**. The iMovie window will open, so you can begin working.

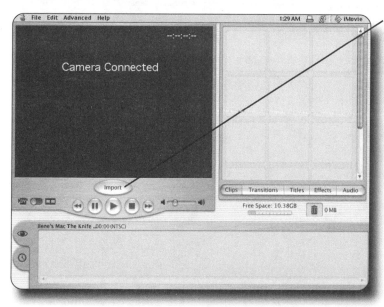

8. Click on **Import** to begin saving your movie to your hard drive. Your movie will start to play and your video clips will appear in the Shelf.

9. Click on **Import** again. Your movie will stop importing.

Before editing your movie, you should look at the available controls and options.

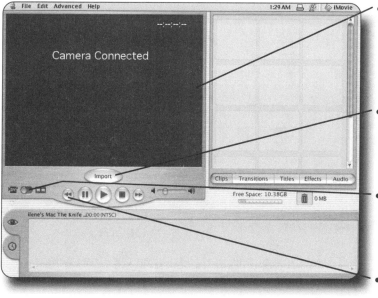

- **Monitor window**. When you are playing or importing your movie, you can view it in the Monitor window.

- **Import**. Click on this button to import your movie into iMovie; click on it again to stop the import.

- **Mode switch**. Set the switch to the left to use Camera mode; set it to the right to use Edit mode.

- **Rewind**. Click on this to rewind your movie while it is playing.

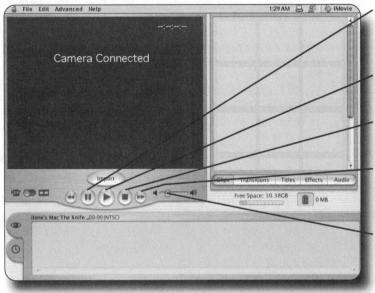

- **Pause**. Click on this button to pause the playing of your movie.

- **Play**. Click on Play to see your movie in action.

- **Stop**. Click on Stop to stop the playing of your movie.

- **Fast forward**. Click on this button to forward your movie while it is playing.

- **Sound control**. Slide the blue button left to raise the volume or right to lower the volume.

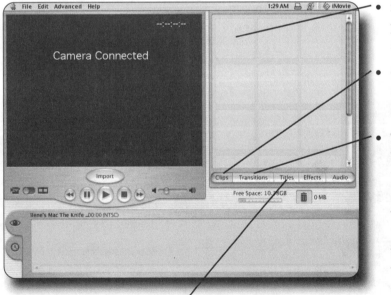

- **Shelf**. The Shelf is where your movie clips are stored.

- **Clips**. Click on this to open the Shelf, if it is not already open.

- **Transitions**. Click on Transitions to open a palette that allows you to choose the type of transition to use between scenes of your movie. A transition is a fluid change from one scene to another.

- **Titles**. Click on this button to open the Titles palette, from which you can choose different title styles to use in your movie.

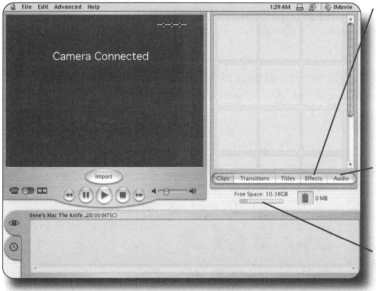

- **Effects**. Click on Effects to open the Effects palette, from which you can adjust your movie's visual appearance. You can add sepia tones, sharpen your movie's appearance, or adjust colors.

- **Audio**. Click on this button to open the Audio palette, from which you can add sounds to your movie.

- **Free Space**. The Free Space bar shows you how much space is available for use on your hard drive. Green is normal, yellow means your space is waning, and red means you are running out of hard drive space.

NOTE

You should always keep at least 100 MB of space available on your hard drive for movie editing.

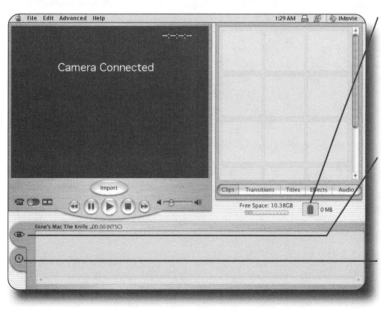

- **Trash can**. Use the Trash can to dispose of any unwanted movie clips. Always empty the trash when you start to run out of room on your hard drive.

- **Clip Viewer**. Drag movie clips from the Shelf to the Clip Viewer to edit them and make them part of your saved movie.

- **Timeline Viewer**. Use the Timeline Viewer to edit and synchronize video and audio.

Editing Your Movie

Once you have imported all of your movie clips, you can edit them in a variety of ways. You can cut scenes, add music, titles, and effects, and have fun creating your own personal movie!

When you choose a clip to edit, some of the Monitor window controls change and a Scrubber bar appears.

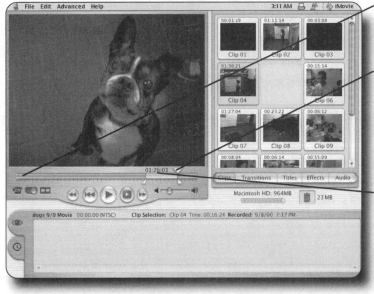

- **Scrubber bar**. This bar shows the duration of the movie.

- **Playhead**. This triangle shows where in the movie you are at any given time. You can drag the Playhead to any point in the movie.

- **Time counter**. This counter shows the time for your movie. The counter will increase as your movies play. The format is minutes:seconds:frames (30 frames per second).

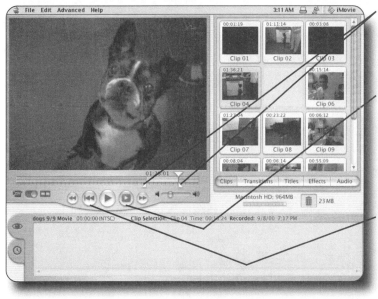

- **Crop markers**. Use the crop markers to select portions of your movie that you want to crop.

- **Full screen**. Click on the Full screen button to see your movie in full screen mode; click it again to return to the standard display.

- **Home**. Click on the Home button to return to the beginning of your movie.

Removing Frames

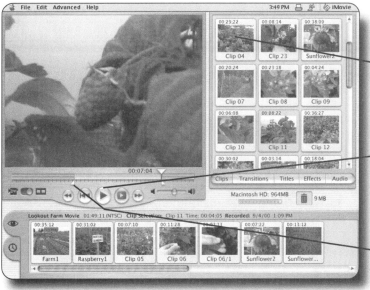

You can easily edit your clips by removing frames.

1. **Click** on the **clip** you want to edit. The clip will appear in the Monitor window.

2. **Click** on the **Play button** to view the clip and decide which frames you want to edit.

3. **Click** below the **Scrubber bar**. The crop markers will appear.

4. **Drag** the **crop markers** to select the area you want to cut. The selected area will become yellow.

TIP

To move through the clip frame by frame, use the right and left arrow keys on your keyboard while your cursor is in the Scrubber bar.

5. **Click** on **Edit**. The Edit menu will appear.

6. **Click** on either **Cut** or **Crop**, depending on which part of the clip you want to remove.

NOTE

There are two ways you can edit frames in your movie. When you select an area and choose Cut from the Edit menu to remove frames (the yellow selected area), the cut portion becomes a separate clip. Alternatively, you can choose Crop to remove the frames that are *not* selected (the blue areas) permanently.

7. Click on the **Play button**. Your newly-cropped clip will play in the Monitor window, and you can check to be sure that you've edited out the correct frames.

NOTE

If you've made a mistake in your cropping, click on Undo to return the clip to its original format.

Renaming Clips

To keep track of your movie files, it is sometimes helpful to rename the clips.

1. In the Clip Viewer, **double-click** on the **movie clip** whose name you want to change. The Clip Info dialog box will appear.

2. Type the **new name** in the Name text box.

3. Click on **OK**. The new name for your clip will be saved.

Moving Clips

If you want to change the order in which your clips appear in your movie, you can rearrange them in the Clip Viewer.

1. Click on the **clip** you want to move. The clip will be selected.

2. Drag the **clip** to the new location and release the mouse button. The clip will be placed in the new location.

NOTE

You cannot move a clip between two other clips that have a transition between them. You must first delete the transition and move the clip, then add the transition again. Transitions are covered more in the next section, "Adding Transitions."

Adding Transitions

Transitions provide a visually pleasing flow between different scenes in your movie. In iMovie, transitions are *rendered*, which is the process of putting elements in a movie together. You can experiment with the different transitions iMovie offers and create some interesting effects for your movies.

1. **Click** on **Transitions**. The Transitions palette will appear.

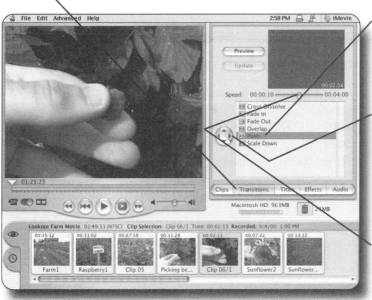

2. **Click** on a **transition effect**. The effect will appear in the preview window.

3. **Click** on an **arrow** to choose the transition direction, if the direction wheel is enabled. (Some transitions only proceed one way.)

4. **Move** the **Speed slider** to set the time for your transition. Remember that a slow transition will require more time to render.

5. **Click and hold** the **mouse button** on the transition. The transition will be selected.

6. **Drag** the **transition** from the Transitions palette and **drop it** on the Clip Viewer, between the movie clips to which you want to apply the effect. A red progress bar will appear beneath the transition, showing you that the transition is rendering.

7. **Click** on the **transition** when it has finished rendering. The transition will be selected.

8. **Click** on the **Play button**. Your transition will play in the Monitor window.

NOTE

Even small transitions use a lot of hard drive space, so check your available space after you add each transition. You might have to make your transitions smaller to avoid using up all your available hard drive space.

Adding an Audio Track

Adding audio to your movie can be as simple or as complicated as you want. You can extract sound from your video, record music from an audio CD, or even record your own narration. In addition, iMovie provides sound effects for you to use. You can move the audio file, crop it, paste it, and even lock it in position.

Adding Sound Effects

iMovie makes adding sound effects amazingly simple.

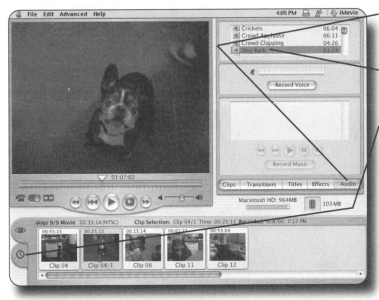

1. Click on **Audio**. The Audio palette will appear.

2. Click on a **sound effect**. The sound effect will play.

3. Click on the **Timeline Viewer tab**. The Timeline Viewer will move to the front.

4. Click on the **audio track icon**. The audio track will be selected.

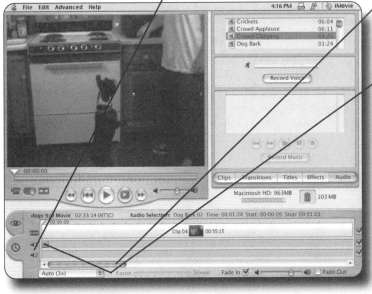

5. Drag the **scroll bar** to the location where you want to insert your chosen sound.

6. Drag the **sound effect** to the audio track and **drop it** at the desired location.

NOTE

You can adjust the volume of a sound so that it plays in the background and add narration in the foreground.

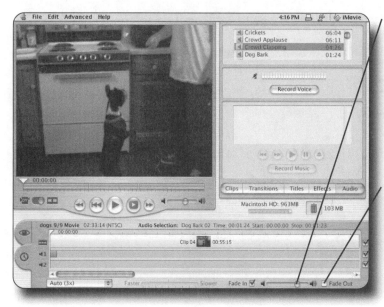

7. **Drag** the **Clip Volume slider** to adjust the volume of your sound effect.

8. **Click** on the **Fade In check box**. The volume will fade in when the sound effect plays.

9. **Click** on the **Fade Out check box**. The volume will fade out gradually as the sound effect ends.

10. **Click** on **Advanced**. The Advanced menu will appear.

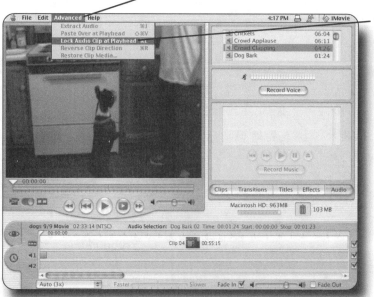

11. **Click** on **Lock Audio Clip at Playhead**. A small tack icon will appear on your sound effect to indicate that it is secured.

Adding Recorded Music

You can also easily add pre-recorded music to your movie.

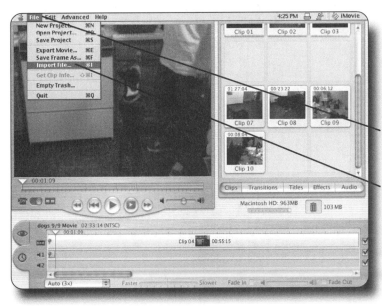

1. In the Timeline Viewer, **click** on the **Playhead** and **drag it** to the location where you want to insert your music.

2. **Click** on **File**. The File menu will appear.

3. **Click** on **Import File**. The Import File dialog box will open.

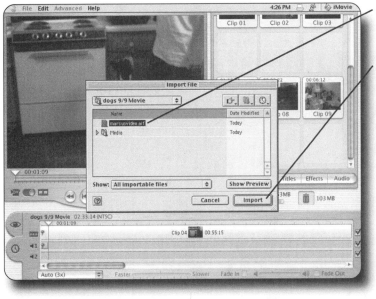

4. Navigate to your **AIF or MP3 audio file**.

5. Click on **Import**. Your music file will appear in the Timeline Viewer.

6. Adjust the **clip's volume** using the Clip Volume slider.

7. Click on the **clip speed slider** and **adjust** the **speed** at which the clips are played in the movie. This will help coordinate your movie clip with your sound file.

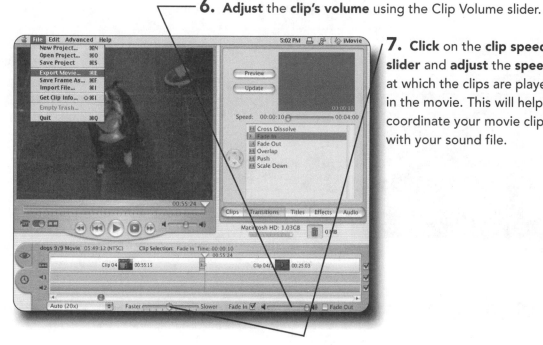

Exporting Your Movie

When you have finished editing your movie and adding transitions, sounds, and music, you can export it back to digital video tape or to a QuickTime file. In this example, you'll export your movie to QuickTime.

1. Click on **File**. The File menu will appear.

2. Click on **Export Movie**. The Export Movie dialog box will appear.

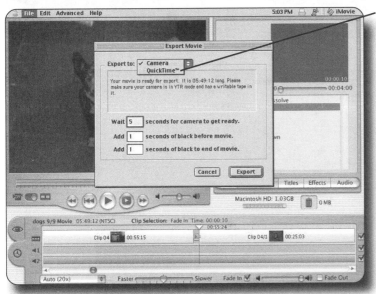

3. Click on **QuickTime** in the Export to pop-up menu. The Export Movie dialog box will change, offering you some format options.

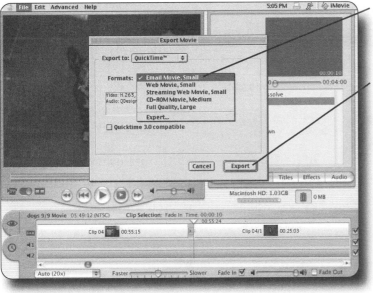

4. Click on the **format** you want to use for your movie in the Formats pop-up menu.

5. Click on **Export**. The Export QuickTime Movie dialog box will open.

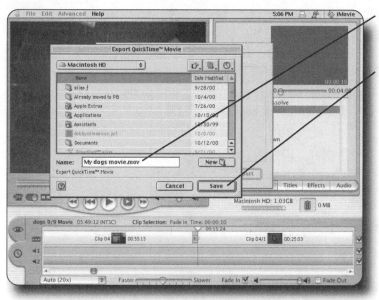

6. Type a **name** for your movie in the Name text box.

7. Click on **Save**.

An export progress bar will appear while your movie is processed. (It can take a long time to export a movie.)

8. Locate your **movie** on your hard drive and **double-click** its **icon** to play it.

Congratulations, you are now a movie producer!

10

Working with QuickTime

QuickTime is Apple Computer's multimedia player. It can be used to work with video, music, animation, text, sound, and virtual reality documents on and off the Web. QuickTime can be used to open over 240 kinds of digital media, including the most popular file types: AIFF, MIDI, PICT, WAV, and MP3. In this chapter, you'll learn how to:

- Use the basic controls of QuickTime Player
- Play movies in QuickTime Player
- Listen to streaming audio on the Web
- Update QuickTime
- Use Picture Viewer
- Manipulate pictures with Picture Viewer

NOTE

You can find a list of file types supported on Apple Computer's Web site at http://www.apple.com/quicktime/specifications.html.

The QuickTime Player

QuickTime and all of its associated files come installed on your iMac. These files are stored in your Applications folder.

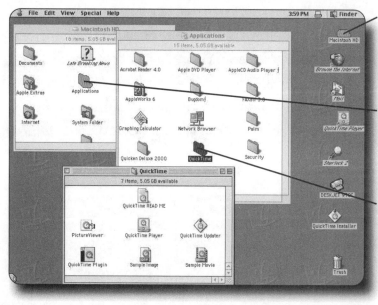

1. Double-click on the **Macintosh HD icon**. The Macintosh HD window will open.

2. Double-click on the **Applications folder**. The Applications window will open.

3. Double-click on the **QuickTime folder**. The QuickTime window will open.

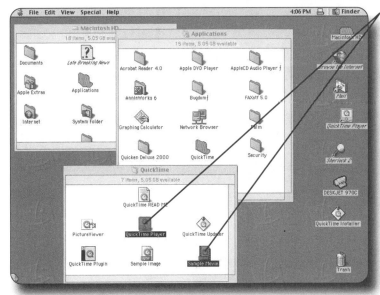

4. **Drag** the **Sample Movie file** onto the **QuickTime Player icon**. When the QuickTime Player icon is highlighted, release the mouse button. QuickTime Player will launch and the movie will be ready to be played.

Before playing the sample movie, look at the parts of the QuickTime Player. All of the controls can be used while working with movies, sounds, or music.

• **Movie Title**. The name of the movie that is currently open

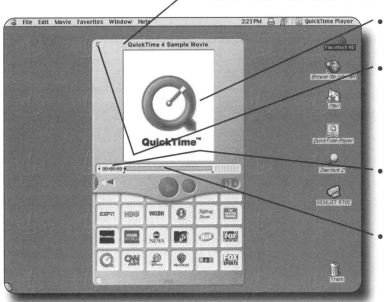

• **Movie**. The area in which the movie is played

• **Close Box**. Click on the close box to close the movie. Remember that QuickTime Player is still open in the background.

• **Time**. The time counter shows the length of the movie as it plays.

• **Time Line**. The diamond displays the progress of the movie as it plays.

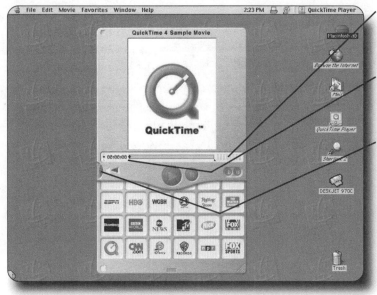

- **Graphic Equalizer**. This display shows the sound of the movie.

- **Chapter Marker**. Drag the triangle to mark a spot in the movie.

- **Volume Control**. Drag the dial to control the volume.

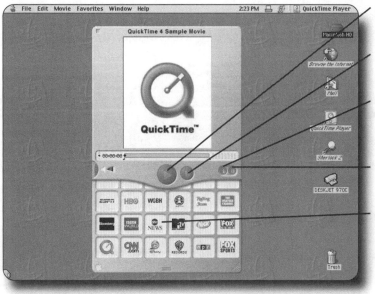

- **Play Button**. Click here to play a movie.

- **Pause Button**. Click here to pause the movie.

- **Info Button**. Click here to get information on the movie.

- **Controls**. Click here to open the sound controls.

- **Favorites**. Bookmarks for your favorite QuickTime movies, radio stations or TV channels are stored here.

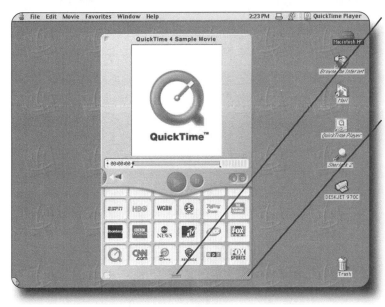

- **Drawer Pull**. Drag the pull downward to open your Favorites drawer (also accessible from the Favorites menu)

- **Resize Control**. Drag on the corner to make the movie larger or smaller

Playing Media Files with QuickTime Player

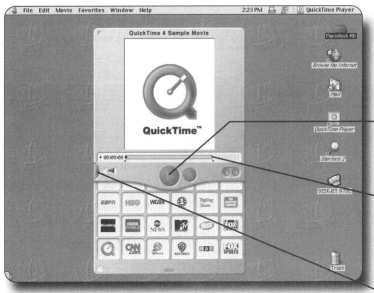

Playing a movie or sound in QuickTime Player is easy. If you've closed the Player, repeat steps 1 through 4 above, then continue.

1. **Click** on the **Play button**. The QuickTime movie will play.

2. **Click** on the **diamond** and **drag it** across the **Time Line**. The movie will play in slow motion.

3. **Click** on the **Volume control** and **drag it up or down**. The dial will turn and the volume will be adjusted.

QuickTime Player Controls Tray

Although Apple doesn't include any sound files to try with QuickTime Player, you will most certainly want to use the Controls tray to adjust sound. As you discover sound files such as WAVs and MP3s, the Controls tray will come in very handy. The controls are very similar to a tape deck or CD player and will work with all media that QuickTime plays.

1. Click on the **Controls button**. The controls tray will slide down.

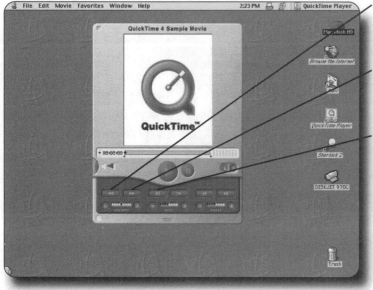

- **Fast Rewind**. Click here to play your media file backwards very quickly.

- **Fast Forward**. Click here to play your media file forwards very quickly.

- **Step Back**. Click here as many times as needed to incrementally move the media frame by frame, back to the beginning of the file.

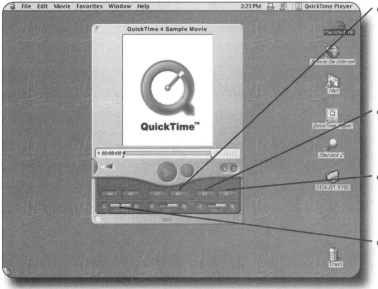

- **Step Forward**. Click here as many times as needed to incrementally move the media forward through the file.

- **Go To Start**. Click here to move to the beginning of the media file.

- **Go To End**. Click here to move to the end of the media file.

- **Balance Slider**. Drag the black square to change the speaker balance to the left or right channel.

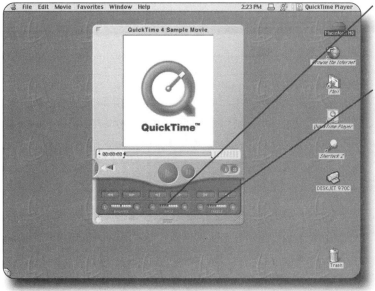

- **Bass Slider**. Click in the black squares to give your sound greater or fewer low bass tones.

- **Treble Slider**. Click in the black squares to give your sound greater or fewer high treble tones.

2. Click on the **Controls button again**. The controls tray will slide up, saving any changes you made in the sound levels.

Using QuickTime on the Web

QuickTime is used on many Web sites. Apple has provided some pre-installed TV and radio stations in your Favorites Drawer. You can either view QuickTime files through your Web browser or directly through the QuickTime Player.

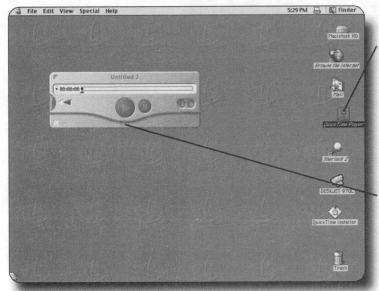

1. Double-click on the **QuickTime Player alias icon** on your desktop. An untitled QuickTime movie will open— notice that the new file does not show a movie area because no movie is open.

2. Click and drag the **Drawer Pull down**. The previously installed favorite locations will be visible.

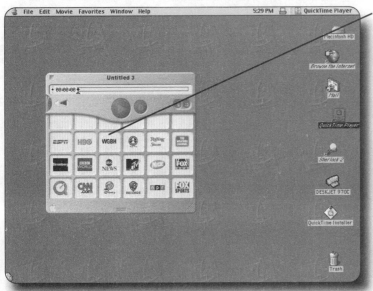

3. Click on the **WGBH bookmark**. Your iMac will open a QuickTime movie and automatically connect you to the Internet and to the WGBH Educational Foundation. From here, you can choose to watch TV or listen to the radio on your iMac using QuickTime video or audio streaming.

TIP

Apple Computer, Inc. works with many movie companies and provides fun movie trailers done in QuickTime on their Web site. You can usually find a listing of the newest trailers at http://www.apple.com/quicktime/hotpicks, or by clicking the Q bookmark in your Favorites Drawer.

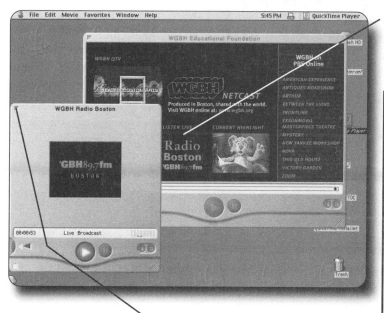

4. **Click** on a **link** of interest and enjoy the show. A new QuickTime movie will open.

NOTE

If you connect to the Internet through a modem and telephone line, you may find the audio and video slightly choppy. This is due to the speed of your connection. Cable modems and DSL Internet connections are much faster.

5. **Click** on the **close box** when you are done. The QuickTime movie will close.

6. **Click** on **File**. The File menu will appear.

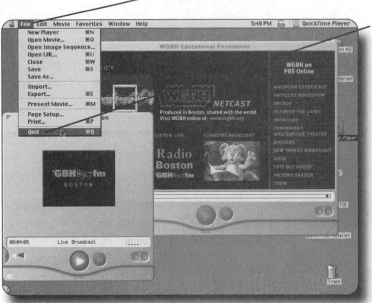

7. **Click** on **Quit**.
QuickTime Player will close.

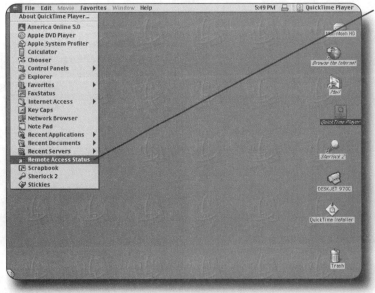

8. **Choose Remote Access Status** from the Apple Menu. Remote Access Status will open.

9. **Click** on **Disconnect**. You will be disconnected from the Internet.

Updating QuickTime

Apple has built smart technology into QuickTime. If you have ever played a QuickTime movie on the Apple (or other) Web site, you are notified automatically when a

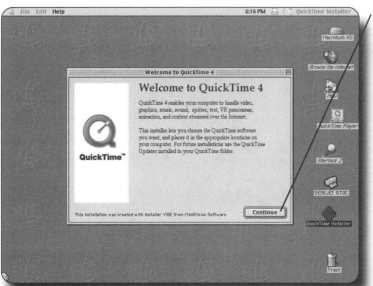

QuickTime update is available. QuickTime is updated regularly.

If an update is available, you receive a notice in the form of a dialog box across your browser screen.

1. Click on **Update**. A notice that your Internet connection must be active will appear. If your connection is not active, reconnect now. The Welcome to QuickTime 4 screen will appear.

2. Click on **Continue**. You will proceed to the License screen.

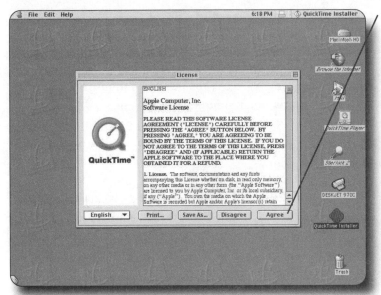

3. Click on **Agree** (after reading it, of course). You will continue to the Choose Installation Type screen.

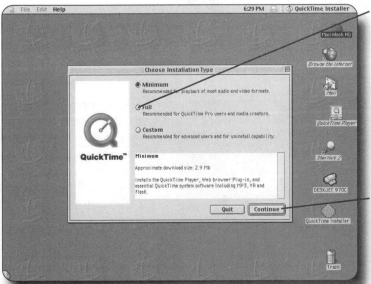

4. Click on the **radio button** for the type of QuickTime installation you want. If you have purchased the QuickTime Pro package in the past or expect to purchase it, click on the Full radio button. The radio button will be selected.

5. Click on **Continue**. The Quicktime Installer screen will appear.

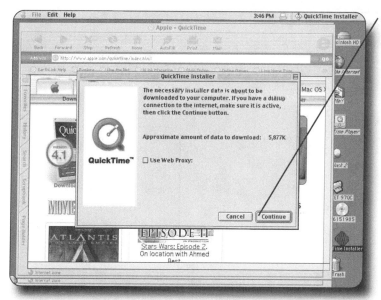

6. Click on **Continue**.

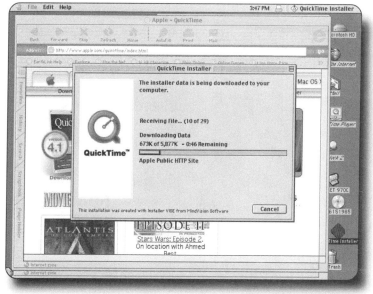

Your computer is automatically connected to Apple's File Transfer site. You can watch the progress of the download process. A dialog box will appear when the download and the installation is complete.

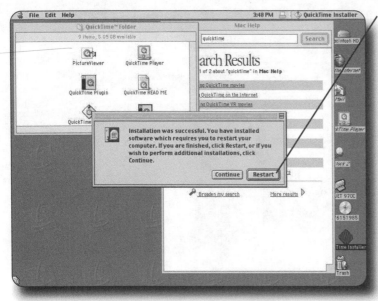

7. **Click** on **Restart**. If you have other work open, you can click behind the dialog box and save your files first. Your iMac will restart.

NOTE

Once your computer has restarted. You will see that your old QuickTime files have been sent to the Trash. This is normal. Empty the Trash before you proceed.

Using PictureViewer

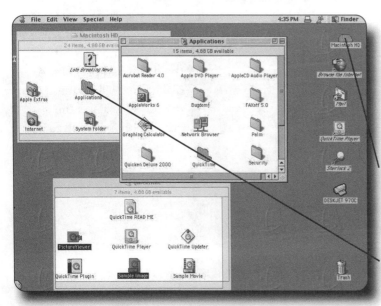

PictureViewer is a program that comes with QuickTime. It is used to view any picture that is compatible with the QuickTime format. PictureViewer also allows very basic editing of an image.

1. **Double-click** on the **Macintosh HD icon**. The Macintosh HD window will open.

2. **Double-click** on the **Applications folder**. The Applications window will open.

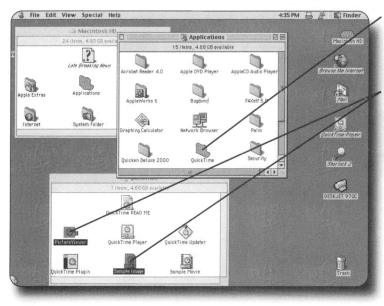

3. Double-click on the **QuickTime folder**. The QuickTime window will open.

4. Click and drag the **Sample Image** and **onto** the **PictureViewer icon**. The sample image will open in PictureViewer.

5. Click on **Image**. The Image menu will appear

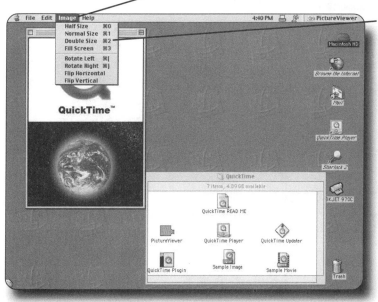

6. Click on the **options**. PictureViewer will allow you to resize or change the orientation of the sample image.

When you are done making changes to your image, you can save it in a number of different file formats.

7. **Click** on **File**. The File menu will appear.

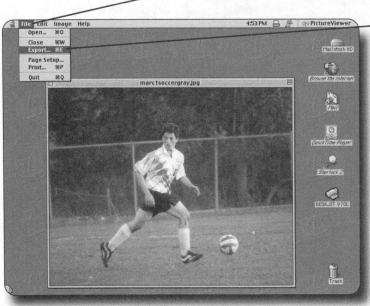

8. **Click** on **Export**. A dialog box will appear.

9. **Click** on the **Save Image as pop-up menu.** The pop-up menu will open.

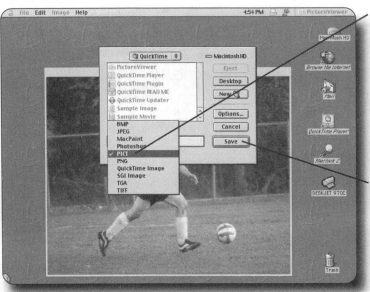

10. **Click** on a **file format** for your revised picture. The format will be selected. Notice that the file name for your picture will change for each file type.(See more information on file types below.)

11. **Click** on **Save**. Your file will be exported into the new format and saved to your hard disk.

File Formats in PictureViewer

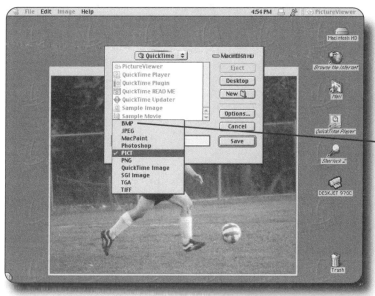

The different file formats in which you can store documents allow you to open your pictures in different kinds of photo editing software.

- **BMP** is a bit-mapped Windows format for use on PCs. It is not a native Macintosh format. Pictures are converted to a series of dots, which is not very good for photographs.

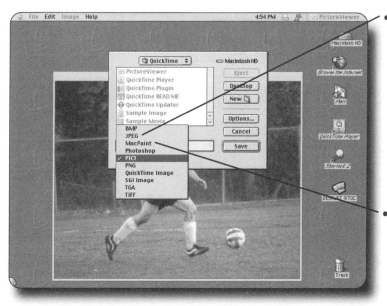

- **JPEG** (*Joint Photographic Experts Group*) is a compressed image format. It is best used for compressing color photographs, as it retains color information well. Use JPEG to make photographs for your web page or to print.

- **MacPaint** is a bitmapped format. It is best used for line art and simple artwork to be used in a wordprocessor or newsletter.

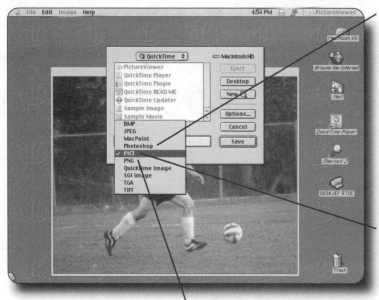

- **Photoshop** is the native format for Adobe's Photoshop software. It can be opened by many different other programs as well. These files tend to be very large, and include all the original color information, which make it a good choice for editing pictures.

- **PICT** is a native Macintosh format often used for Desktop pictures.

- **PNG** (*Portable Network Graphics*) is a relatively new graphic compression format, designed to replace GIF and TIFF formats on the World Wide Web.

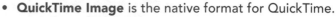

- **QuickTime Image** is the native format for QuickTime.

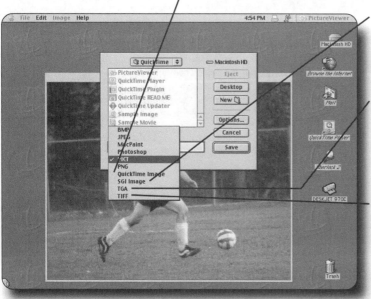

- **SGI image** (*Silicon Graphics Image*) is a format for use on Silicon Graphics computers.

- **TGA** (*TrueVision Targa*) is a graphic file format for video, which a home user would probably never use.

- **TIFF** (*Tagged Image File Format*) is an older format, still used for printing materials or scanned images.

PART V

Your iMac on the Internet

11

Wandering the World Wide Web

The Web was created to provide a way to deliver linked text and graphics over the Internet, which previously contained only text documents. Today the Web has evolved far beyond simple document transfer. It spans the entire globe, contains a wealth of information, allows us to shop for just about anything that can be delivered, and supports real-time audio and video as well as text and graphics. The Web was designed to relate similar and complementary information in a simple fashion to everyone. In this chapter, you'll learn how to:

- Launch a Web browser
- Search for information the Web
- Follow linked text (hyperlinks)
- Save the location of your favorite Web pages
- Electronically register your iMac

Introducing the World Wide Web

The bulk of the Internet's information content is provided over the World Wide Web. When a company or individual wants to make Web content available to the world, they create a *Web site*—a collection of documents that can be viewed using a Web browser. Web documents are formatted using a language called HTML (*Hypertext Markup Language*). Each document is known as a *Web page*; the first page that you see when you reach a Web site is usually called the *home page*.

Looking at Web Activities

An enormous amount of content is available on the Web. On the Web you can

- Research any subject

- Make a purchase

- Look up information for a school paper using one of the many homework helper sites

- Get technical support for hardware and software by sending a question to the manufacturer

- Track a package that has been sent by a major courier such as UPS or Federal Express

- Find the lowest available airplane fare and book a flight

- Get software updates for products such as QuickTime and other software that came with your iMac

- Play games

- Read information about your hobby, a favorite recreation, or your favorite entertainer

- Listen to music

- Obtain tax forms

- Find a weather forecast and weather maps

This list could go on for pages! The Web is an excellent source of information for many subjects, but you should be aware that there is no guarantee that precisely what you need will be available. You should also be aware that not every page of information contains guaranteed expertise on a subject; many pages are created by hobbyists who might not be professionals in their fields.

Understanding URLs

Each Web page has an address called a *Uniform Resource Locator*, or URL. Assuming that you are connected to the Internet and your browser is open, you can reach a Web page by typing the URL of the page you want to view.

URLs for Web pages generally begin with *http://*. This signifies that the part of the Internet being called up is the *Hypertext Transfer Protocol*. The characters that follow specify exactly which page you want. The first part of many addresses is *www*, which refers to the World Wide Web. The location after that is usually the site or company name.

Some Web sites you might want to explore are:

- Macintosh hardware and software sellers: http://www.drbott.com, http://www.belkin.com, http://www.maczone.com, http://www.cc-inc.com/ macmall, http://www.macconnection.com

- Homework helper sites: http://www.bigchalk.com, http://www.familyeducation.com

- Apple Computer: http://www.apple.com

NOTE

The end of an address is usually .com, .org, .net, .gov, or .edu. These abbreviations denote company, organization (usually a non-profit), network, United States government, or educational institution. Foreign countries each have their own abbreviation, such as .ca (Canada), .fr (France), .it (Italy), and so on.

- Hardware and software help: http://www.macfixit.com, http://www.macintouch.com

- Home networking help: http://www.farallon.com/homenet

<table>
<tr><td>

NOTE

If you have chosen a local ISP, you may need to make the connection manually. Check with the ISP's technical support personnel to be sure.

</td></tr>
</table>

Making the Internet Connection

Web browsers assume that your computer is already connected to the Internet. If you're using America Online (AOL) as your Internet Service Provider (ISP), you need to sign on to AOL before launching a browser. If you are using EarthLink, the first Internet application you use, such as a Web browser, makes the connection for you.

<table>
<tr><td>

NOTE

AOL's software includes its own browser, which is based on Internet Explorer. However, the AOL browser is more limited and may have some compatibility problems with some Web sites. Therefore, you may want to use a separate browser rather than relying on AOL's implementation.

</td></tr>
</table>

Launching Your Browser

The iMac comes with two Web browsers: Microsoft Internet Explorer and Netscape Navigator, both located in the Internet folder on your Macintosh hard drive. They are very similar. Internet Explorer is often made the default browser. You may want to experiment with both before deciding which one you like best, but this chapter covers Internet Explorer.

Logging on to the Web with EarthLink

If you use EarthLink as your ISP, follow these steps to launch your browser:

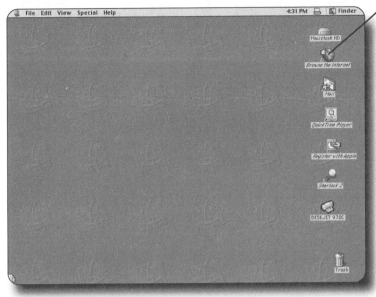

1. Double-click on the **Browse the Internet alias** on the Desktop. Internet Explorer will launch. Your modem will automatically connect to EarthLink and a dialog box will open, asking if you want Internet Explorer (IE) to be your default browser. This dialog box will open only the first time you launch Internet Explorer. When IE starts, it will display the Web page that is stored in your software as your home page, most likely: http://apple.excite.com.

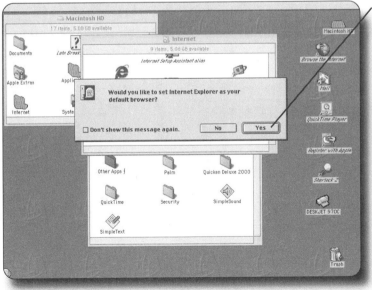

2. Click on **Yes** if you want to use Internet Explorer as your default browser. The EarthLink Personal Start Page Sign Up/Log In page will appear. You can use this page to personalize your home page, which will be set to an EarthLink/Apple page.

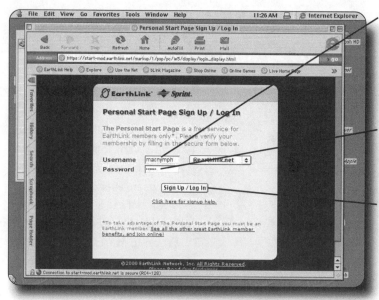

3. Type your **EarthLink user name** in the Username text box and **press Tab**. The cursor will move to the Password text box.

4. Type your **EarthLink password** in the Password text box.

5. Click on **Sign Up/Log in**.

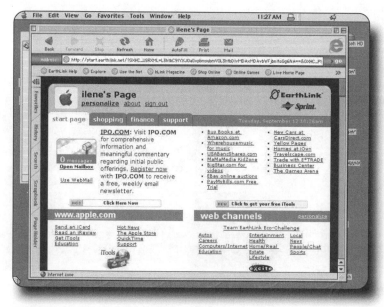

Your personalized home page will appear. Using links on this page, you can access hundreds of popular Web sites.

Navigating the Web

The Web is made up of millions of Web sites. Once you are taken to the page that has been designated as your browser's home page, you can move from page to page following trails of information. To navigate the Web, you have many choices, several of which are discussed in this section.

Following a Hyperlink

The most common way to move from one Web page to another is to click on a text hyperlink. The hyperlinks used in Web pages function exactly like those in the Apple Guide; you click on underlined text to be transported to the location linked to the text.

1. **Move** the **mouse pointer** over the underlined text that represents a hyperlink. The mouse pointer will change to a hand with a pointing finger. The URL of the linked location will appear at the very bottom of the browser window.

TIP

When you launch Netscape Communicator for the first time, you must create at least one user profile. Follow the instructions on each of the ten screens presented and use the Next button to move from screen to screen. If you want to use Netscape as your e-mail program, you must type mail.earthlink.net in screens 5 and 6 to identify your incoming and outgoing mail server. A similar Apple/Excite page will open as your home page, which you can then choose to personalize.

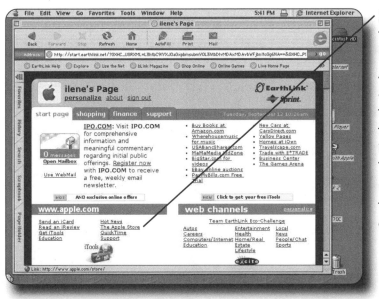

2. **Click** on the **hyperlink.** The URL of the linked location will appear in the Address line of the browser, and the browser will begin to transfer that Web page from the computer on which it is stored to your screen. This process is called *downloading* (transferring a file from some other computer to yours).

3. Click on **Back**. The browser will return to your home page (or the page you were previously viewing).

Searching a Site

Many Web sites are made up of hundreds of pages. If you go to a site looking for some specific information, following the hyperlinks through the entire site is often tedious. Fortunately, most large sites make it possible for you to search through the site by supplying a search box where you can type in what you seek.

1. Scroll down and **find** the **Search section** in your home page. It should contain a text box in which you can enter a search term.

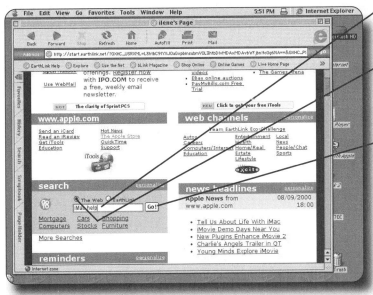

2. Type the **search term** in the text box.

3. Click on **The Web** to search the entire World Wide Web.

4. Click on **Go!**. The Security Notice dialog box will open.

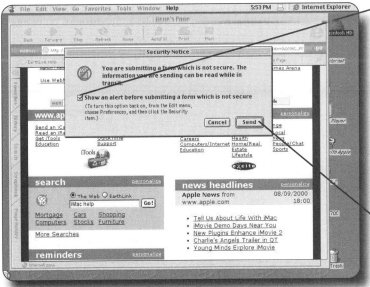

5. Click on **Show an alert before submitting a form which is not secure** to turn off the appearance of this dialog box. EarthLink is set, by default, to alert you when the information you send is not protected. You can turn on this feature again later if you like.

6. Click on **Send**. A list of hyperlinked matches for your search term will appear.

TIP

There is no official standard for the design of Web sites or Web pages. You might find that instead of a Go! button, there is a Search or an Enter button.

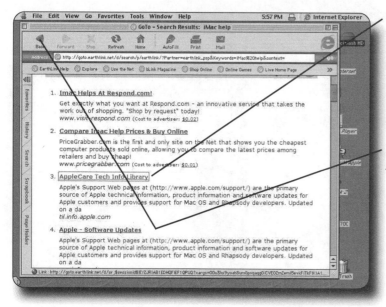

7. Click on a **hyperlink** to reach the designated Web page. The link will change color (indicating that it has been followed) and the linked page will open.

8. Click on **Back** to return to your personal home page.

Submitting a Form

Some Web pages are designed to gather information from you and send that information to the person or company who owns the Web site. Such pages contain *forms*. You fill out the information and use a Submit button to send the information over the Internet to its destination. One such form is used when you register on Apple's newly-designed technical support site. To do so, follow these steps:

1. Type http:// signin.info.apple.com in your browser's Address text box and **press Return**. The browser will download the Web Page and display it.

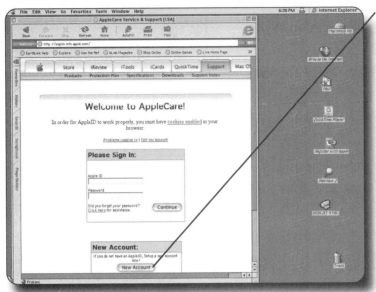

2. Click on **New Account** near the bottom of the page. The Apple ID page will appear.

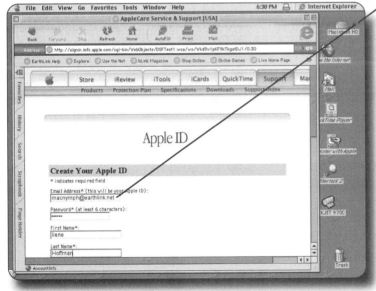

3. Enter the **requested information** in the appropriate text boxes.

NOTE

Usually, required pieces of information are starred or appear in red.

---

4. Click on **Continue** at the bottom of the form when you have finished filling in the information. You data will be sent, and you will probably see a confirmation that your data has been sent. You might be presented with the Forms AutoFill dialog box.

NOTE

Many Web sites, especially those from which you can make purchases, have implemented security measures to protect your credit card number and other sensitive information while it travels over the Internet and when it is stored on a Web server. When you submit a form to a secure site, your browser may display an alert telling you what security is being used. It's better to place an order using the telephone than risk sending your private information to an unsecured site.

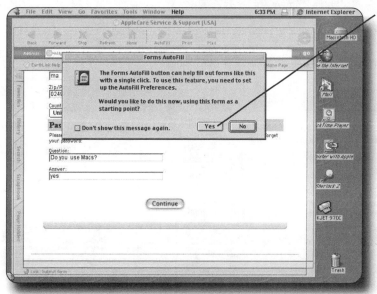

5. Click on **Yes** in the Forms AutoFill dialog box if you want to use AutoFill, and then complete any requested information. If you click on No, you can also click on the check box, so that Explorer does not show the dialog box again.

Using Bookmarks

As you navigate the Web, you will often visit Web sites that you want to visit again. The easiest way to keep track of these sites is to *bookmark* them in your Favorites menu. You can then access your bookmarked sites simply by going to the Favorites menu.

NOTE

Bookmark is a Netscape Navigator term. Internet Explorer refers to bookmarks as *favorites*.

1. **Click** on **Favorites**. The Favorites menu will appear.

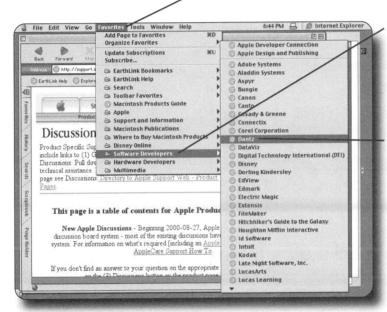

2. **Move** the **mouse pointer** to Software Developers. The list of already marked sites will appear.

3. **Click** on a **site** of interest.

The browser will download the chosen site and display it.

Adding Your Own Favorites or Bookmarks

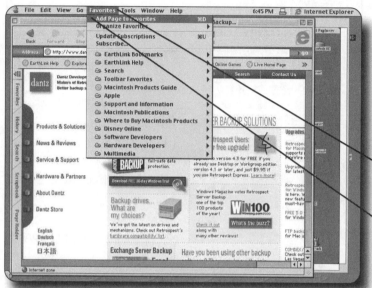

Creating new favorite sites is easy. Simply follow these steps:

1. **Display** the **page** you want to add to the Favorites menu.

2. **Click** on **Favorites**. The Favorites menu will appear.

3. **Click** on **Add Page to Favorites**. The new bookmark will be added to the bottom of the Favorites menu.

Clicking on Image Hyperlinks

Not all hyperlinks are text—many of them are images. At first, this might make it hard for you to find links on a page. However, there is a trick to finding them.

1. **Move** the **mouse pointer** to an image that is a hyperlink. The mouse pointer will change to a hand with a pointing finger.

2. **Click** on the **image**. The browser will download the requested page and display it.

Searching the Entire Web

Probably the biggest problem with the sheer size of the Web is that it can be difficult to find exactly what you need. *Search engines*—Web sites that index other Web sites— have been developed to provide some global search capabilities. Search sites use different ways to search and index sites, but the result is a large list of topic-related sites.

One of the first search sites was http://www.yahoo.com. It is still a good site for finding educational resources or commercial information that is organized into business categories.

1. **Type http://www.yahoo.com** in the Address box in your browser and **press Return**. The browser will download the Web page and display it.

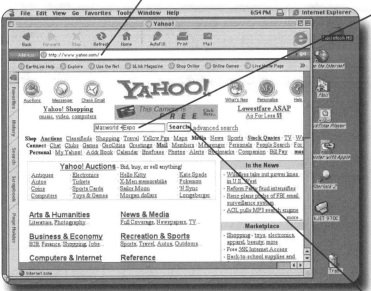

2. **Type** a **search term** in the text box at the top of the page.

TIP

If you have more than one search term, put a plus sign (+) in front of each term. That will instruct Yahoo to retrieve only those sites that contain *all* of your search terms.

---

3. **Click** on **Search**. Yahoo will search its database to find Web sites and categories of Web sites that include your search term. It will then displays the results of the search on a new Web page. Yahoo results include hyperlinks to categories and individual Web sites.

TIP

Do not bookmark pages that contain results produced by a search engine. Those pages are usually temporary, and are generated by your search and then discarded when you are done with them. If you try to return to one via a bookmark, you will often get an error message indicating that the URL doesn't exist.

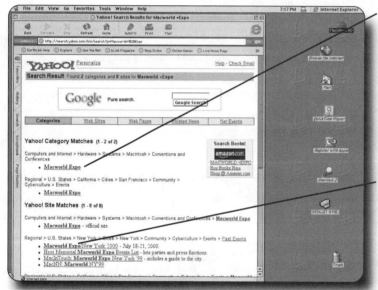

4. **Click** on the **hyperlink** to a category to view the Web sites in that category. Yahoo will display a list of individual sites on a new page.

OR

4b. **Click** on the **hyperlink** to an individual site to go directly to a Web page. The browser will download the page and display it.

TIP

For serious research on the Internet, you may want to consider using a *metasearch engine,* a search engine that searches many other search engines for you. Two excellent sites are http://www.dogpile.com and http://www.search.com.

5. **Click** on **File**. The File menu will appear.

6. **Click** on **Quit**. Your browser will close.

12

Getting out Your iTools

iTools are a suite of Web utilities designed to make your Internet browsing experience easier and more fun. iTools are part of Apple's Web service, which allows you to create a home page, set up a free e-mail address, store files on your own remote disk on Apple's Internet servers, or control Internet access for your children. The iTools features became available with Mac OS 9.0.4. This means that you cannot set up an iTools disk or use other iTools features unless you use Mac OS 9.0.4 or later. In this chapter, you'll learn how to:

- Set up iTools on your iMac
- Set up a Mac.com e-mail account
- Set up an iDisk
- Create a home page

Introducing iTools

You need to register before using any of the iTools services. The Apple iTools services include:

- **E-mail**. You can set up a free e-mail address at Mac.com. This address can be used with any e-mail software and any Internet Service Provider. You can also forward this mail to your regular e-mail box if you like. Setting up an account is easy; in fact, Apple even walks you through creating a second e-mail account in Outlook Express.

- **KidSafe**. Apple's parental controls include access to educator-selected sites. Parents can customize access to make sure that the content their children see is appropriate, according to their values. You can set up controls to cover chat rooms, file transfers, e-mail messages, and games access.

- **iDisk**. iDisk gives you extra storage space, similar to your hard drive. You can use it to store your Web files for your Mac.com home page or to easily share files with others.

- **HomePage**. You can use Apple's servers and templates to create and store your own personal Web site. Apple includes easy-to-use templates that require no knowledge of HTML (the Web page language) and make publishing the page a snap.

- **iCards**. iCards are Apple Computer's answer to sending birthday, greeting, and other types of cards you might normally buy in a store. A variety of high quality pictures are available along with "canned" messages. Every card can be personalized with your own words, too!

- **iReview**. If you want to find quality Web sites to peruse, what better way than to read brief descriptions with reader reviews? Apple provides capsulated descriptions and ratings of reviewed sites. Plus, you can add your own review and suggest sites.

Setting up iTools

To set up iTools, you must first launch your Web browser. The following instructions assume that you have set up an Internet connection as described in Chapter 2 "Mac OS Setup Assistant."

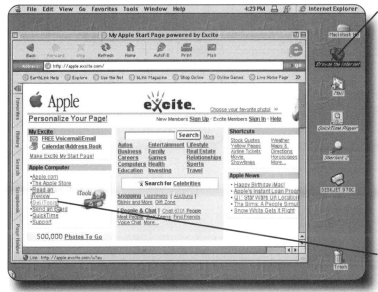

1. Double-click on the **Browse the Internet alias** on the Desktop. Internet Explorer will launch. The iMac will automatically connect to the Internet and display the Web page that is stored in your software as your home page, which was set up in Chapter 11 "Wandering the World Wide Web".

2. Click on the **Get iTools link**. The Apple - iTools home page will open.

NOTE

If you are using a different home page or a different browser, you can go to the iTools page by typing www.apple.com/itools/ in your address bar, then pressing Return.

3. **Read** over the **Apple - iTools page** and **decide** which **features** you want to use.

4. **Click** on **Free Sign Up**. The iTools page will open.

TIP

You can add this page to your Favorites list for easy access later. Click on Favorites and choose Add Page to Favorites. The page will be added to the bottom of your Favorites list.

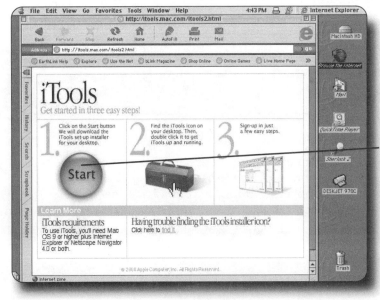

Step 1

The first step is the easiest—just download the iTools installer to your iMac and go.

1. **Click** on **Start**. The iTools Installer program will begin to download. Microsoft Internet Explorer will open the Download Manager window to display the download progress.

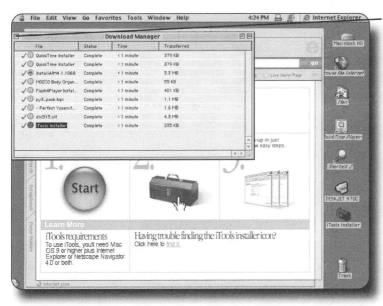

2. Click on the **close box** when the download is complete. The Download Manager window will close.

Step 2

The second step will automatically configure your web browser to use iTools and get you started with the sign up process.

1. Double-click on the **iTools Installer icon** on the Desktop. Your browser will open the iTools setup page.

2. Click on **Continue**. You will proceed to the next setup page.

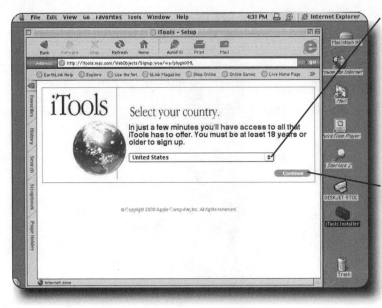

3. Click on the **pop-up menu**. The pop-up menu will open.

4. Click on your **country**. (The default is the United States.) Your country will be selected.

5. Click on **Continue**. You will proceed to the next page.

Step 3

Now it's time to provide your personal information and complete the registration.

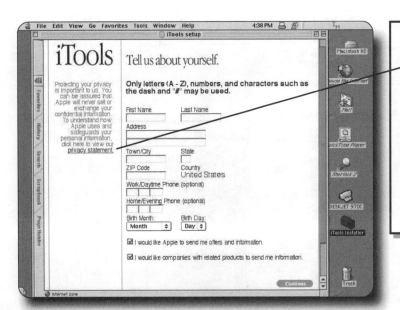

NOTE

Although people rarely read the privacy information on a site, it's a good idea to review it. Also, click on and read the information about Cookies. Use your browser's Back button to return to the Apple Customer Privacy Policy.

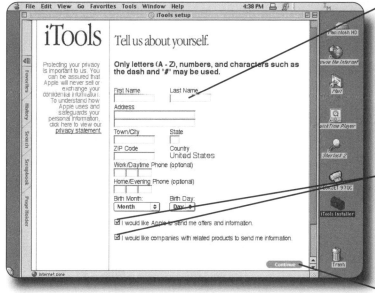

1. Fill out the **iTools form**. You can use the Tab key to move from field to field. (Since Apple doesn't explain why your birthday is needed, we can only hope it means you will get a birthday card from them.)

2. Click in the **check boxes** if you want to receive e-mail from Apple and other companies. Checks will appear in the check boxes.

3. Click on **Continue**. The Terms of Agreement form will appear.

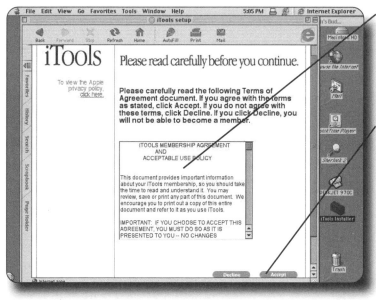

4. Read the **Terms of Agreement form**. Use the scroll bar on the form to move through the entire document.

5. Click on **Accept** if you agree to these terms. You will proceed to the next page.

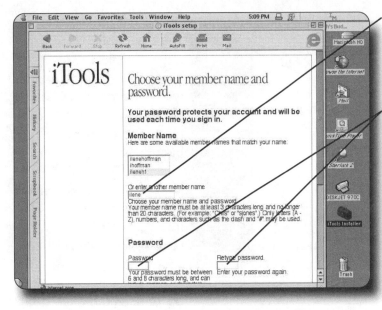

6. **Type** the **name** you want to use on your e-mail messages into the first text box.

7. **Type** the **password** you want to use into the Password and Retype password text boxes. Use the scroll bar to move down the page.

8. **Type** a **question** that Apple can use to verify who you are, in the event you forget your password, into the next text box. If needed, scroll down the page to see this information.

9. **Click** on **Continue**. You will proceed to the next page, where your account information will appear.

NOTE

If you cannot use your preferred e-mail name, Apple will tell you. Follow Apple's instructions to go back and choose a different name. Some variation of your name or a different name is better than one with a stream of numbers after it. Be creative—think different!

10. **Click** on **File**. The File menu will appear.

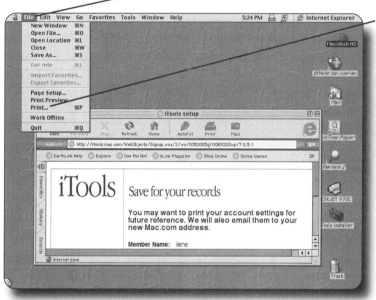

11. **Click** on **Print**. Your iTools account information will print on your printer.

12. **Click** on **Continue**. You will proceed to the next page.

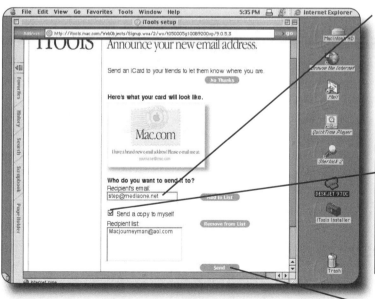

13. **Type** a **friend's e-mail address** into the Recipient's email text box if you wish to let a friend know you've set up a new account.

TIP

Be sure to check the Send a copy to myself check box. This is a good way to see Apple's iCard service in action!

14. **Click** on **Send**. A message will be sent to yourself and your friend and the Login page will appear.

Signing in to iTools

Now you get to sign in as an officials iTools user!

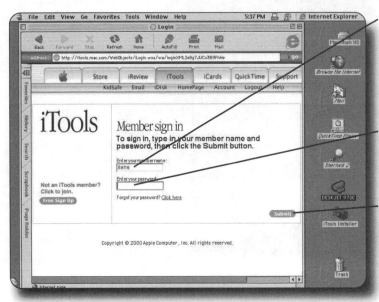

1. Type your **member name** if it does not already appear in the Enter your member name text box and **press** the **Tab key**.

2. Type your **password** into the Enter your password text box.

3. Click on **Submit**. The iTools start-up page will appear. You are now done setting up your e-mail account (and logging into iTools).

4. Click on the **Logout link** on the iTools menu bar. Your session will end and you will return to the Apple Computer main page.

To continue setting up your iDisk, don't log out yet and continue to the next section.

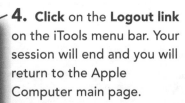

NOTE

If you close the browser window now, remember to repeat steps 1 and 2 to log back in.

Setting up an iDisk

The iDisk is 20 MB of storage space provided for registered users on the Apple servers. The disk is good when used as a temporary holding area for files, permanent storage of a Web site, or to share files with others.

1. Click on **Go** at the bottom of the iDisk section. The iDisk page will open.

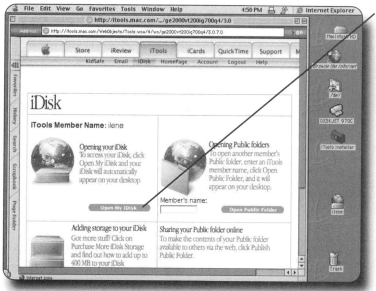

2. Click on **Open My iDisk**. An iDisk icon with your mac.com user name will appear on the Desktop.

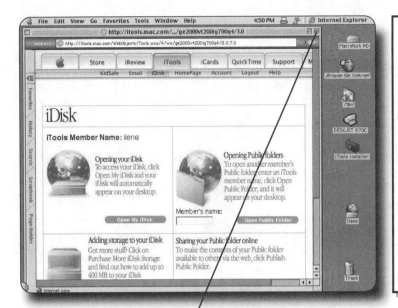

NOTE

It may take a little time for your iDisk to appear on your Desktop. Remember, you are accessing Apple's servers over the Internet remotely and you have to account for delays in the worldwide Internet network. This volume will not open or save files as quickly as the hard drive inside your iMac.

3. Click on the **rollup box** to minimize your browser window so that you can see your Desktop.

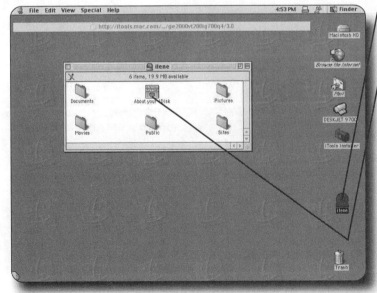

4. Double-click on the **iDisk icon**. The iDisk folder will open.

5. Double-click on the **About your iDisk icon**. SimpleText will launch so you can read about your iDisk.

NOTE

The iDisk does not stay on your Desktop permanently. You must open the iDisk each time you want to use it. The iDisk connection only lasts one hour.

Your iDisk Folders

There are five folders in your iDisk. These folders are provided for very specific tasks. You can create folders inside these folders, but not on the top level.

- **Documents**. This folder is for storing documents of any type. This is a private folder and is only accessible by you.

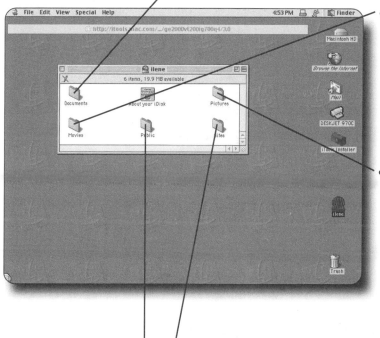

- **Movies**. This folder is for storing movie files. After you create movies with iMovie, you can store them here and use them on your Web page. Any QuickTime movie can be stored here.

- **Pictures**. This folder is for storing picture files that you use on your Web site. Pictures should be in JPEG or GIF format for best viewing on the web. (You can save almost any picture in these formats using PictureViewer.)

- **Sites**. This folder is for Web pages.

- **Public**. This folder is for public viewing of your documents. Anyone who knows your iDisk name can open and view the contents of this folder. The files can also be moved to another user's computer.

1. **Click** on the **iDisk icon** and **drag it** to the Trash when you are done using it.

Creating a Home Page

Creating a personal home page has never been easier for Mac users! Apple has provided all the tools you need. If you have disconnected from the Internet, you must reestablish your connection before you can set up your home page on Apple's iDisk server.

1. **Type www.apple.com/itools** into your browser and **press Return**. The Apple iTools page will open.

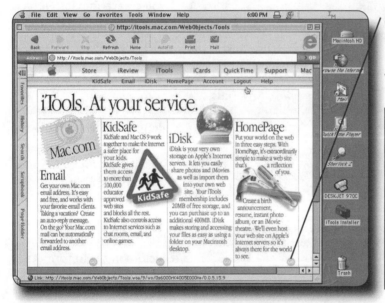

2. **Click** on **Go** under the HomePage section. The HomePage Welcome page will open.

NOTE

If you have previously logged out of iTools, you will be presented with the Member sign-in page before you can open any iTools pages. (Refer to the "Signing in to iTools" section.)

Apple provides many templates you can choose to create your page.

3. Click on the **style button** for the type of home page you want to create. You can click on each button to see the many different page styles available. A selection of samples of the style you chose will appear on the screen.

NOTE

You can learn more details about Apple's HomePage tools and other iDisk possibilities by clicking on the icons that appear at the bottom of the Home-Page Welcome page.

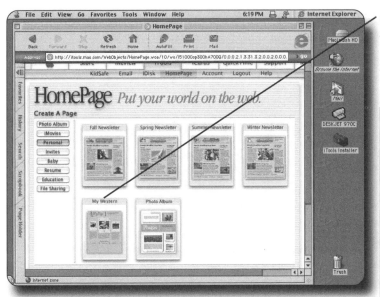

4. Click on a **page style** from the templates presented on the page. The next page will appear.

NOTE

Each page is slightly different. You can follow the directions for each page style to create your page. However, each page has the options discussed in the remaining steps.

5. Click on **Edit Text**. All of the available text areas can now be edited.

6. Click in any **text area** and **type** your replacement **text**.

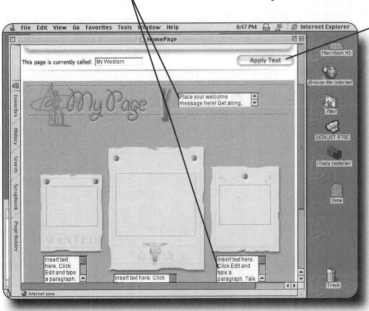

7. Click on **Apply Text** when you are done. The page will refresh and your new text will be displayed.

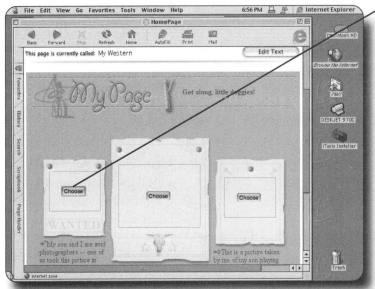

8. Click on **Choose** if you want to add a picture to your page in the space provided. The image page will open.

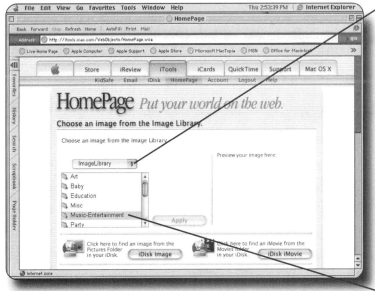

9. Click on the **pop-up menu**. The pop-up menu will open.

10. Click on **ImageLibrary**. The list box will display the available image categories.

TIP

You can also click on iDisk Image to choose a picture from your iDisk.

---

11. Click on an **image category** you like. The category will be selected.

12. Click on **Open Folder**. A list of images in the category you selected will appear in the list box.

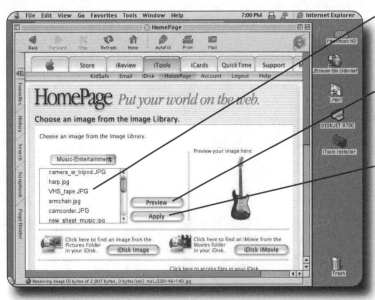

13. **Click** on any **file name** in the list box. The file will be selected.

14. **Click** on **Preview**. The image will appear on right side of the page.

15. **Click** on **Apply**. The edited page will appear. Repeat steps 9-15 for each image area.

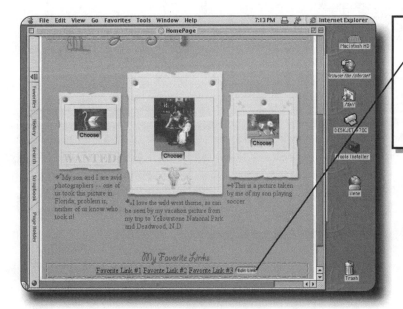

NOTE

Use the Edit Link button at the bottom of the page to add your own favorite Web sites to your home page.

Finishing your Home Page

After you create your Web site, you will have it out on the Internet for all to see in just a few clicks.

1. Click on **Preview**. Your finished home page will appear.

2. Click on **Edit** and **repeat** the **procedures** in the "Creating a Home Page" section. You will be able make any needed changes.

3. Click on **Publish** when you are satisfied with your page. Your HomePage will be posted on the Internet and the Congratulations page will appear.

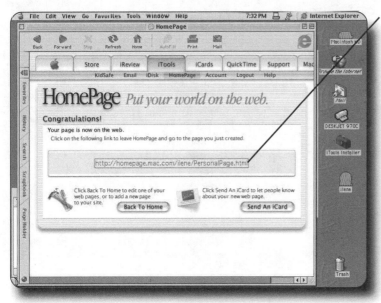

4. **Write** down the **address** of your new HomePage.

5. **Click** on the **address**. Your page will open in your browser.

NOTE

Any pictures you insert are shown in a small size. To see the picture in its original size, just click on it and another window with your picture will open.

13

Using E-Mail with Outlook Express

E-mail is a free way to send messages and files across the Internet to one or more people. There are many e-mail programs available, Outlook Express and Netscape come installed on your iMac. If you're using EarthLink or a local ISP, you might use Outlook Express to send and read e-mail messages. However, if your ISP is AOL, you use AOL's e-mail program to manage your e-mail messages. This chapter uses Outlook Express as an example of how e-mail works, but covers some AOL commands when they differ significantly. You can then apply what you have learned to almost any e-mail software. In this chapter, you'll learn how to:

- Set up an EarthLink e-mail account
- Create and send e-mail messages
- Read e-mail that has been sent to you
- Handle unwanted e-mail and e-mail attachments

Setting up an EarthLink E-Mail Account

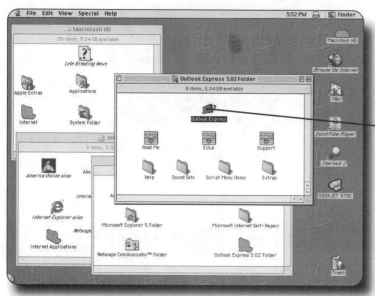

Composing and sending e-mail messages is a simple process. But, before you can work with e-mail, you need to have an e-mail account.

1. **Find Outlook Express** on your hard drive and **double-click** on its **icon**. Outlook Express will launch, and the Outlook Express Setup Assistant dialog box will open.

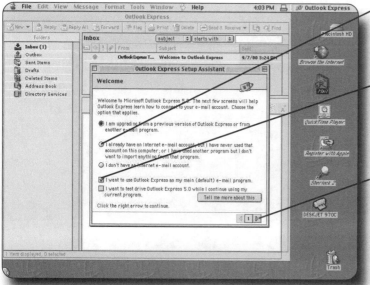

2. **Click** on **I already have an Internet e-mail account**. The option will be selected.

3. **Click** on **I want to use Outlook Express as my main e-mail program**. The option will be selected.

4. **Click** on the **right arrow button**. The next page of the Outlook Express Setup Assistant will appear.

Using the Outlook Express Setup Assistant

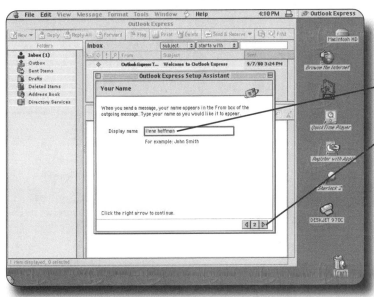

Outlook Express automates setting up your new e-mail account.

1. **Type** your **name** in the Display name box.

2. **Click** on the **right arrow button**. The next page of the Outlook Express Setup Assistant will appear.

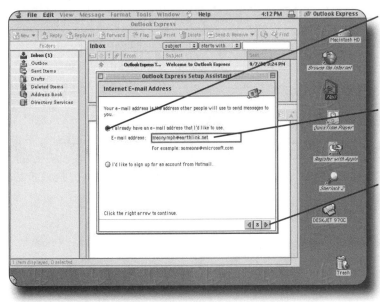

3. **Click** on **I already have an e-mail address that I'd like to use**. The option will be selected.

4. **Type** the **e-mail address** you chose when you set up your EarthLink account.

5. **Click** on the **right arrow button**. The next page of the Outlook Express Setup Assistant will appear.

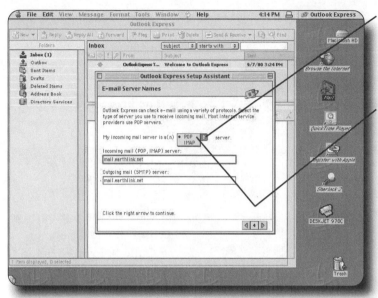

6. Click on the **My incoming mail server is an pop-up menu**. The pop-up menu will open.

7. Click on the **type** of mail server you use. The option will be selected.

NOTE

Most mail servers use POP (Point to Point) servers.

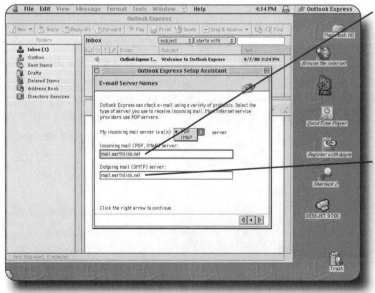

8. Type your incoming **mail server** in the Incoming mail (POP, IMAP) server text box, if necessary. (Outlook Express usually inserts the correct server addresses automatically.)

9. Type your outgoing **mail server** in the Outgoing mail (SMTP) server text box, if necessary.

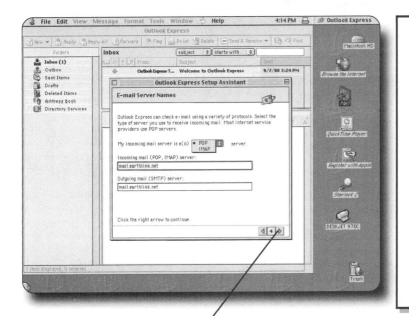

NOTE

If you use an e-mail account that is not part of the EarthLink network, you can get the correct mail server addresses from your ISP. Your incoming mail server is usually called something like, pop.mail.servername. Your outgoing mail server name is usually smtp.mail.servername. SMTP means simple mail transfer protocol

10. Click the **right arrow button**. The next page in the Outlook Express Setup Assistant will appear.

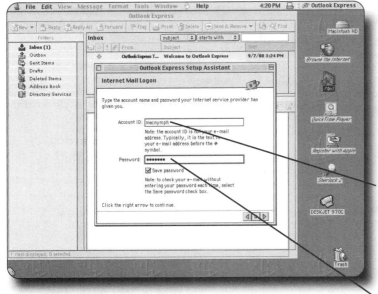

Finishing Your Account Setup

You may want to write some of the information you provide to the assistant down on paper at this point. You may need to reference it later.

1. Type your **account name** in the Account ID text box. This is the name you chose when you signed up on EarthLink.

2. Type your **Password** in the Password text box.

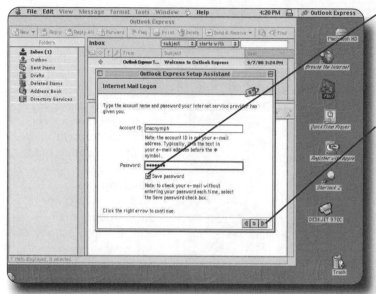

3. **Click** on the **Save password check box** if you do not want to type your password each time you use your e-mail service.

4. **Click** the **right arrow button**. The next page of the Outlook Express Setup Assistant will appear.

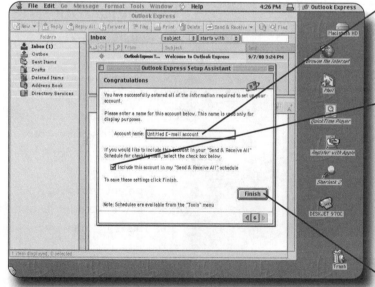

5. **Type** the **name** you want to use to identify this particular e-mail account in the Account name text box.

6. **Click** on the **Include this account in my "Send & Receive All" schedule check box**. The option will be selected. Now, when you pick up or send mail, this account will always be checked.

7. **Click** on **Finish**. Your e-mail account will be created.

Creating an E-Mail Message

An e-mail message is essentially a text document. It has two unique parts: the address of the recipient and a subject. Once these items have been entered, you can work on the content of the message.

You can create e-mail either *online* (connected to your ISP) or *offline* (not connected to your ISP). If you create the message while you are online, you can send it immediately. If you create it offline, you can't send it until you connect to your ISP. Composing e-mail offline has a definite advantage if your home has only one telephone line—you don't tie up the phone line while you're typing. Offline message creation is also a good idea if you are sending a large number of messages. However, if you are just typing a fast reply to someone, it may be just as easy to create the reply online.

Although Outlook Express and America Online look very different, you can use some of the same commands to compose and send e-mail messages.

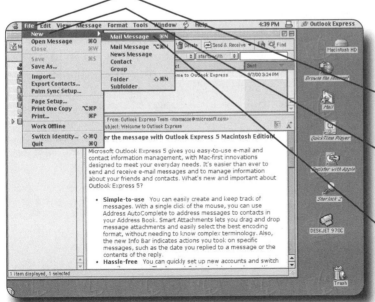

Creating a New E-Mail Message

1. Click on **File**. The File menu will appear.

2. Move the **mouse pointer** to New. The New menu will appear.

3. Click on **Mail Message**. A new, blank e-mail message will appear.

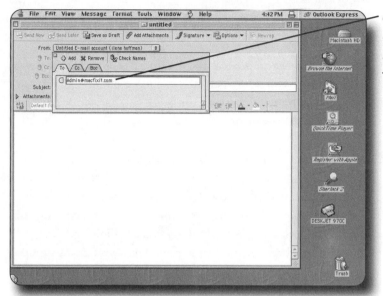

4. **Type** the **e-mail address** of the person to whom you are sending the mail in the To text box and **press Return**.

TIP

If you want to send your e-mail to more than one person, you can click on the Cc tab. (Cc means carbon copy—a leftover from the days when carbon paper was used.) The person specified in the To text box can see the e-mail address of the person receiving the copy.

If you want to send your e-mail to more than one person, but you don't want the person in the To text box to see who else is receiving the e-mail, choose Bcc. (Bcc means blind carbon copy.) Then, the only address that appears on all copies of the e-mail is the address in the To text box.

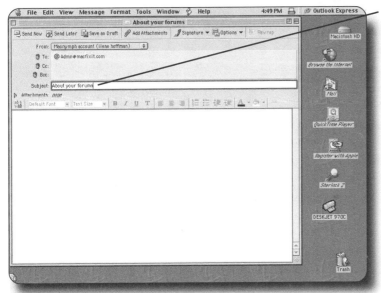

5. Type the **Subject** of your e-mail in the Subject text box and **press Tab**. The cursor will move into the main message space.

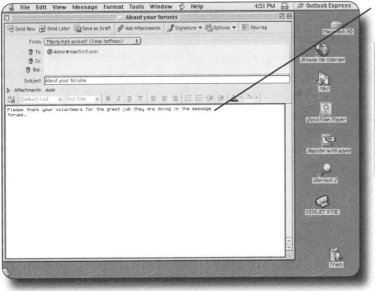

6. Type your **message**.

NOTE

If you have Microsoft Office installed on your iMac, you can use its dictionaries to spell check your e-mail.

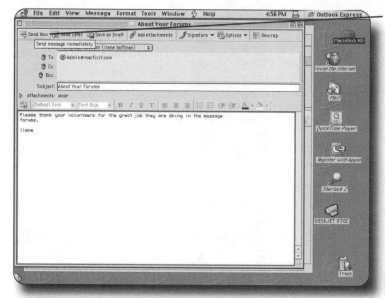

7. **Click** on **Send Now** when you have finished creating your e-mail message. Outlook Express will send your e-mail message, if you are already online.

NOTE

If you click on Send Now when you are working offline, Outlook Express will dial the ISP, open an Internet connection, and send your e-mail message.

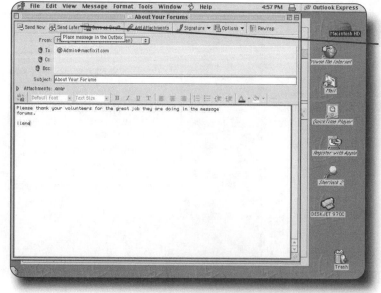

OR

7b. **Click** on **Send Later**. Your e-mail will be saved in your Outbox and a message box will appear, telling you that your message will be sent the next time you connect to the Internet.

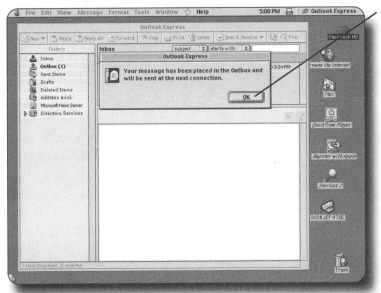

8. **Click** on **OK**. The message box will disappear.

9. **Click** on **Tools**. The Tools menu will appear.

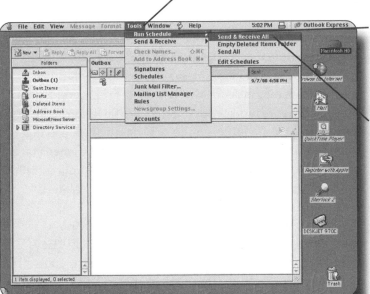

10. **Move** the **mouse pointer** to Run Schedule. The Run Schedule menu will appear.

11. **Click** on **Send & Receive All**. Any messages in your Outbox will be sent, and you will receive any new e-mail messages sent to you.

Understanding E-Mail Addresses

Internet addresses have the form user_name@location_name. The user_name is your AOL screen name or the account name you gave your ISP. You get the location_name from your service provider. Typically, location names end in .com or .net, unless the address is outside the United States. For example, AOL's domain name is aol.com; therefore, JDough5248's Internet e-mail address is jdough5248@aol.com.

Where can you locate e-mail addresses? If you know someone's AOL screen name, you can create his or her e-mail address by adding @aol.com to the screen name. Or, if you don't know the correct e-mail address or service provider, you can search for the e-mail address. A great place to search for e-mail addresses is http://www.infoseek.com.

Entering the Subject

When e-mail messages arrive at their destination, all recipients see is the address of the sender and the text of the subject line. A great deal of junk e-mail messages are sent (called *spam*), which may include advertisements for pornographic Web sites, get-rich-quick schemes, and chain letters. Therefore, you should be sure to provide a subject line that identifies your message as legitimate—especially when you are sending it to someone who might not recognize your e-mail address. Otherwise, the message might just be deleted.

For example, if your e-mail message is announcing a meeting, make sure the subject says exactly that: "Boys Club Meeting on 10-30-00." When you introduce yourself in a message, steer away from subject lines such as "Hello" or "Greetings." Bulk e-mailers often use such subjects to disguise junk e-mail. Instead, use something like "Introduction of Jane Dough" or "Recommendation from

John Doe" or "Application for Clerical Position." Whenever possible, use something that is personally meaningful to the recipient of the message.

Writing the Message

Writing the body of an e-mail message is usually like working with a text editor. You can use any of the text handling techniques you learned in Chapter 8, "Working with AppleWorks." How much you can format the text depends on the e-mail software you use. AOL's software, for example, lets you set the font, type size, and type style along with the alignment and text color. However, if the recipient of the e-mail message is not another AOL subscriber, there is no guarantee that the recipient will see the formatting. The recipient's e-mail software may not support formatted text and will therefore present the message in plain text. Some programs support using HTML (*Hypertext Markup Language*), the language used in Web pages, in e-mail. Again, not all software supports HTML mail, and your recipient may get a lot of text with visible HTML code. When in doubt, send e-mail messages in plain text.

NOTE

Once you send an e-mail message over the Internet, it cannot be recalled. (You can retrieve a message to another AOL user only if the user has not read the message.) Queuing mail to send later is a good idea if you aren't sure you want to send a message. A good tip to remember is: If you are angry at someone, write the e-mail message and let it sit a day—and then reread it before sending the message.

Working with E-Mail Attachments

E-mail has become an important vehicle for the delivery of many kinds of files. You can attach any file to an e-mail message and the file will be sent when the message is sent. Such *attachments* are often compressed so they are as small as possible and, therefore, take the minimum amount of time to send. In addition, multiple files being sent at the same time can be combined into a single, compressed file called an *archive*. This simplifies the sending of multiple attachment files.

Attaching Files

To attach one or more files to an e-mail message, you should first compress them. Your iMac comes with two free programs from Aladdin Systems, Inc. for stuffing (compressing) files: Aladdin DropStuff and Stuffit Expander.

1. Double-click on **Macintosh HD** on your desktop. The Macintosh HD window will open.

2. Double-click on the **Internet folder**. The Internet window will open.

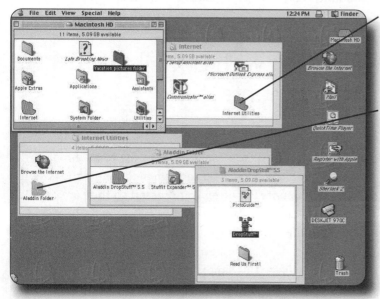

3. Double-click on the **Internet Utilities folder**. The Internet Utilities window will open.

4. Double-click on the **Aladdin folder**. The Aladdin window will open.

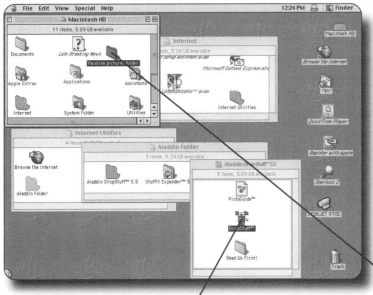

TIP

This would be a good use for Sherlock2. An alternative to all this double-clicking is to open Sherlock2 from the Apple menu, type DropStuff, and then simply double-click the Aladdin DropStuff folder from inside Sherlock 2.

5. **Locate** the **file or folder** you want to attach to your message.

6. **Drag** the **file or folder** to the DropStuff icon and **release** the **mouse button** when the DropStuff icon is highlighted.

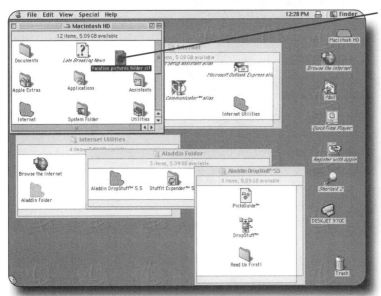

DropStuff will compress your file into a file with the same name appended with .sit at the end.

NOTE

If DropStuff presents you with a Registration alert, just click the Not Yet button to dismiss it.

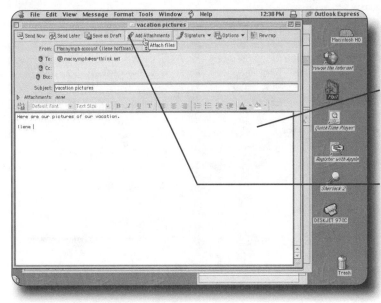

7. Return to **Outlook Express** (or your current e-mail program).

8. Create a new **e-mail message**, as you did in the "Creating an E-Mail Message" section.

9. Click on **Add Attachments**. The Choose Object dialog box will open.

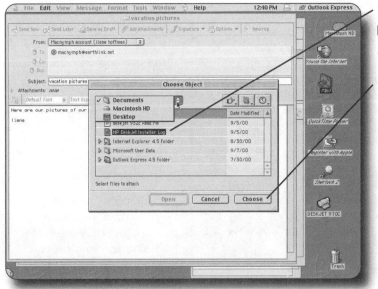

10. Navigate to the **location** of your compressed .sit file.

11. Click on **Choose**.

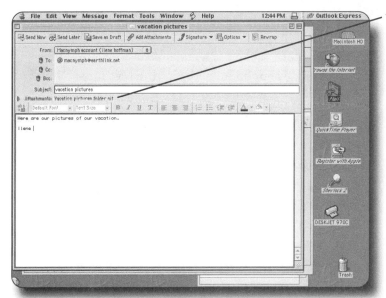

Your file or folder will be attached to your e-mail message.

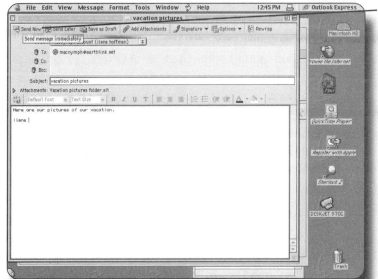

12. Click on **Send Now.** Your modem will connect to the Internet (if you are not already connected) and your message and file will be sent.

Understanding Archives

When you send multiple file attachments, you'll need to compress them, as you did in the previous section, "Attaching Files."

NOTE

AOL automatically compresses files into an archive for you. This may not be what you want, especially if the files are going to a Windows user rather than a Mac OS user.

There are three major types of file archives currently in use:

- **StuffIt**. StuffIt Deluxe is a commercial archiving utility that was developed primarily for the Macintosh. StuffIt Expander™ is a free program that will remove and decompress files from an archive. It is supplied with AOL, and DropStuff™ is used by AOL to create an archive when you send multiple attachments. StuffIt Expander is available for Windows, but is not yet commonly used by Windows users. Therefore, if AOL creates a StuffIt archive and sends it to a Windows user, it is possible that they won't be able to extract the files from the archive. You may want to suggest to your Windows-using friends that they get Aladdin Expander™ for Windows.

- **Zip**. Zip is primarily a Windows archiving format produced by the shareware programs PKZip and WinZip. Most Windows users will have WinZip, so they can decode Zip archives. The Macintosh version is ZipIt. If you need to send multiple attachments to a Windows user, go to AOL's keyword Software and search through the shareware library for ZipIt. You can then download the file and try it out. You can use it both to create Zip archives and to extract files from them. The latest version of Stuffit Expander for Macintosh can extract Zipped files. It's free on Aladdin Systems' Web site, at http://www.aladdinsys.com.

- **MIME**. MIME (often abbreviated MIM) is an Internet archive created by many e-mail programs when a user sends more than one attached file. To decode a MIME archive, you need the MIME Decoder shareware utility, which you can find by searching the shareware library at AOL's keyword Software or on the Internet at http://www.versiontracker.com. MIME Decoder only removes files from archives; it does not create them because MIME archives are generally handled by e-mail software rather than by users.

Receiving and Reading E-Mail

To read e-mail messages, you must first connect to your mail server and pick them up. When you first sign on to AOL, you hear a male voice say "Welcome." Then, if you have mail that has not been read, you hear that famous phrase "You've got mail!" At that point, you can click on your mailbox and read the messages.

Even if you're not using AOL, receiving and reading e-mail is a simple process. To get e-mail on EarthLink using Outlook Express, just follow these steps:

1. **Click** on **Tools**. The Tools menu will appear.

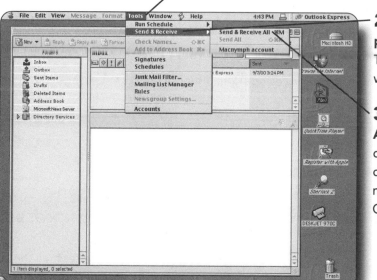

2. **Move** the **mouse pointer** to Send & Receive. The Send & Receive menu will appear.

3. **Click** on **Send & Receive All**. Outlook Express will connect to EarthLink to check for new mail, and any messages waiting in your Outbox will be sent.

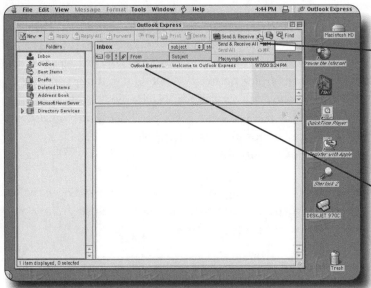

TIP

Alternatively, you can click on Send & Receive in the toolbar and select Send & Receive All from the pop-up menu that appears.

4. Click on a **message** in your Inbox. The message will be displayed in the text box below it. You can double-click on a message in your Inbox to read it in its own window.

NOTE

If you are using AOL, double-click on a message to read it.

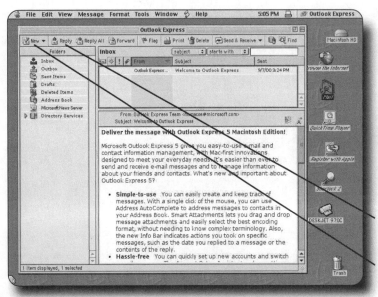

Handling Messages in Outlook Express

In Outlook Express, all the buttons needed to handle mail appear in the toolbar at the top of the Outlook Express window.

- **Reply**. Click on Reply to reply to a message.

- **New**. Click on New to create a new message.

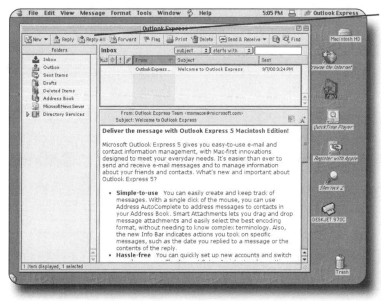

- **Reply All**. Click on Reply All to reply to all of the message recipients (if the message was sent to more than one person).

TIP

Use the Reply All feature carefully. Be certain that the reply is of interest to everyone in the list. Otherwise, you run the risk of people becoming angry with you for filling up their mailboxes with unnecessary messages.

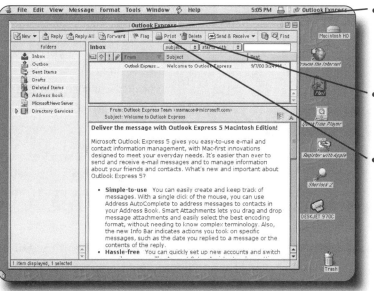

- **Forward**. Click on Forward to send a received message to someone else.

- **Delete**. Click on Delete to move a message to the Deleted Items folder.

- **Print**. Click on Print to print a hard copy of a message.

NOTE

To delete Outlook Express messages from the Deleted Items folder, hold down the Control key and drag the Deleted Items folder to the Trash.

Handling Messages in America Online

The AOL Mailbox window and the windows that contain e-mail messages provide tools for handling messages. You can do the following from the Mailbox window:

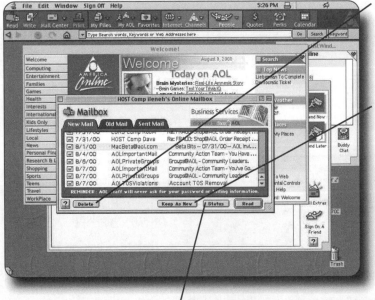

- **Delete a message**. Select one or more messages and click on Delete to remove the message or messages.

- **Leave a message as unread**. When you read a message, AOL automatically transfers it to the Old Mail section of the Mailbox. If you want to leave it in the New Mail section after it has been read, click on the message and click on Keep as New.

- **Check the status of a message**. You can check the status of messages that you have sent to other AOL users. (You cannot check the status of Internet e-mail.) Click on the message and click on Status. You can then see whether the mail is unread, has been read, or has been deleted.

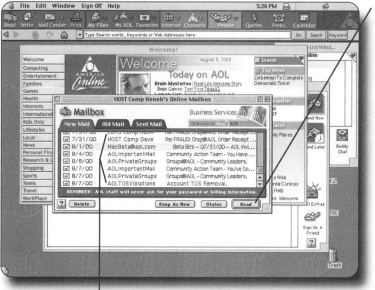

• **Read** a **message**. As an alternative to double-clicking on a message, you can read your mail by clicking on a message and then clicking on Read.

NOTE

Notice the five e-mails in my Online Mailbox that start with AOL—all of these are fraudulent e-mails sent to look as if they are official AOL mail. All of them contain links, which are outside of the AOL service. Hackers use e-mails like these to get you to go to Web sites that have password detection programs on them. Most do not work on the Macintosh platform. If you think an e-mail message might be fraudulent, it probably is. You can forward such mail to TOSE-mail1 (Terms of Service E-mail violations).

Handling Attachments Safely

Just as you can send attached files to other people, they can send attachments to you. Given the climate of today's e-mail, you must be very careful with attachments. If you receive any attached files that are from someone you do not know and that you did not expect, don't download the attachment.

NOTE

On AOL, forward messages with suspicious attachments to TOSFiles. If you are using another ISP, check with them to see what address to use for reporting problematic attachments.

Why all the caution? Because sometimes unexpected attachments from strangers are password-stealing scams or *viruses*. A virus is a malicious program that causes damage to your computer, often by erasing part or all of your hard drive. You will read more about protecting your iMac from viruses in Chapter 18, "Protecting Your iMac." It is true that most password-stealing and virus programs are designed for the Windows operating system and do not affect a Macintosh. However, there are enough Mac OS viruses on the Internet to make caution extremely important.

If you know the sender of an attachment or if the attachment is something that you expected to receive, you can download that attachment to your computer.

14

Sending and Receiving Faxes

Your iMac's modem can send and receive faxes, along with the help of the FAXstf software that is preinstalled on your hard disk. In this chapter, you'll learn how to:

- Set up the fax software
- Send a fax
- Set up the computer to receive a fax
- View a fax that you have received

Setting up the Fax Software

For the most part, the FAXstf software is preconfigured for you on your iMac. There are two groups of settings that you may want to customize, however. The settings are available through the Fax Browser application.

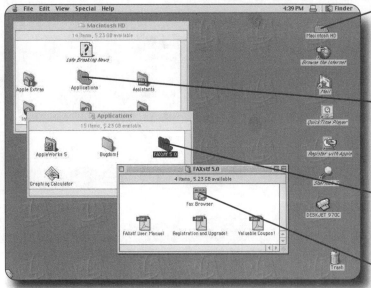

1. Double-click on the **Macintosh HD icon**. The Macintosh HD window will open.

2. Double-click on the **Applications folder**. The Applications window will open.

3. Double-click on the **FAXstf 5.0 folder**. The FAXstf 5.0 window will open.

4. Double-click on the **Fax Browser icon**.

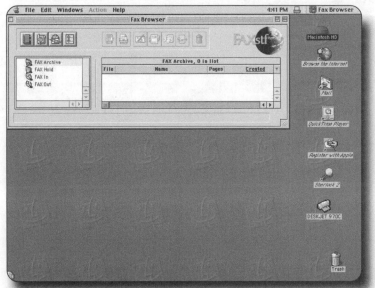

The Fax Browser program will launch and its menus will appear in the menu bar.

5. Click on **Edit**. The Edit menu will appear.

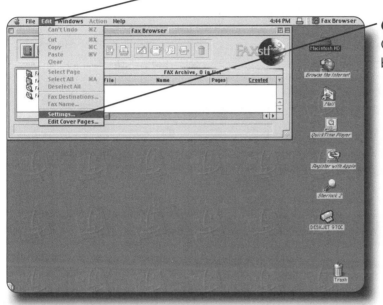

6. Click on **Settings**. The Cover Page Settings dialog box will open.

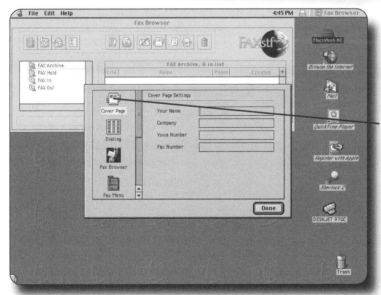

The icons in the scrolling panel at the left of the dialog box are switches that change the contents of the right panel.

7. Click on the **Cover Page icon**. The Cover Page Settings panel will appear.

NOTE

A *cover page* is the page that is sent just before the pages of a document being faxed. Most of the time you want the cover page to contain your name and contact information.

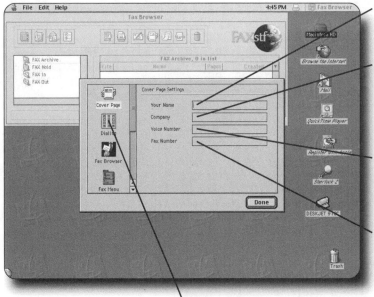

8. **Type** your **name** in the Your Name text box.

9. **Type** your **company name** in the Company text box, if the fax is being sent on behalf of a business.

10. **Type** your **telephone number** in the Voice Number text box.

11. **Type** your **fax number** in the Fax Number text box.

12. **Click** on the **Dialing icon**. The Dialing Settings panel will appear.

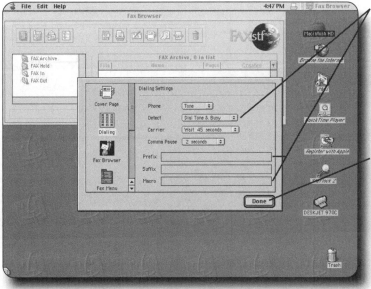

13. **Change** any of the **settings** that are not correct for your situation using the pop-up menus and the text boxes. The default settings should be fine for most situations.

14. **Click** on **Done**. The setting changes will be saved and the Settings dialog box will close.

15. **Press Command+Q**. The Fax Browser program will quit.

Sending a Fax

Sending a fax is very similar to printing a document on a printer. The major difference is that you have to let the fax software know the fax number of the receiving fax machine.

Setting up your iMac to Send a Fax

You must use the Chooser to prepare your iMac for faxing.

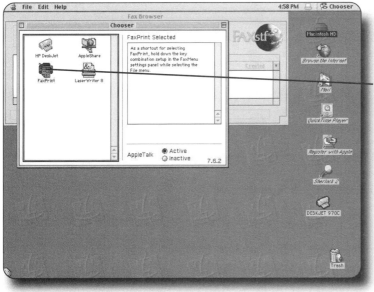

1. **Select Chooser** from the Apple menu. The Chooser dialog box will open.

2. **Click** on the **FaxPrint icon** in the list of printers. The FaxPrint icon will be selected.

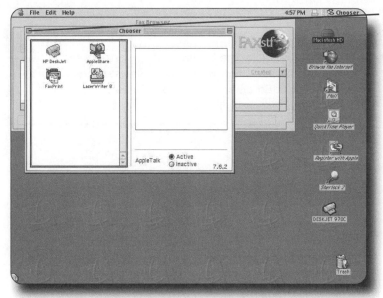

3. **Click** on the **close box**. The Chooser will close and an alert will appear notifying you that your printer settings have changed.

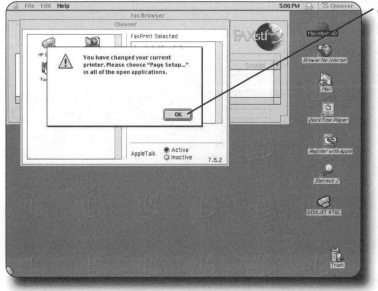

4. **Click** on **OK**. The alert box will close.

Preparing a Fax

Any document that you can print on your iMac can be sent as a fax.

1. Open the **document** you want to fax. The program which you used to create the document will launch and the document will appear.

TIP

You don't need to save a document to fax it. You can therefore create and fax something that you don't intend to keep.

---

2. Click on **File**. The File menu will appear.

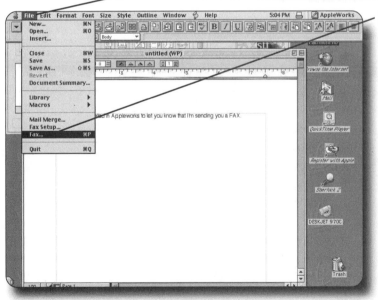

3. Click on **Fax**. The FaxPrint dialog box will open.

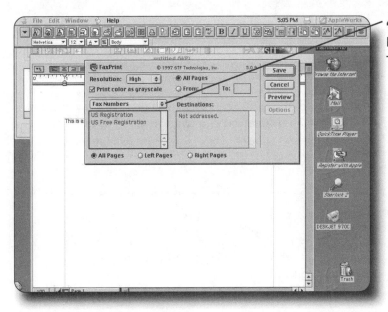

4. Click on the **Fax Numbers pop-up menu**. The pop-up menu will open.

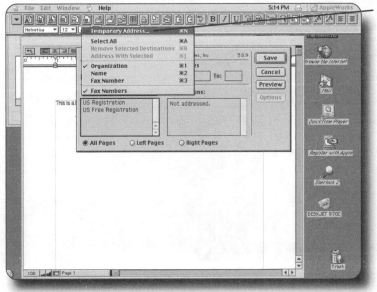

5. Click on **Temporary Address**. A dialog box will appear.

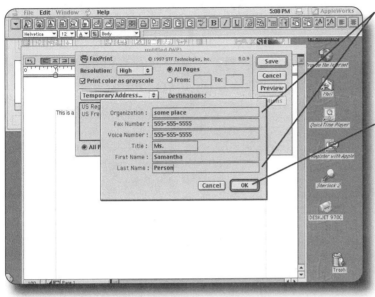

6. Type the **fax recipient's information** into the text boxes. The only value that is required is the fax telephone number.

7. Click on **OK**. The dialog box will close and the FaxPrint dialog box will be the active window again.

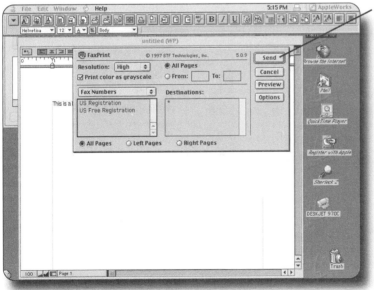

8. Click on **Send**. FAXstf will save the fax document to the hard disk and immediately attempt to send the fax. The Fax Options dialog box will open.

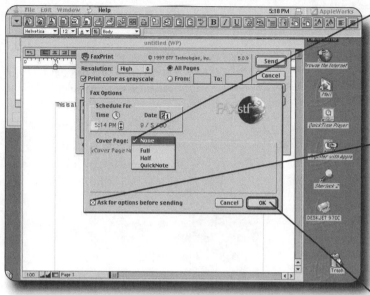

9. **Click** on the **Cover Page pop-up menu**. The pop-up menu will open.

10. **Click** on the **type** of cover page you want.

11. **Click** on the **Ask for options before sending check box**, if you do not want to see this options screen each time you send a Fax. A check will appear in the check box.

12. **Click** on **OK**. The Fax Options dialog box will close and the FaxStatus window will appear.

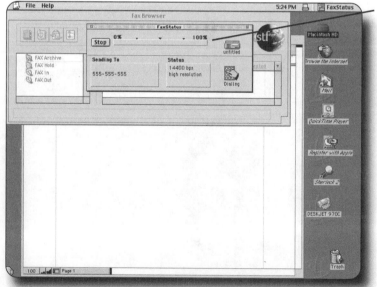

13. **Monitor** the **status** of the fax in the FaxStatus window. When the fax transmission is complete, the FaxStatus window will close.

Receiving Faxes

You don't have to do anything except turn on your iMac to receive a fax. As long as there is a telephone line connected to the iMac's modem, it will automatically answer incoming calls and save incoming faxes.

NOTE

Choose Show Browser from the Windows menu if the Browser window is not on the screen.

Using the Fax Browser

FAXstf's Fax Browser provides an easy way to manage faxes.

1. **Launch** the **Fax Browser application**. The Fax Browser will appear.

The Fax Browser organizes faxes into four categories:

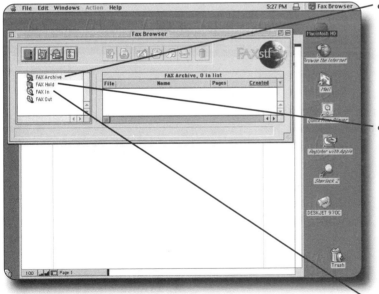

- **FAX Archive**. This category contains incoming faxes that you have read and want to leave on the computer's hard disk.

- **FAX Hold**. This category contains outgoing faxes that FAXstf has been unable to send successfully. A fax might end up in this category because the recipient fax machine was busy, for example.

- **FAX In**. This category contains incoming faxes that you have not read.

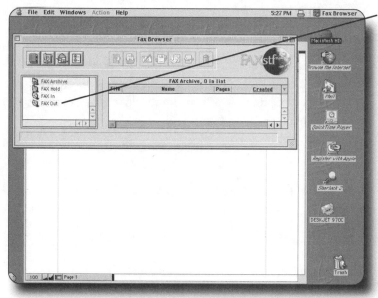

- **FAX Out**. This category contains outgoing faxes that have not been sent.

Click on a category name to see the faxes in that category. Then, highlight (select) a fax to do any of the following:

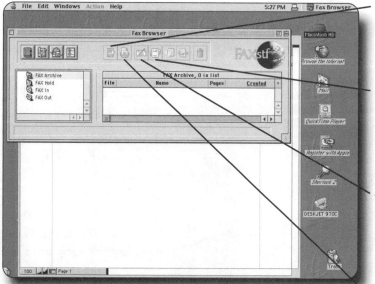

- **View a fax**. Click on the View button. You can read faxes in any of the four categories.

- **Create a cover page**. Click on the Cover Page button. You can create or edit cover pages only for outgoing faxes.

- **Edit a fax**. Click on the Edit button. You can change only outgoing faxes—those in the Hold or Out categories.

- **Print a fax**. Click on the Print button. You can print faxes in any of the four categories.

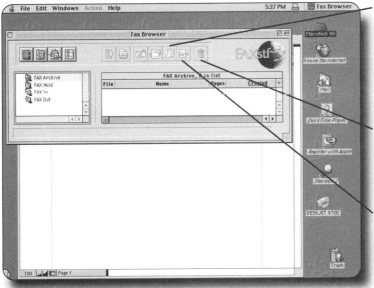

- **Schedule a fax**. Click on the Schedule button. You will be able to set the time at which the fax will be sent. You can schedule only outgoing faxes.

- **Delete a fax**. Click on the Delete button. You can delete faxes from any category.

- **Send a fax**. Click on the Send button. The fax software will attempt to send the fax immediately. You can only send faxes that are in the Hold or Out categories.

TIP

You do not have to remember the command to which each icon refers. When you move the mouse pointer over the icons, a text explanation appears on the bottom of the window as a reminder.

PART VI

Maintaining Your iMac

15

Adding Software

The iMac's hard disk is preloaded with a number of programs, but others can be found in the wallet of discs (CD-ROMs) that is included in the Accessories box of your iMac's packaging. To use them, these programs must be manually installed.

CD-ROMs are the most common method of distributing software. To obtain free updates, visit the Web sites of software companies. In this chapter, you'll learn how to:

- Install software from a CD-ROM
- Find and download software updates via the Web
- Install updates downloaded from the Web.

Installing Software from a CD-ROM

In most programs, such as Quicken 2000, the installer program copies all the software you need onto your hard disk. Other programs, such as dictionaries, encyclopedias, and many games, install only the portion of the software that is required to access data on your hard disk. The rest of the program data remains on one or more discs because of the enormous amount of space the data would take up if loaded fully onto your hard disk. Consequently, you must have the disc in the CD-ROM drive to access (use) and view all parts of the software.

Since most users buy a printer to go with their computer, this chapter will walk you through the installation of a printer driver—the software needed to talk to the printer. As an example, the driver for a Hewlett Packard 932C ink jet printer will be installed. This installer is representative of most , so you can follow these instructions to install almost any program.

> ### NOTE
>
> Some installations require that no other program be running except the installer. It is always wise to save all files and quit all programs before updating or installing any new software.

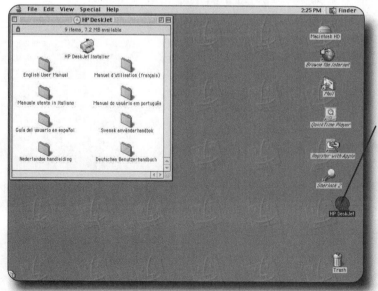

1. Insert the **disc** in your iMac's CD-ROM drive. After a few seconds, the CD-ROM's icon appears on the desktop.

2. Double-click on the **CD-ROM icon**. The disc's folder window will open. Usually, one of the first visible items is the installer program for the software. The icon typically includes the word "Install" in the file name.

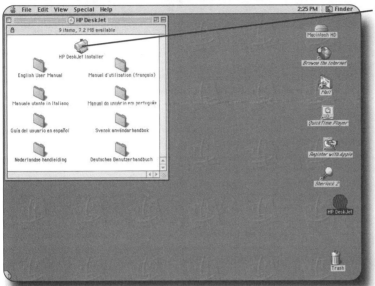

3. Double-click on the **installer icon**. A splash screen will appear, identifying the software that you are installing.

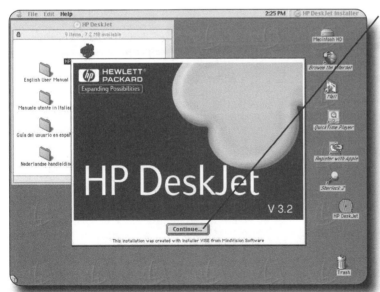

4. Click on **Continue**. The License window will appear.

NOTE

Exactly what license windows opens varies somewhat from one installer to another. What appears in this chapter is a typical example.

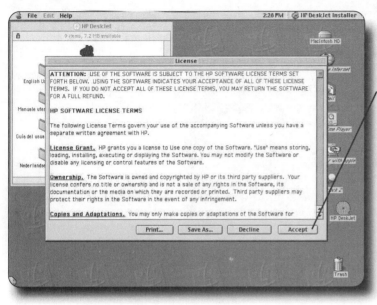

5. **Read** the **license** to make sure the terms are acceptable.

6. **Click** on **Accept** if you agree to the license agreement. A Read Me window will appear.

7. **Click** on **Continue** after reading the information. This screen is particularly helpful and is not included in most installer programs. You can also save this document to your hard drive. You will proceed to the Installer dialog box.

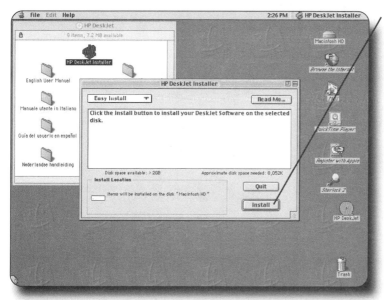

8. **Click** on **Install**. An alert will appear.

You will also see several other options available in the Installer dialog box.

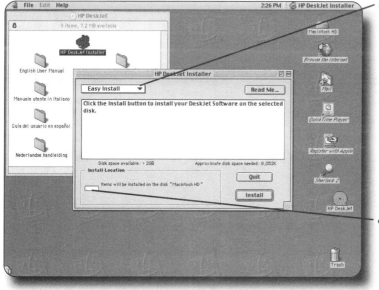

- A pop-up window where you can choose the type of installation. If you choose Easy Install, the installer will give you the most commonly used files. If you want to select your own files, choose a Custom Install. In most cases, however, Easy Install is the best choice.

- The location where the software will be installed. Unless you tell it otherwise, an installer places the new software in a folder on the top level of your hard disk. (If you have more than one hard disk, it uses the one that contains the System Folder.) A lot of software only allows installation to the top level of System drive, but you can move the application to another folder or drive after installation.

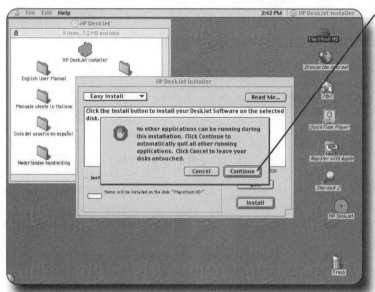

9. Click on **Continue**. The installer program will now quit all of your running applications and a window will open that displays a progress bar to illustrate the progress of the installation.

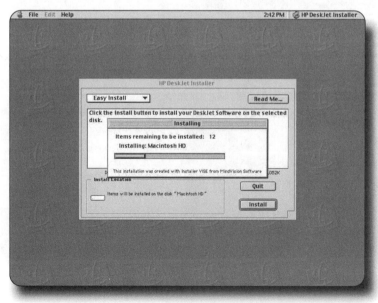

Some software, especially utilities, games, and educational software may show you graphics or pictures while you wait for the install to finish.

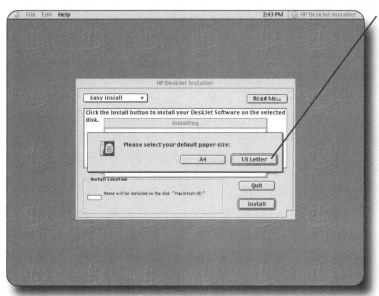

10. Click on **US Letter**, the preferred paper size. An alert box will appear.

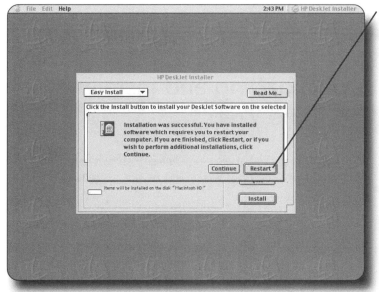

11. Click on **Restart**. Your iMac will restart.

Finishing the Installation

The final step in installation may require that you complete one or more of the following tasks, depending on the individual installer program:

- **Registration**. Many installers allow you to register your software automatically. You fill in your information in a series of dialog boxes and the installer dials a toll-free number that sends it to the software manufacturer. Optionally, you can decline automatic registration and then mail in your registration.

- **Quit or Continue**. If the software you just installed does not require that you restart the iMac before using the software, you can choose to continue with further installations or quit the installer and return to the Finder.

- **Set Up**. After you restart your computer, some installation programs launch a small application requesting that you set up the software for your own iMac configuration.

Downloading and Installing from the Web

There is a great deal of excellent Macintosh software available on the Web. Some good, reasonably safe sources are:

- Apple Computer (http://www.apple.com/)

- Download.com (http://www.download.com/)

- VersionTracker.com (http://www.versiontracker.com/)

- The InfoMac archive (http://hyperarchive.lcs.mit.edu/HyperArchive.html)

Checking the Apple iMac Web Pages

The Apple Computer iMac Web pages are a great source of iMac information and software updates. To return to the site quickly, add a bookmark to your Web browser.

To visit the iMac Web pages:

1. **Connect** to the **Internet** if necessary.

2. **Launch** your **Web browser**.

3. **Type http://www.apple.com/support** into the Address box.

4. **Press Enter**. The Apple Support page will display.

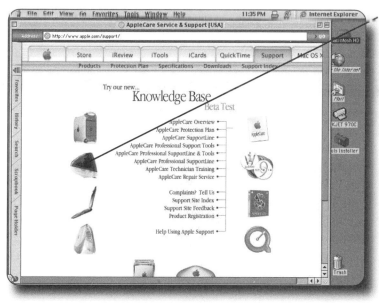

5. **Click** on the picture of the iMac. Apple's support site front page changes periodically, so the page may not look exactly as shown here.

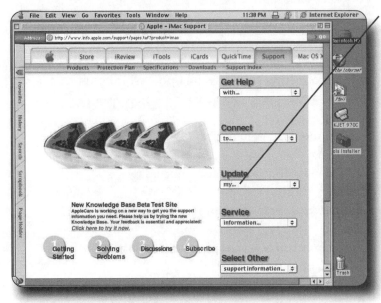

6. **Click** on the **my pop-up menu**. The pop-up menu will open.

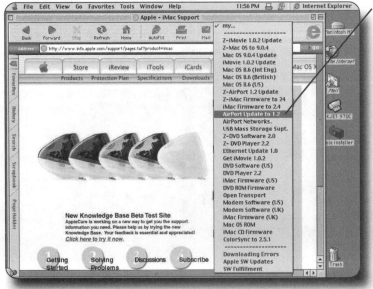

7. **Move** the **mouse pointer** to the desired update and release the mouse button. The Software Downloads page will appear.

NOTE

Only those updates relevant to the iMac are listed in the pop-up menus. Read update information carefully, as not all updates apply to all iMacs. The newer your iMac, the less likely an update is relevant within 30 days of your purchase. Go to http://til.info.apple.com/techinfo.nsf/artnum/n58174 (an Apple's Technical Information database article) to read which updates are relevant for your iMac.

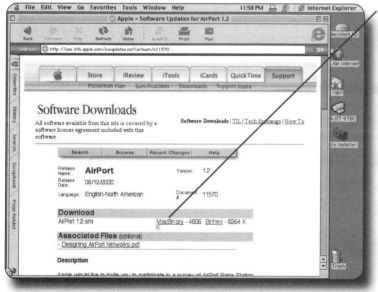

8. **Click** on the **hyperlink** for the MacBinary download. The Download Manager will open and display the progress of the download.

TIP

MacBinary (a program in compressed form) usually provides the smallest file for downloading and is usually a better choice than BinHex (a program translated into text characters).

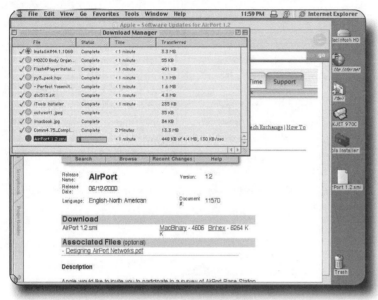

The result of the download of an update is a new icon on your Desktop. The icon may be for a Stuffit archive, a self-mounting disk image, or some other type of archive. Stuffit Expander will automatically extract most archive types and place the uncompressed file or folder on your Desktop. However, if you've downloaded a self-mounting image, you may need to go through a few extra steps to get to the update's installer program.

Handling a Self-Mounting Image

A *self-mounting image* is a compressed file containing all of the documents you need on a virtual disk. The name always ends in .smi to indicate it is a self-mounting image. Disk Copy is the application that opens these files. It is stored in the Utilities folder on your hard drive.

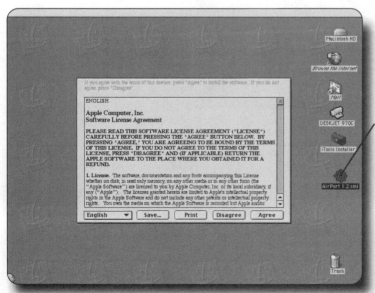

1. Double-click on the **icon** of the downloaded file. A license agreement will appear.

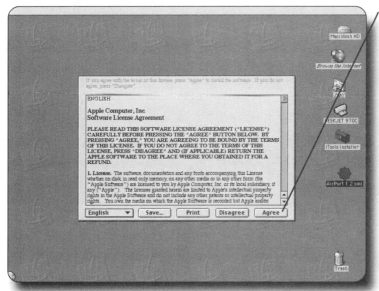

2. Click on **Agree**. The license agreement dialog box will disappear and a new icon in the shape of a floppy disk will appear on the Desktop.

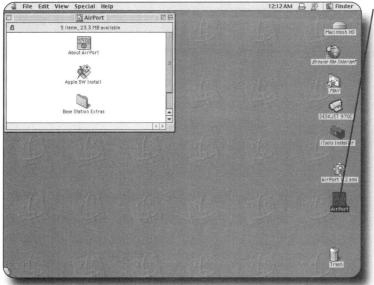

3. Double click on the **disk icon**. The folder window will open to show the contents of the disk, including an installer file.

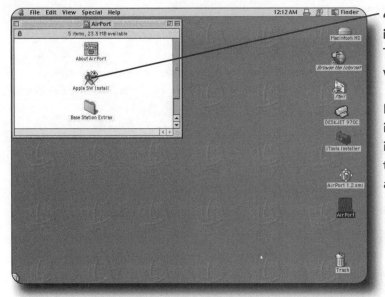

4. Double-click on the **installer or updater file**. The installer or updater will launch.

In some cases, an update installs itself without any intervention needed. When the update is completed, an alert appears.

TIP

You may want to download all the recommended update files before installing any of them because system software updates typically require you to restart the machine for the updates to take effect.

16

Adding Peripherals

The iMac is a major change from earlier Macintoshes in terms of what hardware is included and what ports are available. The floppy disk drive, the old standby ports for keyboard and mouse (ADB), the serial ports (for modems and printers), and ports for adding hard disks and scanners (SCSI) were eliminated. Instead, new connection ports called Universal Serial Bus (USB) and FireWire are used for all of these. In this chapter, you'll learn how to:

- Choose a printer you can use on your iMac
- Determine which add-on devices you can connect to your USB ports
- Select add-on devices you can connect to your FireWire ports

The USB port has several advantages over the older connections. It has the ability to add many devices to the same computer, and you can plug and unplug them at any time with no worry of damaging the computer. USB is not as fast as SCSI, although it can be as fast as serial and ADB ports (the old keyboard and mouse ports). Using a hub, you can add up to 127 USB devices to your iMac (see the "Hubs" section later in this chapter for more information).

The FireWire port has the same advantages as USB, but is much faster, and you can daisy chain 16 FireWire devices (or 63 devices if you use a tree arrangement). You can also unplug and plug in FireWire peripherals while the computer is on, as long as the external device is not reading or writing data. The iMac's FireWire port only accepts 6-pin connectors, so make sure you plug the correct end of the cable into the computer. Apple Computer cautions not to use cables over 15 feet (4.5 meters) long.

NOTE

The discussion throughout the rest of this chapter includes a price range for most types of devices. Keep in mind, however, that prices on computer hardware are always dropping so use these prices as relative indicators of cost.

Other connections to the iMac are Ethernet (10/100BaseT); the modem; sound in and out; and, on the early (Bondi-blue) iMacs, an *IrDA* infrared port and a non-standard internal connector called the Mezzanine port. There are also two slots so that you can add more memory (RAM). iMacs use different types of RAM. The original iMac (Tray Loading) uses DRAM Form Factor SO-DIMMs. The iMac (Slot Loading) computer uses standard PC-100 DIMMs .

Printers

One of the first peripherals you are likely to add is a printer. Printers vary widely in the interface they use, the quality of their output, and their price. In general, the higher the print quality, the more costly the printer. Color printers always costs more than black-and-white printers of the same quality.

HP LaserJet 1100se Photo courtesy of
Hewlett-Packard.com.

Network (Ethernet) PostScript Laser Printers

At the high-end of the printer world are laser printers, which use a technique similar to photocopy machines to place an image on paper. Some laser printers can print in black-and-white only; others can print in color. Laser printers provide the best possible output from your iMac.

Price Range: $429–$5,000

Driver: Included with the Mac OS

Accessories required for use with iMac: Ethernet crossover cable ($25 and up, depending on length) *or* Ethernet cable ($15 and up, depending on length) and Ethernet hub ($50).

Sample manufacturers: Hewlett-Packard (http://www.hewlettpackard.com), Brother International Corporation (http://www.brother.com), Xanté Corporation (http://www.xante.com), GCC Technologies, Inc., Lexmark International, Inc. (http://www.lexmark.com).

DeskJet 932C Photo courtesy of
Hewlett-Packard.com.

USB Printers

The easiest and most inexpensive printers to use are those that have a USB interface. You just plug them in, install the driver software, and print. The output is excellent and the color is vibrant, and often of photographic quality. If you plan to print photographs, look for a printer that is designed specifically for photo quality output.

Price range: $89–$500

Driver: Included, or available for download from vendor Web site

Accessories required for use with iMac: USB cable ($10) or FireWire cable ($14–$40)

NOTE

The DeskJet 932C is not only very quiet and fast, it comes with an attachment to print 4" x 6" photos. Be forewarned that the color ink cartridges can be expensive, though.

Sample manufacturers: Canon, Inc. (http://www.canon.com/index.html), Hewlett-Packard (http://www.hewlettpackard.com), UMAX (http://www.umax.com), Epson (http://www.epson.com).

Scanners

CanoScan D660U 932C Flatbed Scanner Photo courtesy of Canon Computer Systems, Inc.

A *scanner* is a device that digitizes printed matter. You can use scanners to load photographs or other documents onto your iMac's hard disk.

NOTE

When you scan a page of text, the text is not editable with a word processor or text editor because a scanner produces a graphic image. If you want to "read" the text and turn it into an editable text document, you need *optical character recognition* (OCR) software, such as OmniPage Pro from ScanSoft (http://www.scansoft.com).

NEC Technologies PetiScan, an excellent portable scanner, the size of a large paperback book.(http://www.petiscan.com)

USB and FireWire Scanners

Price range: $50–$300

Accessories required for use with iMac: USB cable ($10) or FireWire cable ($14–$40)

Sample manufacturers: Canon Computer Systems, Inc. (http://www.ccsi.canon.com), NEC Technologies (http://www.petiscan.com), Hewlett-Packard (http://www.hewlettpackard.com), UMAX (http://www.umax.com), Epson (http://www.epson.com), Agfa Division, Bayer Corporation (http://www.agfa.com), Microtek (http://www.microtekusa.com).

SCSI Scanners

Price range: $50–$500

Accessories required for use with iMac: SCSI cable or SCSI-II connector (see the "Port Adapters" section below).

Sample manufacturers: Canon Computer Systems, Inc., (http://www.ccsi.canon.com), Heidelberg Color Publishing Solutions (http://www.linocolor.com), Hewlett-Packard (http://www.hewlettpackard.com), UMAX (http://www.umax.com), Epson (http://www.epson.com), Agfa Division, Bayer Corporation (http://www.agfa.com), Microtek, (http://www.microtekusa.com), Acer Peripherals, Inc. (http://www.acerperipherals.com).

Input Devices

Apple's original iMac round mouse

Macsense's iCatch, available from Belkin
(http://www.belkin.com)

Contour Design's Perfit Mouse,
available in different hand sizes

USB has been welcomed by many Mac users because it makes available a wide range of input devices—for example, keyboards, mice, trackballs, trackpads, graphics tablets, and game controllers—at a price that's lower than the price for similar ADB devices. If you don't like the Apple Pro Keyboard or Pro Mouse that came with your iMac, you can pick up another style for a rather reasonable price. For example, at the time this book was written a combination extended keyboard and oval mouse were available for around $50. There's even a little sock attachment called the iCatch that covers the round iMac mouse to make it oval (at a cost of about $10). There are even mice made specifically for left-handed people, and mice made for people with different hand sizes.

NOTE

If you plan to use a joystick or gamepad, you'll want to install Game Sprockets from the iMac Install CD-ROM that came with your iMac (in the CD Extras folder) or download the latest version from Apple's Web site (http://asu.info.apple.com). If you choose to download the latest version from Apple's Web site, type "sprockets" in the Search box.

Sample manufacturers:
Logitech (http://www.logitech.com),
Contour Design (http://www.contourdesign.com),
MacSense (http://www.macsense.com),
Wacom (http://www.wacom.com),
Altek Corporation – Kurta Division
(http://www.kurta.com),

Keyspan, a division of InnoSys, Inc.
(http://www.keyspan.com), XLR8 (http://www.xlr8.com),
Ariston Technologies LLC (http://www.ariston.com).

Data Storage

One of the greatest criticisms of the iMac has been its lack
of removable storage, especially the omission of a floppy
disk drive. Given that you need some form of external
storage for backup, adding a disk drive is something you
are likely to do.

Several types of USB drives are available, including
hard drives.

TIP

Belkin Components (http://apple.belkin.com) and
Dr. Bott LLC. (http://www.drbott.com) both carry full
lines of Macintosh peripherals, cables, and other
devices. Both provide excellent service and support.

Floppy Drives

Floppy drives store 1.44 MB on an inexpensive disk (less
than $1 per disk). Working with floppies is inexpensive and
the format is compatible with the floppy drives used by
most of today's computers. Having a floppy disk drive also
makes it possible to install software that is supplied on a
floppy disk. However, the limited storage capacity makes a
floppy drive unsuitable for little else other than the transfer
and backup of small files.

Price range: $75–$150

Sample manufacturers: VST (http://www.vsttech.com), Newer Technology, Inc. (http://www.newertech.com), Microtech International, Inc. (http://www.microtech.com), iMation (http://www.imation.com).

SuperDisk

A SuperDisk drive can read and write 1.44 MB floppy disks as well as its own 120 MB SuperDisks. The major drawback to the SuperDisk is that the 120 MB disks can be read *only* by another SuperDisk, and this is not a standard format adopted by a large number of vendors. It is, therefore, great for backup purposes and installing software from floppies, but not necessarily for file exchange.

Price: $150

Sample manufacturers: iMation (http://www.imation.com), VST (http://www.vsttech.com).

Zip Drives

The Zip drive uses a 100 MB or 250 MB cartridge, but cannot handle 1.44 MB floppy disks. The Zip 100 MB format has become a de facto industry standard and many computers come equipped with Zip drives. The Zip disk is well suited for both backup and transferring files. It does not, however, allow you to install software from 1.44 MB floppy disks.

Price range: $150–$200

Sample manufacturers: Iomega (http://www.iomega.com), Microtech International, Inc. (http://www.microtech.com), VST (http://www.vsttech.com).

CD-RW Drives

A CD-RW (read/write) drive allows you to burn your own CD-ROMs, as well as reuse read/write discs that were erased. Most discs store about 650 MB and can be used for backup. You can even create discs from which you can boot your iMac in the event of a start-up problem.

> **Price range**: $200–$400

> **Sample manufacturers**: VST (http://www.vsttech.com), Iomega (http://www.iomega.com), Sony (http://www.sony.com), LaCie (http://www.lacie.com), iMation (http://www.imation.com), APS Technologies (http://www.apstech.com), Yamaha (http://www.yamaha.com).

Hard Drives

USBFW60 External Drive (USB and FireWire compatible). Photo Courtesy of VST Technologies.

USB hard drives make it easy to expand your hard disk storage. However, they are much slower than the iMac's internal hard drive and therefore are best suited for backup, rather than day-to-day processing.

> **Price range**: $250–$350

> **Sample manufacturers**: VST (http://www.vsttech.com), LaCie (http://www.lacie.com), Fantom Drives (http://www.fantomdrives.com), APS Technologies Inc. (http://www.apstech.com).

Flash Memory/SmartMedia Readers

Many of today's digital cameras and hand-held computing devices use tiny storage media known as *flash memory* (or simply, flash cards) or *SmartMedia*.

Price range: $50–$100

Sample manufacturers: Newer Technology, Inc. (http://www.newertech.com), SanDisk (http://www.sandisk.com), Microtech International, Inc. (http://www.microtechint.com).

Audio and Video

There are now peripherals that are designed for hobbyists and casual business use, including different kinds of cameras, speakers, and MIDI keyboards. Prices are constantly going down as new products are released, so do your research well.

Video Cameras

Canon ZR-10 Digital Camcorder.
Photo Courtesy of Canon.com.

To have a small video camera for video conferencing, Web video, or still photos for the Web, you can use a USB or FireWire version that works smoothly with the iMac.

Price range: $80–$130

Sample manufacturers: CanonDV USA, Inc. (http://www.canondv.com), iRez (http://www.iRez.com), Logitech (http://www.logitech.com), Sony Electronics (http://64.14.40.97:80/index.jsp), Kensington Technology Group of ACCO Brands Inc. (http://www.kensington.com).

iRez The Kritter USB. Photo courtesy of iRez.

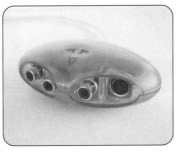

iRez CapSureUSB. Photo courtesy of iRez.

Video Capture and TV Tuner

Video capture devices grab a single image from a live motion video source such as a VCR or video camera using composite or S-video, audio in and out, a TV tuner, and a TV port.

Price: $150

Sample manufacturer: iRez (http://www.iRez.com), Logitech (http://www.logitech.com), Kensington Technology Group of ACCO Brands Inc. (http://www.kensington.com).

Still Cameras

Some digital cameras are beginning to appear with USB and FireWire ports, eliminating the need for a separate storage card reader.

Price range: $400–$1100

Manufacturers: Most major still camera manufacturers are now in this market. Check Macworld magazine online for the latest reviews of products (http://www.macworld.com).

USB Speakers

The iMac is equipped with stereo speakers, but if you're an audio buff, you'll probably cringe whenever you hear sound coming from them. Fortunately, you can purchase external USB speakers to provide better sound quality.

Price range: $50–$250

> **Sample manufacturers**: PELE Enterprises, LLC (http://www.pelezone.com), Harman Multimedia (http://www.harman-multimedia.com), Altec Lansing Technologies, Inc. (http://www.altecmm.com).

MIDI

MIDI (*musical instrument digital interface*) provides a means of connecting a MIDI-compatible instrument to a computer so that the computer can either capture what is played on the instrument or play music through the instrument.

> **Price range**: $150–$500

> **Sample manufacturers**: Mark of the Unicorn, Inc. (http://www.motu.com), Midiman (http://www.midiman.net), Opcode Systems, Inc. (http://www.opcode.com), Emagic Soft- und Hardware GmbH (http://www.emagic.de).

Standard Audio Input and Output

As noted earlier, the iMac includes two built-in stereo speakers with Surround Sound technology. It also contains a microphone port, two front headphone jacks, and two "minijacks" for CD-quality sound input and output. Connect a couple of "minijacks" to RCA stereo connectors, and you can hook the iMac into a stereo system, home theater system, boom box, and so on. Regular computer speakers also work fine, as will an external Apple PlainTalk microphone, or Griffin's NE microphone.

Hubs

A *hub* is a piece of hardware that distributes signals between hardware devices that use the same type of connection to a computer. Both USB and Ethernet use hubs to connect multiple pieces of equipment.

USB Hubs

Your iMac can have up to 127 USB devices connected at the same time. However, devices must be attached to the iMac itself in some way, either directly or indirectly through a hub that is connected to the iMac. The iMac has two USB ports along with a two-port hub on the keyboard. Therefore, with the keyboard and mouse plugged in, you only have two ports left.

If you want to add more than two additional USB peripherals, you'll need to add a hub. Some devices such as printers and scanners tend to pull quite a bit of power from the USB circuitry. You'll run into problems getting the hardware to function properly if you don't have a powered hub. Powered hubs usually have small "brick" style power supplies. Hubs typically have four or seven ports.

> **Price range**: $40–$150

> **Sample manufacturers**: Dr. Bott LLC (http://www.drbott.com), Belkin Components (http://apple.belkin.com), XLR8 (http://www.xlr8.com), Keyspan, a Division of InnoSys, Inc. (http://www.keyspan.com), MacSense (http://www.macsense.com), Xircom, Inc. (http://www.xircom.com).

Ethernet Hubs

To connect more than one Ethernet device to the iMac, you'll need an Ethernet Hub. A 10BaseT 5- or 8-port hub can be found for under $50 and is probably large enough for a home network. Hubs that allow you to interconnect 10BaseT and 100BaseT devices (the iMac can run at either

TIP

Farallon (via Ask Dr. Farallon) provides useful networking guides and answers to questions on their Web site (http://www.farallon.com).

speed) will cost significantly more. Cables are also needed between each device and the hub, which can cost from $10 to $25 dollars depending on length.

Price range: $30–$500

Sample manufacturers: Asanté Technologies, Inc. (http://www.asante.com), Farallon Communications, Inc. (http://www.farallon.com), Kingston Technology Corporation (http://www.kingston.com), SonicWALL Inc. (http://www.sonicsys.com).

Port Adapters

Although Apple Computer would like to see everyone using USB peripherals, the truth is that there's a lot of existing hardware that people want to use that cannot be connected via USB. To provide access to these devices, you can purchase a port adapter that converts the USB signals to the signals required by some other type of hardware interface.

USB to ADB

This converter allows you to use Apple Desktop Bus peripherals, such as older Mac keyboards, mice, joysticks, and ADB "dongles" (copy protection devices required for some software to operate). Unless you already have ADB devices that you want to use, you'll probably find less expensive USB devices that do the same thing.

Price: $35

Sample manufacturer: Dr Bott, LLC (http://www.drbott.com/prod/alist/compatibility.html)

SCSI Adapters

SCSI adapters allow the use of SCSI devices (such as SCSI Zip drives, external hard disks, and SCSI scanners with USB) on the iMac. However, because the USB data speed is much slower than even the slowest SCSI speed, this isn't a very good solution unless you already have SCSI equipment you need to use.

Price range: $70–$80

Sample manufacturers: Adaptec, Inc. (http://www.adaptec.com/mac), Microtech International, Inc. (http://www.microtech.com), Orange Micro (Orange Micro, Inc.), Sonnet Technologies, Inc. (http://www.sonnettech.com), Belkin Components (http://apple.belkin.com).

USB–Serial

USB to serial adapters allow various serial devices to work with the iMac. Adapters have from one to four serial ports, and various versions have different levels of support. Generally, they support serial printers for which a driver is available (such as StyleWriters), external modems, and digital cameras with serial connections. None of the available adapters will allow the use of LocalTalk or GeoPort functions yet. Because not all serial devices are supported, check with the vendor to see if the product you're considering will work for your particular application.

Price range: $65–$85

Sample manufacturers: Keyspan, a Division of InnoSys, Inc. (http://www.keyspan.com), NewMotion Technology Corp. (http://www.newmotiontech.com), Xircom, Inc. (http://www.xircom.com).

USB–Parallel

Many printers require a parallel interface. You can use them with an iMac if you purchase a USB-to-parallel adapter. However, unlike the adapters discussed previously in this section, these adapters are closely tied to specific types of printers.

Epson and HP, for example, each provide a USB to parallel cable to work with their own printers and include the necessary drivers for those printers. Belkin's product is very similar to Epson's, and includes Epson drivers. InfoWave's PowerPrint includes drivers for hundreds of printers, including many for which no Mac-compatible drivers exist. MacJet's Drivers provide driver software that is similar to those included with PowerPrint—you may need to purchase the drivers with one of the other cables if your printer doesn't have Macintosh drivers available.

Price range: $45–$100

Sample manufacturers: Epson (http://www.epson.com), Belkin Components (http://apple.belkin.com), Hewlett-Packard (http://www.hewlettpackard.com).

17

Protecting Your Files

In some households, multiple people use one iMac. To protect your files from accidental deletion or other forms of tampering, Apple Computer provides password-protected access for your files, while allowing you to have different setups for different users. In this chapter you'll learn how to:

- Set up multiple users
- Set up keychain access
- Enable file encryption

Setting up Multiple Users

One way to protect your files is to create a different working environment for each user. By setting up different user accounts for as many as 40 different users, you can create a customized environment (including appearance options), give access to particular programs, and prevent another user from changing the system folder.

Use the Multiple Users control panel to create user accounts with one of three different access levels. Only the owner account has access to the full system, including the ability to install applications, set up printers, and access other users' documents. The three access levels are:

- **Normal access**. This level allows users to access almost everything on the hard drive, but does not allow them to see other users' documents folders.

- **Limited user access**. This level allows users to access some Finder commands, but to save and open files only in their own folders.

- **Panels access**. This is the most restricted access level. Users' files and documents appear on one panel, and approved applications appear on another panel. This access level provides one-click access to files.

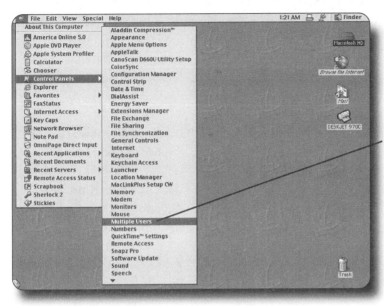

Creating Different User Accounts

Setting up new user accounts is a simple process.

1. Choose Multiple Users from the Control Panels submenu of the Apple menu. The Multiple Users control panel will appear.

2. Click on the **On radio button**. The Multiple User Accounts option will be selected.

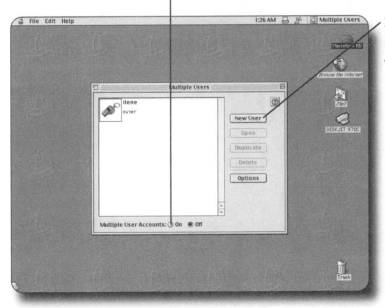

3. Click on **New User**. The Edit "New User" dialog box will open.

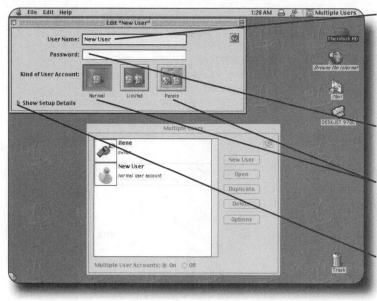

4. Type the **user's name** in the User Name text box and **press** the **Tab key**. The cursor will move to the Password text box.

5. Type a **password** in the Password text box.

6. Click on a **Kind of User Account button**. The option will be selected.

7. Click on the **Show Setup Details triangle** to open the Setup Details panel.

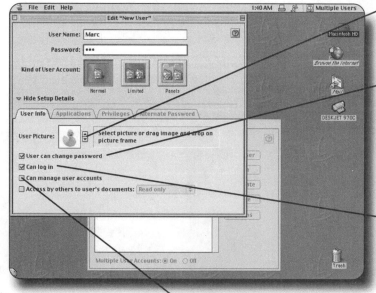

8. Click on the **User Picture up and down arrows** and choose a **User Picture**.

9. Click in the **User can change password check box** if you want the user to be able to change his or her own password. The option will be selected.

10. Click in the **Can log in check box** if you want the user account to be enabled. The option will be selected.

11. Click in the **Can manage user accounts check box** to allow the user access to other user accounts (not including the owner's account). The option will be selected.

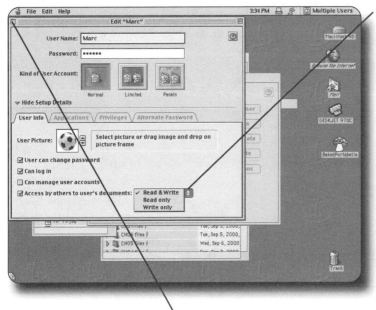

12. **Click** in the **Access by others to user's documents check box** and **choose** an **access level** to determine other users' access levels to this user's files.

NOTE

The other tabs in the Setup Details panel, such as Applications and Privileges, are accessible if you choose other types of user accounts.

---

13. **Click** on the **Close box**. The Edit "New User" control panel will close and the new user setup will be saved.

Global Multiple User Options

You can also adjust the global multiple user options for your iMac.

1. **Choose Multiple Users** from the Control Panels submenu of the Apple menu. The Multiple Users control panel will appear.

2. **Click** on **Options**. The Global Multiple User Options dialog box will open.

3. **Click** on the different **tabs** to see what options are available in each. The tabs will move to the front when you click on them.

There are many options you can set. Since most users do not need to set up multiple user accounts, the options will be covered briefly here.

There are several options you can set in the Login tab.

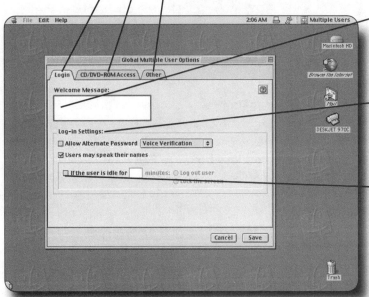

- **Welcome Message**. You can customize a welcome message for the user to see when they log in.

- **Log-in Settings**. You can allow for an alternate password, and even for a voice password.

- **If the user is idle for**. You can specify whether a user should be logged off or the screen locked if the machine remains idle for a certain amount of time.

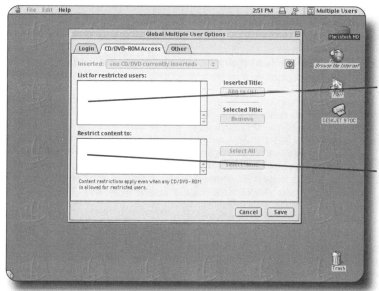

The CD/DVD-ROM Access tab also contains an option you can set.

- **List for restricted users**. You can apply content restrictions to the users in this list.

- **Restrict content to**. You can restrict access to CDs and DVDs by title in this list.

There are a few options you can set in the Other tab.

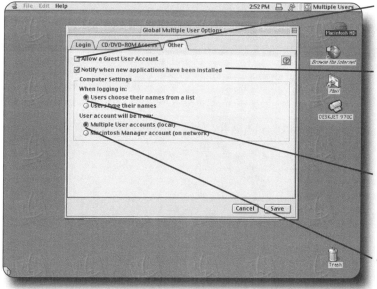

- **Allow a Guest User Account**. You can allow guest user access.

- **Notify when new applications**. You can choose to notify users when a new application has been installed.

- **When logging in**. You can choose whether users must type their names or choose them from a list.

- **User account will be from**. You can choose whether the account is part of a network or resides on one Macintosh only.

Setting up Keychain Access

A keychain is a file where you can store passwords set up for servers, applications, and Internet locations. When you set up your iMac for multiple user access, each user is assigned a keychain.

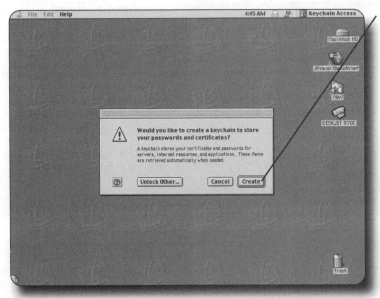

1. Choose Keychain Access from the Control Panels submenu of the Apple menu. The Keychain Access message box will appear.

2. Click on **Create**. The Create Keychain dialog box will open.

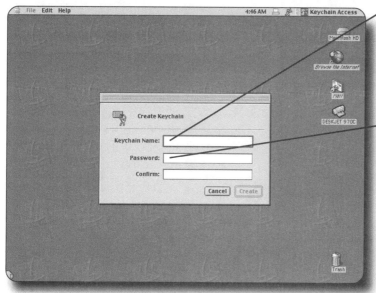

3. Type a **name** for your keychain in the Keychain Name box and **press** the **Tab key**. The cursor will move to the Password text box.

4. Type a **password** and **press** the **Tab key**. The cursor will move to the Confirm text box.

NOTE

A passwords with six or more characters is considered secure, meaning it is harder to guess. Therefore, you'll always want to use at least six characters when choosing a password.

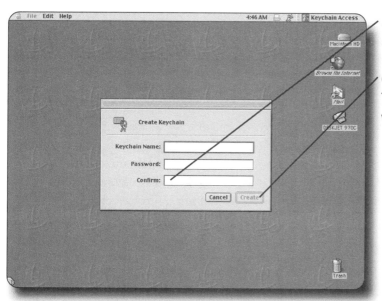

5. Type your **password** again to confirm it.

6. Click on **Create**. The Keychain dialog box will open.

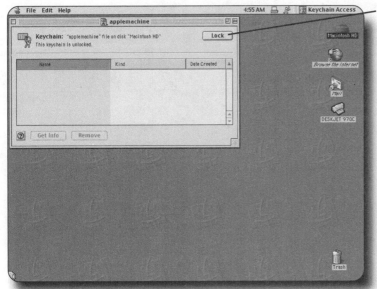

As you use documents, files, servers, and Internet locations, you can add their passwords, when needed, to your keychain. When you unlock a keychain, all of your documents are also unlocked. Therefore, be sure to choose Lock from the Keychain dialog box if you leave your machine unattended. You can also save an Internet site password by dragging the Internet location file to an open keychain window.

NOTE

Keychain files are stored in Preferences folder in your System Folder on your Macintosh hard disk.

File Encryption: Apple File Security

If you want to protect individual files from use by other people, the simplest method is to password protect those files. You can use Apple File Security to encrypt files. You can only protect files, not folders, disk volumes, items in the System Folder, or items that are open or locked.

Password Protecting Your Files

Any file can be password protected.

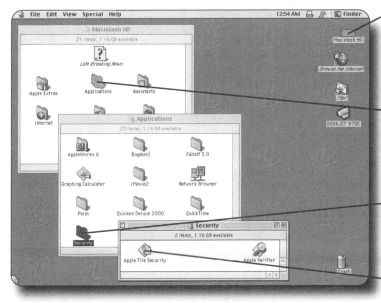

1. Double-click on the **Macintosh HD icon**. The Macintosh HD folder will open.

2. Double-click on the **Applications folder**. The Applications folder will open.

3. Double-click on the **Security folder**. The Security folder will open.

4. Double-click on the **Apple File Security** icon. An Open dialog box will appear.

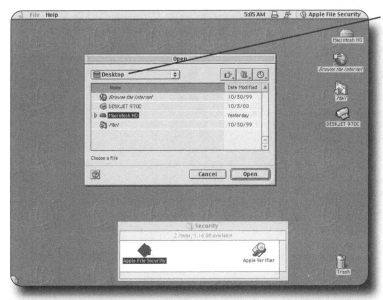

5. Navigate to a **file** you have created on your iMac. The file is probably stored in the Documents folder on your hard drive.

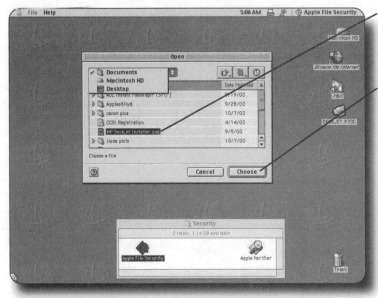

6. **Click** on the **file** you want to encrypt. The file will be selected.

7. **Click** on **Choose**. The Apple File Security dialog box will appear.

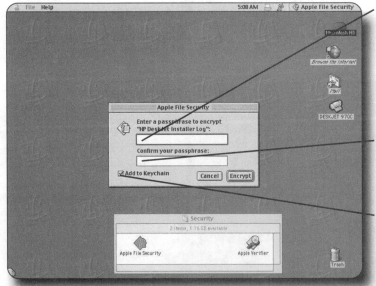

8. **Type** the **password** you want to use in the Enter a passphrase to encrypt text box. The password you choose must be at least five characters long.

9. **Type** the **password** again in the Confirm your passphrase text box.

10. **Click** in the **Add to Keychain check box**. This will add the file to your keychain access.

11. **Click** on **Encrypt**. The file will be protected with the password you specified, and a confirmation message will appear.

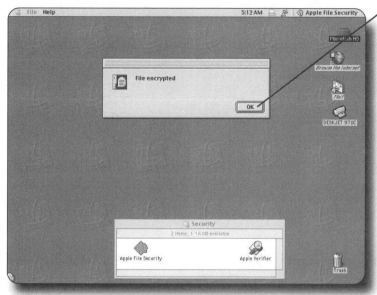

12. **Click** on **OK**. The confirmation message will disappear and the file icon will now include a small yellow key.

13. **Choose Keychain Access** from the Control Panels submenu of the Apple menu.

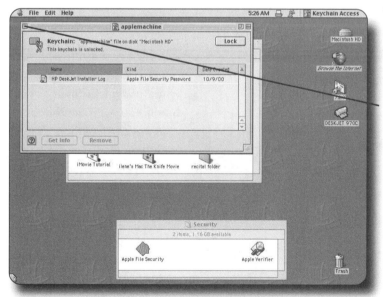

The Keychain dialog box will appear, and you will see that the file has been added to your keychain list.

14. **Click** on the **close box**. The Keychain dialog box will close.

Opening Password-Protected Files

Opening your password-protected files is simple.

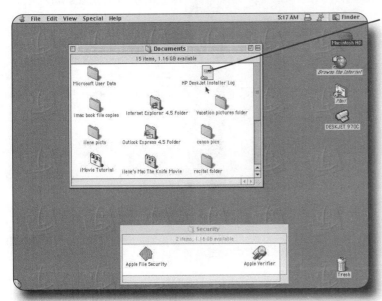

1. Navigate to the **password-protected file** on your hard drive and **double-click** on **it**. The Keychain Access Confirmation dialog box will open.

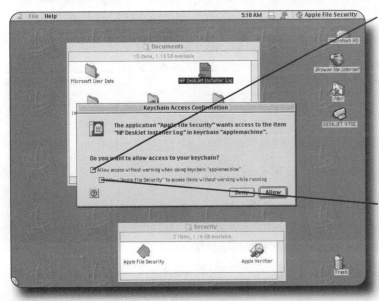

2. Click in the **Allow access without warning when using keychain check box** if you want access to your keychain without first seeing an alert box. The option will be selected.

OR

2b. Click in the **Allow "Apple File Security" to access items without warning while running check box** if you want Apple File Security to work in conjunction with your keychain without displaying any warnings. The option will be selected.

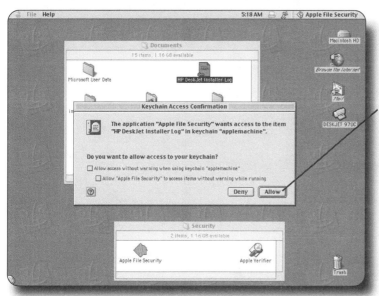

3. Click on **Yes** in the resulting confirmation message box. The message box will close.

4. Click on **Allow**. Your choice in Step 2 will be activated, your document will be unlocked, and a message box will appear, telling you that your file has been decrypted.

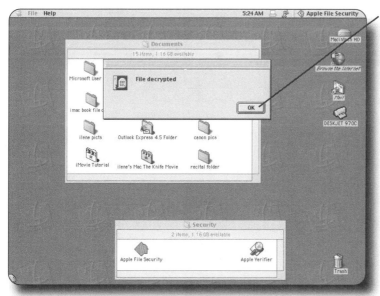

5. Click on **OK**. The message box will close, the file will be removed from your keychain list, and the small yellow key will no longer appear on its icon.

18

Protecting Your iMac

There are three types of danger to your iMac with which you should be concerned: the failure of your hard disk or other major system component; fluctuations in electrical power that can damage components; and viruses, those malicious programs that can infect a computer and destroy the contents of a hard disk. In this chapter, you'll learn how to:

- Make backups of a hard disk
- Protect your iMac from electrical problems
- Handle virus threats

Backing Up

A *backup* is a copy of your files that you keep somewhere safe in case the primary storage media fails—in particular, your hard disk. Although most hard disks run a long time without any problems, you should never trust that your hard disk is going to last forever. To be safe, you must make backup copies of your files regularly.

NOTE

How often should you back up files? That depends on how often you make changes to important files. For example, if you use Quicken as your check register—and no longer keep a manual check register—you can't afford to lose even a single entry. In this case, you should make a backup copy every time an entry is made. In contrast, backing up once a week is probably enough if you use your iMac primarily to access the Internet and rarely download any files or create documents.

What should you back up? The most essential items are the documents you create. If the worst should occur, such as a hard drive crash where you lose all your files, you can almost always reinstall the operating system and your applications from the original CD-ROMs. If you restore by reinstalling from disc, it can take longer than restoring from a complete backup (since the files exist on the original disks), but it does save media costs. Backing up only your documents doesn't take as long as a complete backup and requires much less storage space.

Choosing Backup Media

The first thing to decide is what to use for backup media. The iMac comes with only one hard disk, so an external device is needed. The realistic choices for an iMac include the following:

- **A second hard disk**. Copying files to a second hard disk is fast and easy. The major drawback to this solution is that you are limited by the size of the disk itself. When the backup drive fills up, it can't expand the amount of storage.

- **A Zip disk**. Zip disks are removable disks that hold 100 MB or 250 MB. If you are only backing up your documents because you plan to reinstall application programs from the original CD-ROMs, then this is a good solution. The disks cost about $9-$12 and $20, respectively, and you can always purchase more disks as the number of files goes up. The drawback to this approach is that there comes a point where even a 250 MB disk is too small. Backups may take a long time if you constantly have to switch disks.

- **A SuperDrive disk**. The SuperDrive can read and write floppy disks (a storage capacity of only 1.44Mb) and SuperDisks (120Mb). Like the Zip disk, the SuperDisk is removable and inexpensive.

- **An Orb disk**. Castlewood Systems (http://www.castlewood.com) makes a drive similar to the Zip drive, but the media holds 2.2 GB, which makes it a good solution for large files.

- **A tape drive**. The traditional high-capacity backup media for the Macintosh has been tape, in particular, digital audio tape (DAT). Reasonably priced tape drives have capacities from 2 GB to 24GB. Most come with software to manage the backup process. There is one major stumbling block to using a tape drive on an iMac, however. The vast majority of tape drives use the SCSI interface, which is found on older Macintoshes. The solution is to purchase a USB to SCSI converter. The backup works and is very convenient and reliable, but it's slow.

- **CD-RW**. A CD-RW drive can read, write, and erase CD-RWs. Each disc can store about 650 MB. The discs cannot be reused as many times as the other types of magnetic media, but if you have a limited number of files that don't change daily, a CD-RW drive can be a cost-effective backup medium.

What should you do? In most cases, when people must make a technology decision doing nothing is a viable alternative. However, where backup is concerned, doing nothing is simply begging for disaster to strike. The SuperDrive's low initial prices and reasonable media costs make it a good first choice as a backup device. Consider the second hard drive or tape drive options if the volume of documents grows so large that 100 MB of storage becomes inconvenient.

Storing Backup Copies

Where should you keep backup copies? The most secure backup scheme is to keep a current backup copy in a different location from the computer. For example, if your iMac is at home, you might keep a set of backup disks or tapes in a drawer at the office. Barring that, a fireproof safe or filing cabinet is a good choice. If none of those are available, a drawer safe from magnetic interference (except next to the computer) works well.

Providing Power Protection

The voltages that travel over electric lines usually are not constant. Sometimes they are low; sometimes they are high. High voltages arrive suddenly, in spurts known as *surges*. Although low voltage (often known as a *brownout*) can cause a computer to shut down, it rarely causes any permanent damage to the equipment. In contrast, a power surge can severely damage any piece of electronic equipment connected to the power line. Power surges can also jump from electrical lines to telephone lines running next to them through your walls and destroy modems and fax machines. Just as it is foolish never to back up your hard disk, it is foolish not to provide your iMac with some type of protection against power surges.

Using a Surge Protector

The simplest, and least expensive, type of power protection for your iMac is a *surge protector*, a piece of hardware that

Photo courtesy of Belkin Components

Photo courtesy of Tripp Lite

looks a great deal like a power strip with plug-ins for four or six devices. A surge protector has one function: It isolates equipment plugged into it from power surges.

Surge protectors can cost anywhere from $10 to $50. Generally, you get what you pay for. At the low end, is a device that will stop a surge—at least once. The surge suppression circuitry in an inexpensive surge protector is likely to be destroyed by the first powerful surge that it handles. Often a less expensive device has no indicators on it to tell you if surge protection is still available—you have no way of knowing that it is no longer functional.

More expensive surge protectors provide outlets for telephone lines as well as electrical equipment. They also have indicators that advise whether surge protection is still in effect. In addition, many come with warranties that guarantee against failure of the surge protector itself. If the surge protector fails and equipment is damaged, you'll be reimbursed. If nothing else, a high-end surge protector provides very inexpensive insurance against power surge damage!

Choosing a Line Conditioner

A *line conditioner* combines a surge protector with brownout protection. It has a capacitor that stores a small bit of electricity. When the voltage drops below a threshold level, power is discharged from the capacitor to ensure that the equipment receives a constant voltage. A line conditioner cannot handle a total power outage, but instead is designed to handle normal power fluctuations.

Line conditioners come in various sizes, depending on the number of watts they can handle and cost between $80 and $200. To find out what size you need, check the back of each piece of equipment or the specifications in the users

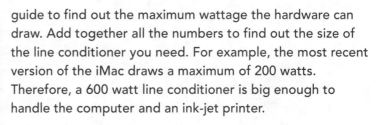

Photo courtesy of Tripp Lite

guide to find out the maximum wattage the hardware can draw. Add together all the numbers to find out the size of the line conditioner you need. For example, the most recent version of the iMac draws a maximum of 200 watts. Therefore, a 600 watt line conditioner is big enough to handle the computer and an ink-jet printer.

Upgrading to a UPS

An UPS (*uninterruptable power supply*) provides battery backup for a computer in case of a total power outage. Most of today's UPSs also include surge suppression and line conditioning, although it is very important to read the specifications of the device to ensure that you are receiving complete power protection.

Photo courtesy of Tripp Lite

The typical UPS is a *stand-by UPS* that runs the computer from the house current until the voltage drops below what the line conditioning circuitry can handle. At that point, the UPS switches the computer to the backup battery. The switchover is so fast that computer operations are not affected. The alternative is a *full-time UPS*—one where the computer always runs directly from the battery. Such UPSs are more expensive than the stand-by products, but do eliminate any chance of problems from power fluctuations because the battery provides a constant voltage.

A UPS battery is not intended to run a computer for a long period of time. It holds just enough charge (usually 5–20 minutes) for you to save files and shut down the computer. The amount of charge depends on the size of the UPS and the amount of power being drawn. UPSs are sized like line conditioners, based on the maximum number of watts they can handle.

In most cases, you plug your computer and monitor (if the monitor is a separate unit) and any external disk drives into a UPS. Other devices—in particular, printers and scanners—are protected by a surge suppressor or line conditioner. You can restart a printing or scanning job without losing anything but time. Since those devices require so much more power than a computer or monitor, they would force you to purchase a much larger and, therefore, more expensive UPS.

UPSs are relatively more expensive than line conditioners. Although you can purchase a 250 watt UPS for about $80, the more powerful models, such as a 500 watt unit, cost between $100 and $500. The price depends on the size of the battery, the number of electrical outlets, surge suppression and line conditioning capabilities, and the type of software included, if any. Prices vary for UPSs to handle desktop computer systems but the high end would be around a 3000 watt model for about $1500.

Making the Final Decision

What power protection should you purchase? If the power coming into your home or office is relatively constant and you're willing to take the risk of losing 15 minutes or so of work (assuming that you save work every 15 minutes), a good surge protector will certainly do the trick. However, if your power is not constant (especially if you suffer from frequent outages), you should consider either a line conditioner or a UPS for the iMac and any external disk drives you might purchase. Use a high-end surge suppressor for the rest of your equipment.

Handling the Virus Threat

Computer viruses have been around since people have been trading files between desktop computers. Every time you download a file over the Internet, there is a risk that a virus program has piggy-backed itself onto the legitimate file.

Viruses don't arise by accident. Someone must write the virus program and send it out over the Internet, either attached to an application program or e-mail message. Once a virus infects a computer, it may do something as benign as displaying a dialog box or as destructive as destroying files on the hard disk.

Because of the current predominance of the Windows operating system, the majority of new viruses affects Windows machines only and do not threaten a Macintosh. Microsoft Word macro viruses can be passed between platforms, however. Some viruses can attack an iMac and, if you happen to send an infected file to someone else, the recipient's computer becomes infected as well! It's therefore wise to pay attention to what you download and occasionally run virus detection software to scan your disk storage.

Practicing Safe Downloading

As you read in Chapter 13, "Using E-mail with Outlook Express," attachments to e-mail and other files for downloading can contain viruses. You can't test for the presence of a virus before downloading a file, but you can minimize the chance of that occurring. Only download files from people or locations that you know. For example, it is fairly safe to download a file from the AOL software libraries because AOL has taken special care to scan all files for viruses and other problems. In addition, the Web sites that have been mentioned throughout this book are relatively safe.

Notice that the phrases *relatively safe* and *fairly safe* appear in the preceding two sentences. It is impossible to be totally immune to a virus threat.

Using Virus Detection Software

Virus detection software is commercial software that can scan a hard disk for the presence of viruses. At the time this book was written, four programs were available for the Macintosh, each costing less than $75: Norton AntiVirus, Virex, Dr. Solomon's Anti-Virus, and MicroMat's TechTool Pro.

Virus detection software works by scanning each file for the presence of a virus it recognizes. If it finds one, it removes the virus from the infected file. The software can only recognize viruses that it has been programmed to detect. When a new virus is released, the developers of the virus detection software must update the software to handle it. Although updates usually appear quickly on a software manufacturer's Web site, it still can't be fast enough to prevent everyone from being affected by the new virus.

As a result, a never-ending cycle of new viruses follows a software upgrade. In fact, a few developers of virus detection software discontinued their products because they felt that virus detection software was issuing a challenge to virus writers, goading them into writing ever more powerful and hard-to-defeat viruses.

If you do a lot of file downloading, you should purchase virus detection software. Although it's not a perfect defense against viruses, it's the best protection available.

Glossary

A

Active window. The window that is currently in use. Only one window can be active at a time, although an unlimited number of windows can be open. Comments issued (such as close) act on the open, or active, window.

ADB. Apple Desktop Bus. A collection of wires designed so that input devices such as mice, keyboards, and trackballs can communicate with the computer. Can support up to 16 input devices at one time. Used on Macintosh computers from the Mac SE until the introduction of the iMac. The ADB port is slower than USB and does not allow plugging in of peripherals while the computer is on.

Alert. A window that appears to notify the user of some condition that must be handled right away. No further work can proceed until a reply button is pressed and the alert closes.

Alias. An icon that points to a file of the same name; it represents the real file. Double-click on an alias to open the original file or application represented by the alias. An alias file name always appears in italics.

Analog signal. A smooth, continuous signal, an analog signal can have an infinite number of values, as *contrasted with* digital signals. (Example: Compare a radio with a tuning dial (analog) and a digital radio with buttons.)

AOL. America Online, the largest Internet Service Provider and on-line service

ARA. Apple Remote Access. The ARA control panel controls remote connections via dial-up (or any connection that is intermittent in nature).

AppleWorks. Formerly ClarisWorks, an application that includes word processing, spreadsheet, data management, paint, draw, and communications capabilities

Application. A computer program used to create specific works. Examples of applications are Microsoft Word, AppleWorks, Adobe Photoshop, etc.

Application software. Software that performs useful work for a user

Archive. Files saved for later use. Compressed archives are files compacted in some way to save space.

Arrow key. A key on the iMac keyboard with an up, down, right, or left arrow on it. Arrow keys can move the insertion point in a text document, or move up and down a list of files in the List view in a Finder window.

ATA. Advanced Technology Attachment. *See* IDE.

ATAPI. An extension of the IDE interface description to allow the use of CD-ROM drives and tape drives

Attachment. A file sent along with an email message. It is attached to the message, therefore called an attachment.

B

Background application. In a multitasking operating system, an application that is running but on which the user is not currently working

Background printing. Printing that occurs while you work on another program or document

Backslash. The slash character (\) on your keyboard. Often used when writing a path name for a file on a hard drive. (Note: colons are also sometimes used for path names.)

Backup. A copy of files typically stored on removable media that is saved in case the original files are damaged

Beep sound. The sound made by the iMac's speaker when an alert appears on the screen. Beep sounds can occur when you press a wrong key, when new mail is available, a process is completed, or any time the computer needs your attention.

Bit-mapped graphics. *See* also pixel. A picture or graphic that is made up of tiny dots

Bookmark. A place holder that saves the address of a Web site. Netscape saves bookmarks in a bookmarks.html document. Internet Explorer bookmarks are called Favorites.

Boot. To start up a computer.

Brownout. A dip in electrical voltage that is not necessarily enough to shut down a computer

Button. A bordered box or oval in a window that triggers program action when clicked with the mouse pointer.

Byte. The basic unit of computer storage, large enough to hold one character. A byte is 8 bits, the smallest unit.

C

Cable modem. A type of modem that connects to your cable TV provider to provide high speed access to the Internet.

Cache. A file that provides temporary storage for a document. Web browsers save pages to your hard drive in cache files, which are automatically removed by the browser.

Carrier tone. An audible electronic tone sent out by a modem that is modulated to carry a digital signal.

Cascading delete. The deleting of everything within a folder, including all other nested folders, that is, folders inside other folders.

CD-ROM. Compact Disc Read-Only Memory. An optical storage disk that uses a laser to read the contents of the disc. Standard CD-ROMs can be read from but not written to.

Central processing unit (CPU). Often known as the "brains of the computer," the CPU is a chip inside the iMac, also called a microprocessor. A CPU can perform mathematical computations. *See* system unit.

Check box. A square that can be empty or checked to select or deselect a program option in a window or dialog box.

Click. A single press and release of the mouse button. To click, position the pointer over an object or screen element, and then press and release the mouse button. Clicking performs an action, such as pressing a button on screen.

Clip art. Usually bit-mapped art, which is often, royalty-free, that is, artwork that can be reproduced with obtaining permission from the artist

Clipboard. An area of computer memory where information is held temporarily. Each new item saved or cut to the Clipboard replaces whatever was there before. Items can be retrieved from the Clipboard and placed elsewhere, even in an application different from the one in which it was created.

Close box. A square at the far-left edge of a window's Title bar. Click on the Close box to remove a window from the screen.

Command key. A modifier key on the iMac keyboard that, when pressed with a letter or number key, can be used as a substitute for making a menu selection.

Contextual menu. A pop-up menu that appears on the Desktop or in a program when the control key and mouse button are pressed together.

Control key. A modifier key on the iMac keyboard

Control panel. A small program used to configure the Mac OS and other software. Control panels are stored in the Control Panels folder in the System Folder and accessible through the Control Panels submenu of the Apple menu.

Control Strip. The Control Strip is a floating pallet of tiles, usually on the bottom-left of the screen. that represent controls for volume, screen resolution, and other commonly used system settings.

Control Strip module. A single tile in the Control Strip

Cooperative multitasking. A type of multitasking in which the operating system and application programs cooperate to determine which program has access to the CPU at any given time.

Copy. To duplicate a selection (text or graphic) and save it temporarily to the Mac's Clipboard.

Cover page. A page that is sent at the beginning of a fax to let the recipient know who sent the fax.

CPU. See Central Processing Unit.

Cross-platform. A program or file that can be used on a Macintosh, a PC of some kind, and or a UNIX computer.

Current folder. The last folder accessed by an application.

Cursor. The arrow on your computer screen which is moved by the mouse, keyboard, or trackpad. The cursor can change depending on the operation you perform, such as a pencil in a draw program, or an I-beam in a word processing program.

Cut. To removes a selection and place it temporarily on the Mac's Clipboard.

Cycle. One tick of the CPU's internal clock

D

Data communications. Using computers to trade information back and forth.

Default. A value or choice that software assumes a user will want to make. Typically, a default choice the most commonly chosen option.

Default button. A button with a heavy border than can be selected by pressing the Enter key.

Demodulate. Remove the carrier tone from an analog signal to retrieve the digital signal that has been imposed on it.

Desktop. The Mac OS interface, which resembles a physical desktop.

Dialog box. A window used to collect information from the user that is necessary to perform a specific task

Digital signal. A signal made up of discrete elements such as 0s and 1s.

Digitize. To transform a paper, film, or audio image into a pattern of 0s and 1s that can be stored and manipulated on a computer.

Directory. A listing of files and folders. It is stored on your hard drive as an invisible file.

Document. The work that a user prepares on a computer such as a letter or an illustration

Document window. Displays the contents of a document regardless of whether it is text or graphics

Double-click. Two quick press and release moves of the mouse button, occurring close together. (See also, click.)

Download. To transfer a file from one computer to another over data communications lines, such as a modem

Drag. To pull the cursor, a file, or a folder from one location to another across the computer screen by holding down the mouse button while moving the mouse pointer.

Drag-and-drop. A technique in which one file is dragged onto another file. Usually used to open a document by dropping it on top of its associated application.

Drawing program. A graphics program in which images are created from shapes that retain their identity as shapes, called objects.

DSL. Digital Subscriber Line. An emerging digital service where data communications signals travel on the same wires as voice telephone signals.

E

Email. Electronic mail. Message exchanges sent electronically to another user, typically over an Intranet or the Internet using an email application.

Earthlink. Earthlink is an American Internet Service Provider whose software is included in the iMac package.

Eject. To remove a disk from the Desktop. When you eject a CD-ROM or floppy, it is also removed from its drive.

Escape (Esc) key. A key that allows the user to cancel an action when working with a program

Ethernet. A type of networking cable provided with the iMac, often used as part of a local area network. The iMac includes an Ethernet port that can use 10BASE-T or 100BASE-T Ethernet transmission.

Extension. A small program that adds functions to the Mac OS and is loaded into main memory (RAM) when the iMac boots.

Extension conflict. A software problem that occurs when two or more extensions don't work correctly when used at the same time.

F

File. A document saved to a computer's hard disk, zip disk, CD-ROM, or any other form of storage.

File management. A type of data management.

File name extension. Characters following the name of a file that indicate the type of application with which it is associated. For example: help.txt indicates that the file named "help" is a text file.

Find and replace. A feature of a word processing application that allows the user to search for words in a document and, if desired, automatically replace them with alternate text.

Finder. The operating system program that manages the Mac OS Desktop.

Firewire. A peripheral bus that allows plug-and-play integration of up to 116 high speed devices daisy-chained together. Devices include digital video cameras, hard drives, printers, etc.

Floating window. A window that appears on top of all other windows, even if it is not the active window.

Folder. A sub-directory on a disk that can hold files and other folders, represented by a graphical representation of a file folder.

Finder window. The top level window that displays all the files and folders stored within a folder or disk icon.

Font. A design for type.

Foreground application. The application with which the user is currently working.

Form. A document with blank spaces (called fields) used to collect information from a user.

Forward. The action of sending an entire e-mail message to another recipient

Freeware. Free software provided by the developer.

FTP. File Transfer Protocol. An Internet protocol for transferring files between two computers.

Function key. One of keys at the top of the iMac keyboard numbered F1 through F12 that is used as a substitute for a menu selection

G

Gigabyte (GB). Approximately one billion bytes

H

Handle. A square that appears in the corner or on the side of a graphics object. Dragging a handle can be used to resize or rotate an object.

Hard copy. A paper copy of a computer document.

Hard disk. High-capacity storage device for programs and data. A hard disk retains its contents even after a computer is turned off.

Hardware. Physical computer equipment, such as a keyboard, mouse, hard disk, or CPU

Home page. Typically, the first page that you see in a Web site, that acts as a directory or introduction to the site.

Horizontal scroll bar. A scroll bar along the bottom of a window that moves the view of a document from right to left.

Host Address. A host address is a hierarchical naming system that uses names separated by periods, going from specific to general. Host names are associated with a particular IP address through the Domain Name Service.

Hot key. A key or combination of keys that starts some action, such as hiding and showing the Control Strip.

Hot swapping. The ability to change out hardware components without shutting down the computer. SCSI equipment is not hot swappable, but you can hot swap USB and Firewire peripherals.

HTML. HyperText Markup Language. The language in which Web pages are written so that they can be interpreted by the World Wide Web. HTML is plain text, with tags offset by a set of brackets (< and >) that affect how pages look. Files that contain HTML code have names that normally end in **.html** (Macintosh) or **.htm** (PC).

HTTP. HyperText Transfer Protocol. An Internet protocol that is the basic method for transferring the content of Web pages across the Internet

Hyperlink. A line of text or a graphic that, when clicked, transfers you to either another portion of the same document or to another page.

I

I-beam (or I-bar). A mouse pointer that looks like an I. Generally used as a text insertion point marker.

Icon. A small picture on a computer screen that represents another object such as folder, document, or hard drive.

IDE. Integrated Drive Electronics. The name for the interface to certain hard disk drives, such as the one in the iMac. Also known as ATA.

Import. To copy the contents of a document into another document or program.

Inactive window. A window that is open on the screen but is not currently in use

INIT conflict. An old term for an extension conflict.

Input device. Hardware that takes data from the outside world and translates it into a form that a computer can interpret, such as a keyboard, mouse or trackpad.

Insertion point. The place in a document where the next typed characters appear, marked by a flashing straight line. (See also I-beam.)

Integrated package. A program made up of tightly connected application modules, such as AppleWorks.

Information service. A service provider that includes its own content accessible by subscribers

IP. Internet Protocol. This is one of several communication standards that allow information sharing on the Internet.

IP Address. An IP address is a set of four numbers, each between 0 and 255, separated by periods, such as 128.158.1.72. All domain names have an IP address, which is assigned from a central source.

IrDA. Infrared Data Association. IrDA is a standard created by the Infrared Data Association for communication between computing devices using infrared signals. IrDA compatible ports may be found in desktop and laptop computers, Personal Digital Assistants, some digital cameras, printers, and even some telephones.

ISP. Internet Service Provider. An organization that provides a connection for a computer to the Internet. The most typical way for the home user to connect is to dial into an ISP's modems. The ISP's modem then routes the transmission to the Internet.

K

Keyboard. An object with letter and number keys used to type text. It is one type of input device.

Kilobyte (K or KB). 1,024 bytes

L

LAN. Local Area Network. A network of computers and other devices that covers a small area (less than a mile radius, generally, and possibly as small as two machines sitting side by side) for relatively high-speed communications between components on the network.

Landscape orientation. A page orientation in which the page is wider than it is tall, available through your printer software or the printer setup selection in your program.

Launch. To start a program

Line conditioner. A piece of equipment intended to stop power surges and increase line voltages during brownouts

M

Main memory. Temporary storage for programs and data while the computer is processing them. The contents of main memory are lost when power is removed from the computer. Also called RAM (Random Access Memory)

Megabyte (MB). A way storage is measured, 1024 kilobytes.

Menu. A list of program options and actions from which a user can choose

Menu bar. The strip at the top of the screen that contains the names of available menus

Metasearch engine. A search engine that searches a collection of other search engines

MHz. Megahertz. One million cycles per second. The unit used to measure the speed of a CPU

MIDI. Musical Instrument Digital Interface. MIDI is the standard by which computers communicate with musical instruments

Modal. A property of a window such that no other actions can take place in the program until the window is closed

Modem. A hardware device that translates a computer's digital signals into analog signals that can travel over standard telephone lines.

Modifier key. A key on the iMac keyboard that, when pressed in combination with another key, changes the original instruction of the other key.

Modulate. To raise and lower the frequency of a carrier tone to impose the pattern of a digital signal.

Monitor. A screen for viewing the output of a computer. The iMac's monitor is built into its system unit.

Motherboard. A computer's main circuit board

Mounted. An active volume (hard drive or disk) recognized by the Mac OS. An icon for the volume appears on the Desktop so the user can access its contents. *See also* Unmount.

Mouse. An input device that, when moved, causes a pointer on the computer screen to move

Mouse pointer. The small pointer on the screen that moves proportionally to the movement of a mouse, track ball, trackpad, or other computer-pointing device.

Multitasking. A feature of an operating system where more than one program can be processing information at the same time.

N

Navigation key. A key on the iMac keyboard that scrolls one page up in a document, one page down in a document, or to the beginning of the document

Network server. A computer on a local area network or Intranet that provides shared files

Non-modal. A property of a window such that other actions can take place in the program while the window is open

Non-printing character. A character that can be generated by pressing keys on the iMac keyboard but for which there is no visible symbol

O

Object graphics. *See* Drawing program

OCR. Optical character recognition. The process of recognizing graphics characters and translating them into editable text

Offline. When you are not connected to an Internet service provider and the Internet, you are "off" the line (refers back to the days when everyone used telephone lines to connect to the Internet).

Online. An active connection to an Internet service provider. See also *Offline*.

Operating system. A collection of programs that manage a computer

Option key. A modifier key on the iMac keyboard.

Output device. A piece of hardware (such as a printer) that takes data stored in the computer and translates it into a form that a human user can understand. Examples are monitors, printers, and fax machines.

P

Page. One visible screen of text; approximately 42 lines, depending on the font used

Paint program. A graphics program in which the image is made up of a pattern of very small dots

Partition. A type of division of hard drive space. This portion of a large hard disk can be mounted as a separate volume.

Paste. To insert the contents of the iMac's Clipboard into the active window at the insertion point

Path name. The route in a disk directory hierarchy to the location of a specific file

PDF. Portable Document Format. A format, developed by Adobe Corp., that preserves the layout of a document and that can be read on any computer using the program Adobe Acrobat Reader.

Pixel. A picture element. One dot on a computer screen

Point. The unit of measurement for the height of type. There are approximately 72 points to the inch.

Pop-up menu. A menu whose options appear when the mouse pointer is held down over the viewable area. Pop-up menus are often found in dialog boxes.

Port. A connector into which external equipment is plugged. Each port is designed to work with a specific type of connection, such as USB, Ethernet, or standard telephone line.

Portrait orientation. When your page is set to be taller than it is wide.

PostScript. A computer language developed by Adobe Corp. that describes the layout of a printed page.

PostScript font. Type that is described by the outline of its characters and designed specifically for printing on a printer that uses PostScript. PostScript fonts require separate screen fonts.

POTS. Plain Old Telephone Service. Standard analog telephone service

Power surge. A sudden increase in electrical voltage in the power entering a piece of electrical equipment

Preferences file. A file stored in the Preferences folder in the System Folder that contains configuration options for a program

Print file. A file in which a print job is stored

Print job. A unit of work sent to the printer to be printed, usually made up of one document or a part of a document

Print queue. The list of jobs waiting to be printed

Printer. An output device that takes a document stored on a computer and copies it to paper or another medium, such as a transparency

Printer driver. Software that acts as an interface between the computer and a printer

Q

Quoting. To repeat what someone else says, and including a portion of an e-mail message in a reply to that message

R

Radio button. A circle that, when clicked on, makes a choice from a group of options (a black dot appears in its center when selected.) Radio buttons are frequently used in dialog boxes and only one radio button in a set can be selected at a time.

RAM. Random-Access Memory. Temporary storage for programs and data while the computer is processing them. The contents of this main memory are lost when power is removed from the computer.

Replace all. A feature of an application where a user can replace all occurrences of an object (such as a word or words) with another object (the replacement text).

Resolution. The amount of detail on a computer screen or printer. The higher the resolution—the more pixels per inch—the more detailed the images.

Rollup box. A square at the far right of a window's Title bar that causes the window to collapse to nothing but the title bar when clicked. Clicking the rollup box a second time returns the window to its original size.

ROM. Read-only memory. Permanent storage inside the system unit that contains programs that start up the computer. When your Macintosh starts up a ROM test is always completed first.

S

Scroll. To move the contents of a long document or window so that a new part of the document or window is brought into view on the screen.

Scroll bar. The shaded bar appearing on the right side or bottom of a window that provides control over scrolling.

Scroll box. A square inside a scroll bar that can be dragged to provide large movement through a document

SCSI. Small Computer System Interface. SCSI is a standard for communication between a computer and its peripheral devices.

Search engine. A Web site that searches the Internet based on a word or phrase that you supply

Select. To choose and highlight something on your computer screen.

Self-mounting image (SMI). A method of storing the entire contents of a floppy disk in a file on a larger disk. A disk image isn't just the contents of the floppy, but every bit of information on the floppy in the same order. When the image launches, an application program in the image fools the operating system into thinking the original floppy disk has been inserted into a "virtual" floppy drive, so that the disk contents appear on your desktop.

Service provider. An organization that provides data communications services to subscribers.

Set. A group of extensions that the Extensions Manager can enable and disable as a unit

Shareware. Software that can be copied and used for a trial period. At the end of the trial period, payment should be made if the user intends to continue to use it.

Shift-click. Click the mouse button while holding down the Shift key on the iMac's keyboard

SimpleText. A text editor that comes with the Mac OS

Software. Computer programs, also called Applications

Spam. Unwanted and unsolicited e-mail messages, also called *junk mail*

Splash screen. The initial screen a program displays when it launches, usually a graphic showing what program it is and who made it

Spool. Save a print job in a disk file temporarily while it is waiting to print

Spreadsheet. The electronic equivalent of an accountant's journal. Spreadsheets manage numeric data, such as analyzing a budget. Most spreadsheet software can also draw graphs from stored data.

Spring-loaded folder. A folder that *springs* open when the user drags and holds an item over the folder

Standard document window. A window with a title bar, zoom box, close box, rollup box, scroll bars, and size box

Stand-by UPS. A UPS that runs equipment off house current until a power failure occurs and then switches immediately to its internal battery

Submenu. A menu whose name is an option in another menu. The submenu's options appear when the user drags the mouse pointer over the submenu's name in its parent window.

Surge. *See* Power surge

Surge protector. A device that is intended to stop power surges before they reach electrical equipment

System beep. The sound that is played when an alert appears on the screen

System extensions *See* Extensions

System software. Software that performs management tasks for the computer

System unit. The case in which the major components of a computer are installed

T

Terabyte. Approximately one trillion bytes

Theme. A collection of settings for the look of the Mac OS Desktop

Thumb. *See* Scroll box

Thumbnail. A small image showing the contents of a graphics file

Title bar. The strip across the top of a window that contains the window's name

Toggle. A switch that is turned on by an action and turned off by repeating the same action

Trash can. An icon on the Desktop into which the user drags icons for files and folders to be deleted. The Trash holds its contents until you choose Empty Trash from the Special menu in the Finder.

TrueType. A type of font in which characters are described by their outlines. TrueType fonts appear smoothly in any size on the screen and provide good printed output.

Typeface. A design for type

U

Unmount. Remove a volume from the Desktop. If the volume is stored on removable storage, unmounting it will also eject it from the drive.

UPS. Uninterruptable power supply. A device that provides surge protection, line conditioning, and a backup battery in case of total power failure

URL. Uniform Resource Locator. An address of a page, site, or file on the World Wide Web

USB. Universal Serial Bus. A peripheral bus that allows plug-and-play integration of many medium speed peripherals at the same time. The iMac has two USB ports, plus a USB keyboard with two more ports, and a USB mouse.

V

Vertical scroll bar. A scroll bar along the right side of a window that moves the view of a document up and down

Virus. A malicious program that causes damage to your computer files. It can often by erase all or part of the hard drive.

Volatile. A property of main memory (RAM) where its contents are lost when electricity is removed

Volume. A disk or portion of a disk that the Mac OS can mount on the Desktop

W

Web page. A single HTML document that is part of a Web site

Web server. A computer on which a Web site resides. Software that transfers HTML pages over the Internet

Web site. A collection of related HTML documents presented over the Web

Window. A container on the screen that allows the user to view something

Window shade. The state of a rolled up window

Word processor. A program for entering, editing, and formatting text. Many of today's word processors also can handle graphics.

Word wrap. A feature of word processors where a word that will not fit on a line is moved to the next line

Z

Zoom box. A box in the top, right-hand corner of most Macintosh windows that looks like a box within a box. Clicking the zoom box once causes the window to expand to fit the screen or as large as necessary to show all the window's content, whichever is smaller. Clicking the zoom box a second time returns the window to its original size.

Index